Loris Malag

and the Teachers

Dialogues on Collaboration and Conflict
among Children, Reggio Emilia 1990

*A Research Partnership between Reggio Emilia Municipal
Infant-Toddler Centers and Preschools and the University of
Massachusetts, Amherst, Illustrating Group Reflective Practice
under the Leadership of Loris Malaguzzi*

by Drs. Carolyn Edwards, Lella Gandini, and John Nimmo,

In collaboration with Tiziana Filippini, Vea Vecchi, and Teachers of the
Diana Preschool in 1990

Compiled and Edited by Carolyn Pope Edwards, 2014
At the University of Nebraska–Lincoln

Zea Books
Lincoln, Nebraska
2015

ISBN 978-1-60962-056-1   paperback
ISBN 978-1-60962-07-8   ebook

Set in Calisto and Segoe Print types.
Design and composition by Paul Royster.

Zea Books are published by the University of Nebraska–Lincoln Libraries

Electronic (pdf) edition available online at
 http://digitalcommons.unl.edu/zeabook/

Print edition can be ordered from Lulu.com, at
 http://www.lulu.com/spotlight/unllib

Preface

In 1990, three of us from the University of Massachusetts in Amherst, participated in an extraordinary research experience with Loris Malaguzzi and the educators of the Diana School in Reggio Emilia. Our focus in this case was "cooperation," how preschool educators promote collaboration and community in their classrooms and schools. We at UMass had been inspired by Joseph Tobin, David Wu, and Dana Davidson's (1989) book, *Preschool in Three Cultures: Japan, China, and the United States*, and wanted to use videotapes of classroom episodes in a similar way to provoke teachers in Reggio Emilia (Italy), Pistoia (Italy), and Amherst (USA) to reflect on the meanings they give to the images, including the actions of themselves and others.

We had noticed the high level of co-action, empathy, and comradeship among preschool children (and among the educators themselves) in the progressive education settings of all three communities, but we also believed there were also interesting cultural differences. We wanted to listen to the specific discourse through which skilled educators, as a pedagogical team, talked about community and cooperation. What was their "distinctive discourse," or "cultural meaning system," (what Jerome Bruner calls a "language of education") for framing issues of getting along, becoming part of a group, and learning to negotiate? Their shared language, we believed, would relate to methods of school organization and grouping of children, as well as to shared beliefs about the roles of the teacher, the nature of the child as learner, rationales for teacher intervention and guidance, and preferred styles of facilitating the learning process. In Reggio Emilia, we initially found that concepts like collaboration and community had a taken-for-granted quality because they were so implicit to the cultural fabric of their pedagogical approach. Our research project provided an occasion for the educators to make their thinking and practice regarding these ideas more explicit and visible – an opportunity they embraced with considerable intensity and complexity. We also realized that the Reggio

educators viewed conflict between children, emotional and intellectual, as integral to collaboration and co-construction – a perspective that was less evident in our research in Amherst, USA.

The analysis of the individual interviews we conducted with teachers was published in an article, first in Italian, then later in English (both are included in this volume). Yet, that short article does not begin to capture the unique experience we shared in October, 1990, when the three of us traveled to Reggio Emilia and spent several days with the Reggio educators. Loris Malaguzzi was a dazzling philosophical intellect, and at the same time such a grounded, empathic, and perceptive person, that even today, we remember the force of his presence and the way he worked with teachers.

This document presents in book form the entire record of the data collection in Reggio Emilia that focused on the Reggio classroom videos and one larger meeting responding to the video edit from the Amherst School, from the initial proposal sent to Sergio Spaggiari (Director of the Municipal Preschools and Infant-Toddler Centers) and Loris Malaguzzi on December 8, 1989; followed by preliminary conversations that took place in February and June, 1990 at the Diana School, including Lella Gandini, Loris Malaguzzi, Sergio Spaggiari, Tiziana Filippini, Vea Vecchi, and others; through all the discussions that took place during an intense week in October, 1990, including Loris Malaguzzi (founding director), Tiziana Filippini (*pedagogista*), Vea Vecchi (*atelierista*), Paola Strozzi, Giulia Notari, Laura Rubizzi, Marina Castagnetti, Magda Bondavalli, Marina Mori (teachers), Lella Gandini (researcher and translator), Carolyn Edwards (researcher), John Nimmo (researcher), and Diana Preschool auxiliary staff. Most of the lengthy encounters during this week were held as round table discussions in the the Diana School *atelier,* with Loris Malaguzzi taking a prominent role as provocateur while teaching teams shared and provided context for video episodes from their classrooms. The dialogues were notable for both the seriousness of preparation and critical engagement *and* the collegial warmth expressed between Malaguzzi and the Reggio educators. We also came to realize that the educators viewed these encounters as powerful opportuntities for their own professional development through the documentation process, rather than passive participation in our research project.

Afterwards, one of us (Carolyn Edwards) safeguarded all of the records, and working with Lella Gandini and other translators, arranged to translate all of the group discussions into English. It is these English translations which constitute the chapters of the compiled document, along with ancillary notes and the observation sheets of the teachers. When we conducted this research, Loris Malaguzzi entrusted us with the videos, tape recordings, and observational notes that the Diana teachers had prepared. We have always honored his trust in our scientific rigor and integrity. Some excerpts of the material have been shared in the three volumes of *The Hundred Languages of Children: The Reggio Emilia Approach*, in the chapters on the role of the teacher and the importance of community (2nd. Edition). Otherwise this superb example of the work of Loris Malaguzzi with teachers, *pedagogiste*, *atelieriste*, and outside researchers has not been available to the scholarly community and the public interested in the history of the Reggio Emilia experience. John Nimmo analyzed the Amherst, Massachusetts, portion of the study for his 1992 doctoral dissertation, *The Meaning of Classroom Community: Shared Images of Early Childhood Teachers* (available from ProQuest, http://search.proquest.com/docview/303992892). In addition, what the three of us heard, saw, and recorded in Pistoia, Italy, has informed many of our presentations and chapters about Pistoia early childhood services (e.g., Cline, Edwards, Gandini, Giacomelli, Giovannini, & Galardini, 2012, available online at http://digitalcommons.unl.edu/famconfacpub/83/, and Edwards, Cline, Gandini, Giacomelli, Giovannini, & Galardini, 2014, available online at http://kellogg.nd.edu/events/calendar/spring2012/learning.shtml).

Given our deep commitment to progressive education and to promoting the rights and potential of all children worldwide, we wish to share the rich record of our research experience in Reggio Emilia, so that current readers and those to come can gain a glimpse of the brilliant minds at work during this era (1990), and as it were, "listen in" on the fascinating discussions that were held on the topic of "cooperation." The Diana School embodies a special place in Reggio Emilia history, including being the subject of the 1991 *Newsweek* article naming the program one of the 10 best schools in the world. While the translation process raises issues of interpretation, we have taken great care as best we could in the translation from the original Italian to protect the integrity and complexity of key ideas and of Loris Malaguzzi's many eloquent metaphors and allegories, often drawn from Italian religious, political, and cultural stories. This volume is a compilation of the actual thoughts expressed—unedited—so that readers can draw conclusions for themselves about the flow of the discussions and the shared meaning created.

We are grateful to the University of Nebraska–Lincoln's Zea E-Books, and to its director, Paul Royster of the University of Nebraska Libraries, for publishing this scholarly record. Copies have been placed in the Documentation and Educational Research Center in the International Centre Loris Malaguzzi in Reggio Emilia. We are pleased that these "traces" of research with Malaguzzi and the Diana School educators will be available on demand, as educators seek out this kind of archival material. For any errors in description, translation, or interpretation, we are entirely responsible.

Carolyn Pope Edwards
Lella Gandini
John Nimmo
2015

Contents

Part IV. "Children Explore Wire"

Part V. "Children Find a Bug"

Part VI. "Children Set the Table for Lunch"

Part VII. Reggio Educators Respond to Video from a Massachusetts Preschool

Part I. Introduction

Background to the 1990 "Cooperation Study" video reflection meetings with Loris Malaguzzi and Diana Preschool educators.

A. Correspondence (English version) by Edwards and Gandini proposing the study to Reggio educators.

B. Preliminary Discussions: Notes (English) of two group reflection meetings that took place in Reggio Emilia, preliminary to the October 1990 meeting.

Stage 1. Notes (English) from meeting 2/6/1990 conducted in Italian by Lella Gandini, with Sergio Spaggiari (director), Tiziana Filippini (*pedagogista*), Vea Vecchi (*atelierista*), about a video that Carolyn Edwards and John Nimmo had compiled from edits taken from Carolyn's 1988 research videotapes made to study "Role of the Teacher."

Stage 2. Notes (English) from meeting 6/15/90 conducted in Italian by Lella Gandini with Loris Malaguzzi, Tiziana Filippini, Vea Vecchi, Magda Bondavalli, and Paola Strozzi, about a set of four videos that teachers had made in preparation for the upcoming October meeting.

Stage 3. Notes (English) from meeting 10/15/90 at 10:15 a.m. This was a small preliminary discussion conducted at Diana School prior to the larger afternoon session. Present were Carolyn Edwards, John Nimmo, Loris Malaguzzi, Vea Vecchi, and Tiziana Filippini. Tiziana acted as translator, and these notes were taken at the event by Carolyn and John.

C. Transcript of entire Cooperation video, translated into English by educators in Reggio Emilia and provided to the American researchers for reference.

9

A. Correspondence (English version) by Edwards and Gandini proposing the study to Reggio educators.

 UNIVERSITY OF MASSACHUSETTS AT AMHERST

Human Services and Applied Behavioral Sciences Division

School of Education
352 Hills South
Amherst, MA 01003

December 8, 1989

Dr. Sergio Spaggiari and Prof. Loris Malaguzzi
Nidi e Scuole dell' infanzia
Comune di Reggio Emilia
Via Guido Da Castello 12
42100 Reggio Emilia, Italia

Dear Sergio and Loris:

Greetings to you and to all of our friends in Reggio Emilia. We hope you are well and planning festive, joyful, and restful holidays.

We are writing to describe our small project involving the videotapes collected in the Diana School several years ago. Our purpose is to use the videotapes as a stimulus and starting point for a more critical, reflective, and provocative dialogue with your teachers than we have yet had. The videotapes contain so many images—layers of meanings—that we in Amherst hesitate to show and "explain" them to American audiences without first gaining your specific interpretations concerning pedagogical objectives that the Reggio teachers and administrators themselves can provide. Here we are guided by an important new methodology from the discipline of Anthopology embodied in a book, <u>Preschool in Three Cultures: Japan, China, and the United States</u>, by Joseph Tobin, David Wu, and Dana Davidson, Yale University Press, 1989. This method is called "multivocal ethnography" and is based on using film and video documents about a culture in a reflexive way to "stimulate the production of a dialogically structured text... an ongoing dialogue between insiders and outsiders, between practitioners and researchers, and between people of different cultures" (Tobin, 1989, in an article on "Visual Anthropology," p. 176).

However, we are not seeking to understand everything about your experience in our current project. Instead, we have a focus on what you call <u>the necessity for the child to participate in the collective life of the classroom, community, and culture, with the teacher serving as guide.</u> Here is an important statement, quoted by Lella Gandini, that seems key to understanding your experience:

Letter to Dr. Sergio Spaggiari and Prof. Loris Malaguzzi - Page 2

The child's potential does not develop in isolation, but rather in interaction with objects,
events, and other people. It is a continuous
transaction with the surrounding world. Images
are used to construct other images--passing through
sensations, feelings, interactions, problems, and
exchanges of ideas. The child needs active co-
participation by peers and adults. The co-parti-
cipation of adults should be competent, not haphazard.
The adults have to construct the occasions of knowledge and then experiment, modify, and widen the
scope and quality of the exploration. There should
be an explicit interaction between the modes and
tensions of the children's exploration, and the
modes and tensions of the adults' researches, in a
continuous process of learning. We thus gain children and adults who look for the pleasure of playing,
working, talking, thinking, and inventing together.
They come to better understand themselves, each
other, how the world works, how it could be made
better, and how it can be enjoyed in friendship.
Children work together, while teachers foster their
cooperation: teachers and children form a partnership.

While this statement no doubt seems obvious to you, we have
found that it eludes North American attempts to translate into
specific pedagogical objectives. North Americans agree in prin-
ciple with the statement, yet their cultural heritage leads them
to emphasize individualism and autonomy often at the expense of
the coming together of young minds in learning and co-thinking.
When viewing slides of Reggio Emilia, American teachers always ask,
"How can the teacher find a goal that will focus the attention of
many individuals?" What if a child doesn't want to join in?"
"Doesn't the teacher limit the creativity of individual children
in the process?" "How about the child whose work is not as imagi-
native and skilled as the others?" "Aren't 3-6 year-olds too young
and too egocentric to be expected to accomodate to one another?"
These are the sorts of questions that guide our study, which aims
toward deeper understanding of the Reggio approach through an interpretation drawn from your own words and insights.

An editted selection of pieces of videotape collected in 1988
in the Diana School will be prepared and then shown in three separate interview sessions regarding each classroom, i.e. one including
Laura and Marina (who worked with the 5-year-olds in 1988), one
including Magda and Marina (who worked with the 4-year-olds in
1988), and one including Paola and Guilia (who worked with 3-year-
olds in 1988). Others, such as yourselves, Vea Vecchi and Tiziana

Letter to Dr. Spaggiari and Prof. Malaguzzi - Page 3

Filippini might desire to participate, too, in one or more of the sessions. These sessions would be conducted at the participants' convenience during the year 1990. During each session we would ask the teachers and other to tell us, as we go slowly through the videotape, whether what they see is significant and "representative" of their children and classroom, then, as moments of particular tension or interest are encountered, we would take the opportunity to tell you some of the ideas we have heard from American educators to provide further richness and provocation to the discourse.

We hope you will give your permission for this study. We hope you will agree it will help us move to a higher level in interpreting and presenting your work, and that the project will prove stimulating and surprisingly informative to yourselves, as well.

Sincerely yours,

Carolyn Edwards, EdD
Professor of Education and
Human Development

CE:ET

B. Preliminary Discussions

Notes (English) of two group reflection meetings that took place in Reggio Emilia, preliminary to the October 1990 meeting.

Stage 1: February 6, 1990.

Discussion conducted at Diana School with Lella Gandini, Loris Malaguzzi, Sergio Spaggiari, Tiziana Filippini, Vea Vecchi, and all teachers of the Diana School, about an edit prepared by Carolyn Edwards and John Nimmo. (Carolyn Edwards and John Nimmo are not present). The decision was eventually made not to use this edit as a basis of further conversations (see Vea's comments below); instead the educators in Reggio Emilia would prepare their own video.

Translated into English by Lella Gandini.

Lella: When we made our original videos (in spring, 1988), our focus had been on the role of the teacher.

Vea: Yes, and that is why these original videos won't work if the goal is to look at cooperation between children. A technical problem with the edit is that it is difficult to hear what the children say. We suggest using an audiocassette backup; and more zoom should be used. But we are very interested in the theme of collaboration or cooperation. Here are several things that we don't like about the video that you prepared at the University of Massachusetts:

(1) Marina Castagnetti is seen helping the kids set up their sculptures on the stick. We all feel Marina is speaking too much. She exerts too much power in setting up the class.

(2) We have no objection to the tape of Laura Rubizzi with the boys and the VCR, drawing the map. But Laura said it was a very difficult day. She waited for them to solve their problems instead of working it out for them.

(3) In the excerpt of the 3-year-olds with the clay, we are very amused by the fact that the teacher Paola Strozzi appears with an apron on. She looks like a cook! It seems unprofessional. However, we are impressed by the children's perseverance; "they are only

three!"

(4) In the excerpt of the 3-year-olds with the leaves, we said to Giulia Notari, "You never crouch down to the level of the children," and then, right away, she does it. But before that, she was sort of hovering over the children. But Giulia was very pleased by what the children did, how long they did it, and so on.

Stage 2: June 15, 1990.

Discussion conducted at Diana School by Lella Gandini (Carolyn Edwards and John Nimmo not present) with Loris Malaguzzi, Vea Vecchi, Tiziana Filippini, Magda Bondavalli, Marina Castagnetti, and Paola Strozzi.

Translated into English by Lella Gandini.

This group has watched together the video they have prepared for the future meeting when Carolyn Edwards and John Nimmo travel to Italy. The video has 4 segments. *First,* three 4-year-old boys work together with clay. *Second,* three 4-year-old girls work together with clay. (In both cases, the teacher had asked the three children to make together an animal. The children could decide together what animal to make.) *Third,* a computer was brought by chance to the classroom and four boys decide to try to make it work. *Fourth,* we see 5-year-old children setting the table. This segment includes a spontaneous event of girls organizing an assembly line to set the table. Videotapes of the 3-year-olds were not ready to show Lella.

Vea notices that collaboration took place in calm moments. She also thought it would be interesting to have some video segment with real conflict. She thinks one must watch a video three times. Also it would be useful to have a transcription of the children's exact words. She would like to discuss these words with Lella and Loris to understand better what were the important aspects. Perhaps also captions on the video of the children's words would be useful.

Tiziana Filippini wants to know if the research team needs one or two episodes at each age (3, 4, and 5).

Vea says she is perplexed about that, because the material with which children are working, or the particular group who are together, can completely change the outcome [i.e. what happens with the group in terms of cooperation]. She notes that when children are 3-years-old, cooperation requires a very long time to happen.

Lella continues speaking about conflict, giving an example of an episode she once witnessed in Pistoia.

Tiziana comments on the fact that children in the videos she has just seen, especially the 4-year-olds interacting with the clay, demonstrate a great quality of civility and kindness to one another. All of the adults were very surprised when they noticed this through looking at the videos.

Loris Malaguzzi listens to Lella's example and begins talking about experiences, purely social experiences, that do not evidence any growth or learning [on the children's part]. He says: These experiences can help children learn how to socialize in the world and get along with other people and participate in everyday life. But these things could happen also in situations where the teacher is not present at all, so what is happening is some kind of ecological, unavoidable process but nothing may be learned. Social interaction of this kind is important, but at least according to some people, there is nothing cognitive happening.

It is important to establish the context of the exchanges that children have. We should control how long the exchange lasts, and the goal of it. Clay is the kind of material that [usually] cannot lead to exchanges that last a long time because after a while there is a lowering of the children's interest. Maybe we should choose materials that can allow for more significant exchanges among the children.

According to some theoreticians, social development is not connected at all to cognitive development; and exchanges which are affective in nature do not produce cognitive growth but instead

> *Just like a ball with which children are playing, the teacher should pick up the idea and throw it back, in order for both to understand what the children are "playing" and also to make the play more significant.*
>
> — Loris Malaguzzi

only a growth in interactive behavior. So it will be very important to record with care what children say in their exchanges, and then for teachers to pick something a child has said and elaborate it and give it back to the child. Just like a *ball* with which children are playing, the teacher should pick up the idea and throw it back, in order for both to understand what the children are "playing" and also to make the play more significant.

Another question is how and when are we to be sure that the children have experienced cognitive growth? And how can we prove it? How can we be sure that in terms of development that the children have arrived to another level? Also if there is an overlap of cognitive and social development, how can we determine how the two overlap and intermingle? That will be something very, very important to discover, and it is a theoretical question.

It is important, furthermore, to notice just when this kind of *sparkle* has occurred that shows intellectual development. When is it evident (or, at least, we have the perception of it, with the presumption the intellectual development has taken place)?

In other words, children can play for hours without this kind of sparkle. What goes on could instead be something that will help toward taking that step, but itself just be a preparatory step.

The infants at the *asilo nido* should be working in pairs. The teacher should create situations in which their behavior has the possibility to be very free and very ample, with lots of possibilities for children to exchange activities in pairs.

In my view, the way to spy on their change (even if one considers gestures and activity) is through the word, which means, if we do not record the words spoken, we do not record anything [meaningful or useful]. This much is absolutely clear... We also should record the quality of silences and the quality of pauses.

The big problem is that if we want to accept the

cooperative experience, we should also accept conflict. Also, it would be very different to see how cooperation works in an activity prepared by the teacher, versus in one that has not been prepared. And to see how the same children who work with clay would behave if they were given the suggestion to make an enchanted mountain; that would be a situation in which the children would be brought to a very strict form of cooperation because they would all contribute by means of materials, objects and activity to make this enchanted mountain. So we should set up a few situations.

It would be important to learn what would be predicted by the children and also what would be predicted by the adults. It would be useful to see, first, what are the individual predictions; then next to start the activity. If a project requires a sort of encounter with certain expectations on the part of the children, then the results—if they have not predicted that—then the outcome will be very different. For example, it is different to say to the children, "Now I am going to give you clay," versus, "We have a plan to do such and such, what do you think about that?" For instance, with the City and the Rain project [a project portrayed in the first edition of the exhibit, *The Hundred Languages of Children,* and the accompanying catalog, *The Hundred Languages of Children: Narrative of the Possible,* 1987, 1996], the children were led to expect something. Also in the case of the Long Jump [a project studied by George Forman, and analyzed in the first edition of *The Hundred Languages of Children: The Reggio Emilia Approach to Early Childhood Education,* edited by Edwards, Gandini, & Forman], the children were asked what they expected and thought about it. The more we succeed to ask the children to participate in this process of prediction and to give information, so that each one gives as much information as he or she knows, then this type of work will also give us the possibility and opportunity to diminish differences among children. That way we can succeed in establishing the participation of all

> So you, the teacher, take these words—this BALL—in your hands and then you repeat the idea in a way that is more clear.
>
> — Vea Vecchi

the children at a higher level. From an educational point of view, this is not a small thing!

Vea intervenes to clarify what Loris has been saying. She says: I want to tell you about something that happened today that relates to what you were saying about each child having a different level of understanding. I have the distinct and clear impression that when a child makes an observation, there is for him a mental image. If this mental image is not also shared by the other child or children, then there arises a problem of communication. I think that one of our roles as a teacher—in order to raise the level of participation—is to take the BALL (that you, Loris, mentioned before), the idea the child has had and that we know is a good ball (a good idea), but which we are not sure that all the children have understood, well, then, we should take it and throw it back to them, maybe even a bit later, but using language that has the very great possibility to be clearly understood.

I offer another example. When the children discover something new, they throw out sentences and words that sometimes are forceful and clear and reach the others, and sometimes are not. Sometimes their comments have just been said in a transitional way because they are about new things—for the person who says them, they are not yet completely acquired. Even to the person himself the idea is almost, but not completely, clear, so to the others the idea is not clear at all.

So you, the teacher, take these words—this BALL—in your hands and then you repeat the idea in a way that is more clear. For example, today we were working with shadows and water, and I said at one point, "Yes, it's true. Look, the reflection seems as if it is going down deep, and the shadow seems as if it is floating." So I gave the children these two terms that had already come out of their words yet had not quite come out. In this way, the play of participation and the play of communication really take place. Of course, communication may take place without your doing this, but it would be important not to miss such a situation.

I think it would be useful to have different phases of this problem of participation. For example, if there is a type of child who has difficulties communicating, then it would be important to create a particular situation. It would be ideal to have a variety of situations so great and terrific that it would be much easier to produce some results that would give us more satisfaction.

Loris agrees with Vea, and then says: It is important to know whether the children have already communicated among themselves, and how they have communicated. So it would be very important to examine what are the expectations of a child for an activity, on the basis of how they have communicated among themselves.

It is also important to have a different methodology for a project (investigation) that is expected to go on for a long time versus a project that is only supposed to last a short time.

One must also take into account the fact that sometimes the children are active but do not produce anything. The teacher should be able to expect this kind of time involving no production, because sometimes there is a sort of pressure on teachers to achieve the things that teachers expect to achieve. Therefore, it would be useful to have videotapes that are in real time—without cuts.

> I realize that with the video, I see much more complexity. And also with the video, we can cheat less with ourselves ...
>
> —Vea Vecchi

Vea: Where we have made cuts, you can always see the time elapsed (the counter) that says how much time has gone by. I think it would be very important to decide, here and now, what should be the structure [of our videotaping], how should be our interventions, and what should be the times involved, so that we all agree about this.

But **Loris** does not respond. Then the group begins to watch the video showing the three boys discussing how to make a dinosaur with clay.

Vea says the boys have worked for 50 minutes, always by themselves in a very civil way. For a while one boy was the leader; and then after making the first dinosaur, they went on to make another and a second boy became the leader. The verbal exchanges were very important, and in order to capture them, the teachers (Laura and Marina) placed a small microphone near the children.

Clearly, Vea, Laura, and Marina are enthusiastic about this videotape they have made.

Vea: I realize that with the video, I see much more complexity. And also with the video, we can cheat less with ourselves, while with slides, we can just take out all but the high points of an experience. Here with the video we can see the whole process and all its complexities.

Loris criticizes a bit the fact that there are too many things on the table and in the background. It doesn't look too clean, he says.

Laura Rubizzi and **Marina Castagnetti** reply that they have improved the visual appearance in subsequent videos.

After the video of the boys, the group watches the video of the three girls that were also required to make an animal together. Apparently the girls took an hour to decide what animal to do. They discussed together for a long time, looking at three or four books, and they asked a lot of questions. They then decided to make a tiger.

Loris notes immediately that probably there were too many things to discuss in this situation [for the girls]. Probably one should have diminished the number of variables, given them fewer paths to follow. The excess of choice could have slowed down and dampened the relevant enthusiasm of the children.

Then followed a discussion between Loris and the teachers about this situation with the girls: whether they had really understood that they were required to make one animal all together, or one animal each. Laura and Marina said that in fact the children were asked to make one animal together. (The teachers even went back a few times saying that.) But even so, the girls started making three different animals. Later, in this video, one of the three girls, who has made a tiger, has great difficulty in making it stand up.

Loris complains about this. He says: You should be aware of whether the children know all the preparatory techniques that would make it possible to solve such a problem. I don't think it is fair to let children get into this state of anguish; it's a sort of cruelty.

So a discussion follows. The teachers (**Laura** and **Marina**) say that this is a situation which is new for the three girls.

Vea: The children have had much experience in working with clay on a horizontal plane, but now for the first time—being 4-years-old—they feel the need to make the animal stand up. So the girls run into new problems, and they are not yet capable of transferring their knowledge of old problems to solve this new one.

Loris continues to criticize the way the teachers have taught.

Vea tries to make her point that this is a sort of more advanced situation that involves new problems to solve.

But the discussion between Loris and Vea lasts a long time.

Vea: I think this highlights the importance and usefulness of video, because it makes us think more. Certain things emerge more clearly than before; we see them in a more complex way.

Loris: Well, but the important thing is to see whether the children have *learned.*

Vea protests once more and tries also to protect Marina and Laura, the teachers under scrutiny.

Loris interrupts and tries to sum up the situation. He says: With the video, you say that you see many more things than you had seen before. The technical aspects of the video have also come under discussion. You have improved your technique; you have tried different methods and used different materials with the children. Now I would like to ask you which of these videos are, according to you, ready to be shown to other people? Do you think they are what you want other people to see—people who work, as you do, with young

children and on matters of cooperation? Because as regards us [the research team], these videos seem very valuable, and just exactly what we would desire for a discussion.

Vea: Well, I would be glad to send them—just taking out a few parts because they are too long. The one of the girls and the clay, especially, I think it is ready to go. I still think the girls needed time to make mistakes, and long times are very relevant [for children]. Yes, I would use these videos as they are.

Tiziana adds that she would like to add the other video which has the children discussing around the computer.

Vea describes this discussion again.

Tiziana: It is very beautiful.

Loris: All of these things are very important—to put these points into discussion, to criticize them—really to discuss, discuss, discuss.

He then goes on to talk about different combinations of children in groups of two, three, and four. He says that this research exercise ought to proceed by means of a series of attempts, in order to represent the best thing for people who work with children.

Stage 3: October 15, 1990, at 10:15 a.m.

This is a preliminary discussion conducted at Diana School prior to the afternoon session. Present are Carolyn Edwards, John Nimmo, Loris Malaguzzi, Vea Vecchi, and Tiziana Filippini. Tiziana acted as translator, and these notes were taken at the event by Carolyn and John. The discussion is about the set of video excerpts from the Common School in Amherst, Massachusetts, that the Diana educators will watch on the last day of work together.

[Editors' note: That video-reflection transcript of the discussion of the Amherst video is included in this volume in Part VII. In this preliminary discussion, which also sets the stage for the days to follow, Loris Malaguzzi speaks clearly about the purpose of teachers analyzing together and reflecting on their own classroom videotapes].

Tiziana describes how, before taping, they had led some meetings with teachers and staff of Scuola Diana and Asilo Nido Rodari, and asked

Malaguzzi to attend. They held two meetings to try to understand what is collaborative learning and what is cognitive conflict—to understand what the research should be looking for and also what kind of methodology could support those goals. Thus, she says, the research served as "a provocation for us."

Loris is concerned about what is their "motivation" for watching and discussing the video. He suggests that it is best to collectively look at a video and then obtain a range of points of view and different interpretations that then need to be discussed to reach a "common point of view." It is best to work toward a theoretical compilation, and obtain a "circle of ideas" to get a common view. This approach is necessary in order to gain further knowledge and improve methodology—to gain an increase of ideas and an improvement of the methodology. Otherwise we find out each other's point of view and if there are differences, we learn this, but we do not progress or move forward. Of course, it is not necessary they we agree on everything. Each event is a story that hangs within a system, in relationship to other events. An event is not just that—what you see in a moment—it is always something that develops as part of other events. If this happens for children, so it does also for adults.

> [I]t is best to collectively look at a video and then obtain a range of points of view and different interpretations that then need to be discussed to reach a "common point of view."
>
> —Loris Malaguzzi

John Nimmo: That's exactly what the Common School teachers in Amherst, Massachusetts, remarked on, also—talking about trying to get past a snapshot feeling about the video segments.

Tiziana nods in agreement.

Loris: The other question is this. When adults look at the video in a critical way ("read critically the video"), we must consider three things, not only the behavior we see. First, we must consider the evolution of the interpersonal relationship among the children. Second, we must consider the evolution of the cooperative learning or thought. And third, we must consider the value of the verbal language they use, because the kind of communication used by the children has a lot of influence on what is going on—at least that is our point of view. We have to avoid analyzing the video only in terms of the behavior seen. There are some events that happen inside the bigger events. I mean, perhaps working with the computer is a big event, but inside this big event are many small events that happen many times. And if we try to understand these, we may generate a new code to read this situation. We have made some attempts, but we are not sure of the results, to make some graphics with the aid of the computer. We have tried to analyze the different categories of words and different categories of thought that we think we see arise at different times in this sequence of children working with the computer. We think that if we can better understand these categories of words and thought, then we will better understand what is going on [in the big event]. So later we will try to explain more clearly what we think about all this.

Tiziana: Yes, while observing the verbal language and watching some particular small events that happen many times within the main situation.

Carolyn: You will explain more of your thinking about what you are telling me now.

Tiziana: Yes.

Carolyn: Now, we share some of those same understandings with you about how things fit into a larger flow.

That was one reason that I was concerned about Loris watching the Common School video before you had heard the background information—

Tiziana laughs.

Carolyn: And this is the script that will provide much of what you are talking about. Indeed, we have exact transcriptions of the words of the children, in case you want to understand more precisely some of the small events and how they fit into the larger picture. (Editors' Note: This transcript was in English and was not drawn upon in the discussions that followed).

Tiziana translates Carolyn's words into Italian for Vea and Loris. She then says: You are right, Carolyn, about this idea of not showing the Common School video to Malaguzzi without having given the presentation about the school. You must keep all of this together and not give him only the video. (She laughs as Loris interrupts). We agree with you! It's a good feeling that Loris is expressing—it's just to try to tell you from what point of view he is trying to work concerning this content.

John: One of the things in the script are quotes from the teachers' own words—what they said when viewing their videos. These provide context to the video pieces.[5 minute pause]

Carolyn: This morning's discussion seems to me an example of the way you work with children—con-tinuing to stick with a discussion until the tension is resolved and there is a solution, not simply quitting after everyone has stated their opinion.

Tiziana: Yes, the important thing is not just to hear diverse points of view, but instead to go so far with the discussion that it is clear that each person has taken something in and moved in his or her thinking, as a result of what has been heard. This involves a sharing of understanding that allows for a joint next step together.

Loris: When the spotlight is first put on an issue—for example, when you first think about videos in terms of collaboration—the spotlight is blinding. We must adapt to the light. So what people first say about the videos is not so interesting. What is more interesting is what people think after they hear one another and move to the next step or the next. This is why we have done so much preparation for your visit.

> *Yes, the important thing is not just to hear diverse points of view, but instead to go so far with the discussion that it is clear that each person has taken something in and moved in his or her thinking, ...*
>
> *— Tiziana Filippini*

C. Transcript of entire "Cooperation" video, translated into English by educators in Reggio and provided to Americans for reference

1. May, 1990

Setting: Table with clay, and boys from the 4-year-old class: Marco M., Filippo and Alan. (Later Tommaso and Alessandro). Teacher, Laura Rubizzi. (Alan is singing) . This episode is discussed in Part II,A.

Alan: Oh! This is the stomach! No, it is a leg, I must finish!

Marco: I am making the body.

Filippo: I do the head.

Alan: What a big ball of clay you took Marco! It is gigantic!

Marco: I do the head that is more better (yes).

Marco: Make it rounder!

Filippo: The eyes…

Marco: Make them narrow, like that.

Alan: Here it is (the leg) I hold it on. Laura, look what a beautiful leg!

Marco: Here I made the food.

Alan: No, you have to make a monster.

Marco: Okay, get ready!

Filippo: The nose, the mouth…

Alan: Square.

Marco: Bravo! Good!

Filippo: Oh! With all those things to eat it will become fat!

Marco: Look what food I made for him!

Alan: Marco, a foot!

Marco: Give it to me, I'll put it on for you, we need an extra piece (he elongates it).

Alan: In the meanwhile I'll do the other.

Filippo: Oh! We should finish it!

Marco: (to Alan) Bigger, bigger!

Filippo: (Makes and attempt to attach the head with the mouth toward the ceiling)

Marco: No stupid, the behind!

Filippo: Ah! (He turns the head around, the impres-sion is that only Marco has clear in his mind how the parts should be put together).

Marco: Is it true that these are the back legs? Now, I am doing the front.

Filippo: Is it the behind?

Marco: Yes, prepare also the nose! Sharp teeth, cut the mouth.

Filippo: How do I do it? You do it.

Marco: Ok! Gimme gimme, I make it rounder! Let's see, let's see!

Filippo: Moustache! (They laugh)

Filippo: I do the nose.

Marco: Let's put the other piece that is finished already, ok! Let's see. (He adds a paw)

Filippo: Let's see our room! (They laugh)

Alan: Ok boss, here is ready another foot.

Marco: To attach.

Alan: Here it is (*Uses the formal verb as to a superior.*)

Marco: Oh thank you! Another foot, we need another foot, damn' foot!

Filippo: Here, where do I put the head?

Marco: Now put it there, not like that (While Filippo had modified the head, by applying the legs he seems to make Marco change his point of view. Now the head is placed more to the left.)

Filippo: Oh! Sorry, like that?

Marco: Turn a little like that. You said a long neck, and now make a long neck.

Filippo: Ah, cute. Sorry!

Alan: But, how can we do now?

Marco: Ah, we forgot that we needed fins. I make marks (Textures the skin).

Filippo: Here is the neck! Gentlemen, here is the long neck!

Marco: No, longer!

Filippo: Long like the school? (He laughs making a funny face.) Lets make it longer! There are two, should we make two heads?

Alan: Let's do two heads? Do you want (agree) to do two heads?

Marco: Ok.

Filippo: Yeah, I agree, one head goes here.

Marco: Oh guys, I forgot the tail, here it is. (They leave the figure to look at the books.)

Alan: Why don't we make this one and then we do another?

Filippo: Should we make it as large as the school?

Alan: How old are you Filippo?

Filippo: Five!

(They speak about toys that Filippo does not seem to know, but Alan seems at a certain point to have found a toy that he has and the other two also have)

Filippo: Come on, the head!

Marco: But I have the head. Why don't we make him mad? So that he can destroy everything, here it is, mad, it seems mad to you? (He shows it to Filippo, then glances at it and says yes with his head)

(Filippo captures the attention of his companions by telling about an adventure he had at the luna-park and then goes on singing)

Filippo: Stop worrying [if] he is my type, stop worrying [if] he is my type…oh! Should we do also drops of dirt? Lets pretend that it was climbing!

Marco: A large volcano.

Filippo: Why worry, here is the neck.

Alan: Should we do four fins?

Marco: (to Filippo) Do you agree?

Filippo: Yes, I agree very much!

Alan: Yes, let's do it!

Filippo: First we finish this on.

Alan: Are we going to do all of them? First we do this one, than this one, than this one…

Filippo: But all the dinosaurs that are in the book will fit?

Alan: Also, this one… you have to make beaks, the little hands, the wings.

Filippo: Why worry, he is my type.

Marco: The last one we do is the mammoth?

Marco: (Working on the dinosaur) To make it stand now I will take the brush. (He wants to layer the mixture of clay and water as if it were glue under the feet of the dinosaur.)

Filippo: But there is already a little of …watch out (why worry) then help us!

Alan: Well, the little nails and the little hands of that bird.

Filippo: Who is going to help me to make this stand?

Marco: But I am still doing the eyes.

Filippo: Oh, it doesn't stand up (tries to make it stand by himself).

Alan: (to the teacher) Laura, it does not stand up.

Teacher: What do you think that you could use?

Alan: That kind of chicken–wire

Marco: That's right, quick!

Filippo: Quick! Oh, can you help me Laura?

Marco: I start making a little small neck (of another prehistoric animal)

Teacher: No, it is almost standing.

Filippo: Here we are!

Alan: How nice, why don't we place another foot so that it can stand?

(They go back to look at the initial stage)

Marco: At the end of the tail it has a sort of nut.

Alan: With spikes.

Marco: We made some marks (on the skin), we'll do what we can do okay?

Filippo: Absolute silence, I said, absolute silence for the workers.

Alan: A point spike? Look, all of you.

Marco: Put it here on the tail.

Filippo: The tail is here. He is my type. We are almost done, is it standing? Yes.

Marco: It is all done, should we make a cross?

Filippo: Laura, if Roberta comes she will be scared by that face!

Alan: Is something missing?

Marco: Wait, I'll do the tongue. (They laugh.)

Filippo: The cheeks, the cheeks! The pupil, I have already made the pupil. Now we can make this one (another animal). Marco, Alan, we can make this one, it is a good one! What a neck! Here I make the wings; gimme I am going to cut it a bit.

Marco: Oh look, put here some sticking glue, now here, enough!

Alan: Another wing?

Filippo: Here Alan, like this one (shows the one he made).

Marco: Make it bigger Alan!

Filippo: We are already almost finished

(Two friends arrive, Tommaso and Alessandro)

Filippo: Tommi, come on, look, we did this one, now we make another one.

Tommaso: Bravo! If you want I can help!

Marco: Yes, we are doing this one...so you should help us do this one if you can!

Filippo: And then this other one, come on quick, otherwise we'll get tired and you will get tired.

Alan: Is this ok?

Marco: Tommi, Look!

2. Spring 1990

Encounter with the computer. Boys from the 4-year-old class-room—who are now Alan 5 [yrs]:4 [mos]; Alessandro 4:7; Marco 5:2; Tommaso 5:2; Teacher: Laura Rubizzi or Marina Castaghetti. This episode is not discussed in the videoreflection meetings.

Tommaso: Why does it not work? Perhaps you do not need this. He strikes a few keys, then goes behind the computer. Here is why! It is the plug! One second I am going to try...why nothing comes up? (Strikes hard the keyboard along with Marco). One second.. (He strikes the key to turn on the video than turn to Alessandro.) Do you see? Nothing happens there.

Marco: Let's try to write: Fifi, our names... Marco, Tommaso, Alan...well where is M?

Marco: This is T (Points to the keyboard)

Tommaso: Why does it not come up? (he turns to the teacher)

Marco: M this is A...

Tommaso: MARCO ARCO

Marco: Then, I did this for this, this or this, then this and this.

Tommaso: Do you need this?

Teacher: Maybe you need to strike all the other keys?

Marco: (gets up and hits the screen with his fists) Ah gear, gears, my father goes always... (going behind the computer) gears, gears, gears (under his breath almost singing).

Tommaso: (goes near M. behind the video) here is why. It is a small light, come and see! It is the blue one, see if I turn it off? Do you see that now it is gone? Do you see the tiny light?

Marco: But I was the one that turned it on.

Tommaso: Here we found it.

Marco: (pointing to the arrows on the keyboard) My father uses these two, this one to go backward and this one to forward, this one to go this way (indicates to the left) and this one go that way (indicates to the right) catch! What the hell did this to me! (points to the screen)

Alessandro: (laughs and all the children strike together the keyboard).

Marco: (strikes with care a few keys without asking) Ah!

Alessandro: Where is X?

Marco: X...I...

Tommaso: E I (he strikes a few keys).

Marco: Enough!

Tommaso: May I sit here a minute?

Marco: Write from there (standing up)

Teacher: No, Marco, let also Tommaso write the right place.

(Tommaso sits at the computer)

Tommaso: Where is E?

Alan: I.

Tommaso: I have to make lots of lots because I am to write a very long word. C is this C?

Alessandro: Yes that is C.

Tommaso: I I I I know I, T...A

Teacher: CITA you wrote cita.

Marco: May I start again when Alan is finished?

(Alessandro sits at the counter)

Alessandro: Where is L L L? Where is E? A A E S S A..?

Alan: ALESA.

Tommaso: Alessandra? (they laugh)

Alessandro: (spells his own name pointing to the letters on the screen) A L E S S three S (they all laugh).

(Alan sits at the computer)

Marco: NNNEN? N A N A (It means midget, they all laugh)

Alan: What is written?

Alessandro: It is written Alan.

Tommaso: Alan Frocesco.

Marco: GGGGGGG

3. Spring 1990

Videogame; the discovery and revision of rules within a group of children from the 4-year-old class: Alan 5:4; Alessandro 4:7; Marco 5:2; Riccardo 5:4; Pierluigi 4; Mariateresa 4:11; Cariaca 4; Filippo 4; Tommaso 5:2; Loriana [age?]. Mariateresa, Cariaca, and Loriana are girls; the others are boys. This episode is not discussed in the videoreflection meetings.

(Marco is sitting at the computer)

Marco: Come on…it fell down!

Tommaso: It was eaten up!

Marco: Nothing.

Tommaso: Jump, Marco, (softly) come on!

Marco: Dang!

Tommaso: (at the computer) (Encouraging) NO NO NO come on come on come on!

Alan: Come on!

Marco: There is only one hope!

Alan: Come on!

Marco: The last one.

Tommaso: No! Eaten up.

(Alessandro explains the ideas to Loriana)

Alessandro: With this one (key) you can jump (shows the screen) only on the empty lines and not on the ones that are full.

Alan: Those (full lines) are cages, you have to tell her!

Alessandro: Jump, Brava! Ah! You will!

(Marco explains the rules to Riccardo)

Marco: This (key) to go this way (points to the screen) when you must jump here, you should not jump these…these…these…you must get here understand?

Riccardo: Yes…I'm gunna to try…I have to press this one, right?

Marco: Right.

Alan: You very very good Richi!

Loriana: Ah, he fell down!

Riccardo: One should have…

Marco: And now you have to go there.

Alan: You very very good.

Pierluigi: You have to go up to there and then you have to go back (turning to Marco), right?

Marco: Yes.

Pierluigi: You must go, Richi, win!

Alan: Bravo!

(Riccardo explains the rules to Mariateresa)

Riccardo: …without letting them get you, you must arrive up here…if you jump one of these small forms you die and if you arrive here you must return there (pointing to the video). Jump!

Mariateresa: Which one is the one to jump? (three of the children point to the key to use).

Riccardo: Do you see there is a monsteroid.

Marco: Is there a monsteroid?

Riccardo: Come on, here it is…there is an ugly one.

Pierluigi: My god…right, Marco?

Riccardo: Well, but I made it!

Pierluigi: You must win!

Marco: (turning to it) Now it is his turn.

Mariateresa: (getting up to leave the place for Pierluigi) Yes.

Marco: Come on!

Pierluigi: You tell me how to do it?

Marco: This key to go this way (to the left) this to go that way (to the right). You must go only on those (he points to the screen) if you don't go you die right away. You must go first there and then come back here. Come on! You can go…no. Just a moment.

Pierluigi: Right?

Marco: Yes, bravo.

(Marco is at the computer. The group is viewed from behind)

Pierluigi: You were here…you must win Richi!

Marco: Then when it is here, it is transformed (singing) into Superbunny!

Marco: Should we have Riccardo always do it? Come on! He is the strongest!

Filippo: Then when he does not win it is still his turn.

Pierluigi: When one dies, it is the turn of another one.

Filippo: So, who will have another turn?

Pierluigi: And the one who loses…another takes a turn?

Filippo: Yes. It is the turn of another one.

Marco: He lost.

Riccardo: And now it is somebody else's turn.

Pierluigi: Somebody else… it is my turn.

(Riccardo starts getting up, but Marco holds him there)

Marco: No, let's do it this way, who loses does it again, who wins, another one does it (leaves the place to another one).

Pierluigi and **Filippo:** Yes, yes.

Riccardo: Who wins all games?

Marco: There are these games; this line here (points to the screen), this line there, and then it is somebody else's turn.

Filippo: Right!

4. Spring 1990

Boys from the 5-year-olds class, setting the table: Christian 5:11; Daniele 5:7; plus those that come in to talk to them. Teacher: Giulia Notari. This episode is discussed in Part VI, A.

Daniele: Here is the parking lot…lets put the table-cloth…sorry it is the wrong side.

Christian: Let's go to this table.

Daniele: No. To that one!

Christian: oh la la…no I will count them (the dishes)…4…5…

(Beatrice comes in.)

Beatrice: Listen, Christian, will you put me near Cecilia, Eleonare and Alice?

Christian: We shall see later.

Daniele: Wait (counts the dishes) 1…2…3…4 (then counts them on the cart) 1…2…3…4

(Andrea comes in.)

Andrea: Will you put me near Gianluca?

Christian: Yes.

Andrea: And near you!

Christian: Yes.

Daniele: No; we cannot do that because Christian goes there and I go there. (It is a table with only two places.) I'll put you here and Gianluca here, ok?

Christian: Or we can put the two of you here (points to the facing table).

Andrea: Okay (she goes away).

Daniele: Who is this? (He tries to read the name of the owner on the envelope that holds the napkin).

Christian: Wait a minute. I have to read here … maybe there is not

Daniele: Yes there is … but it is hard to see …

Christian: Show me … Federico maybe.

Daniele: Federico!

(Elisa comes in.)

Elisa: With whom did you put me?

Daniele: Look by yourself.

Elisa: Well, Daniele, don't you want to tell me where you put me?

(In the meanwhile other children have come in, it is difficult to follow what they say, but they are dealing with the caps of mineral water bottles. This distracts the two boys who are setting the table from Elisa's request.)

Christian: Why should we know?!

Daniele: Is this yours? (He is asking Elisa if it is her envelope with napkin).

Elisa: Yes.

Christian: Near Michele.

Elisa: And I don't like it.

Daniele: (sings) (the five Samurai…)

(Elisa is mad; a teacher, Giulia Notari, comes in)

Daniele: You don't want to stay near Michele?

Elisa: NO! Oh, finally you do understand!

Giulia Notari: Find an agreement among yourselves. Elisa find an agreement with them.

Christian: With whom do you want to sit?

Elisa: With….Francesco!

Christian: No! You stay where we have placed you. (He probably says this mostly because Francesco had been placed at the table of Gianluca and Andrea who had come before to ask to have favored places.)

Elisa: Alright! (Elisa leaves, mad, stamping her feet and slamming the door.)

Christian: (Runs after her, calls her, and gets her in the classroom.) Do you want to stay near Mariagiulia? (He asks this twice.)

Elisa: (mad) Do what you like!

5. Spring 1990

Girls setting the table 5-year-olds class: Elisa F. 5:10; Mariagiulia (no. 1) 5:6; Elisa M. (no. 2) 5:10; Elena (no. 3) 5:6; Francesca (no. 4) 5:6. This episode is discussed in Part VI, A.

Elisa F.: (sings) (Stoppi, stoppi, stoppi stop) Come all here! (Stoppi, stoppi, stoppi stop) Without singing, without whistling, without speaking, only…when I tell you and … pass it on, pass it on, hurry, stop! (La la la la la … li li li li li) Number 1 (she places her friends calling them according to their place in the handing on of dishes) Number 2, number 3 stay there. Number 4 come on, come on, come on! Now we change rhythm…let's sing…come on, come on come on! Without dancing, without musiching (yes), without drawing setting the table with the dishes little dishes…start…stop! Come on Francesca now there remains this to do and now…come, number 1.

Francesca: (singing and spelling) But to Daniele and to Gianluca they are not W A I T E R S ers ers ers.

Elisa F.: In any case we are going to place them just the same…number 1 stay here, number 2 stay here, number 3 stay here, number 4 here…without musiching, without drawing…stop!

(Now Elisa explains to her friends how to sing Papaveri and Papere (Poppies and ducks, a well known pop song).)

Elisa F.: You (to Elisa M.) have to sing with her, with them. (Do you know that the poppies are tall, tall, tall…) and going la, la, la you can sing everything, do you understand? But going; Tra la lala la, do you understand? Together with me! Come on you all sing! Like that!

All: Sing (Do you know that…)

Elisa F.: (But one day a duck asked her father) Come on! (To marry a duck … no a poppy, to marry a duck, how one does? La la la la.)

6. April 1990

In the afternoon two boys from the 5-year-olds class prepare the cots for the afternoon nap. Christian 5:11; Daniele 5:7 (Other children come in to check on them). This epsode is discussed in Part VI, A.

Christian: I think so, I think Gianluca usually sleeps.

Daniele: Then I will put him near Pedrau, I'll make a double bed (two or more cots placed together with one blanket across to keep them together, and another blanket as a cover for both children). The same for us, we are three?

Daniele: I'll place it in the other direction.

Christian: Than mine, then the other and we cover with the blanket of Andrea Campani.

Daniele: Wait, I am going to place it in the other direction.

Christian: And we are going to cover ourselves with the blanket of Andrea Campani?

Daniele: Excellent idea!

Christian: Excellent idea. Let's put three blankets (they place the pillows).

Daniele: Is this right? Is it his pillow?

(In the meanwhile near the cots the children place the favorite toys of the children that are going to use them)

Christian: Under your cot (Daniele is placing his skateboard under his cot).

Daniele: (the Seven Samurai) (Then only his voice is heard) Should we place the toys that the other children have?

(They both sing a song)

Daniele: Wait before…I'll tell when you have to put things.

Christian: I'll put it now. (They sing)

Daniele: Whose pillow is this?

Christian: (singing) I do not remember.

Daniele: (singing) My God, we are in serious trouble.

Mariagiulia: (Comes in to check where they placed her.) Daniele, near whom did you put me?

Daniele: Do you know whose pillow is this?

Mariagiulia: That one is mine!

Daniele: And this one? (It is a large bag with pillow and blanket.)

(In the meanwhile also Chiara and Cecilia have come in.)

Cecilia: It is mine!

Chiara: And where is my blanket?

Christian: Ah! Let's make for everybody a double bed!

Part II. "Clay Animals"

A learning encounter led by teacher Laura Rubizzi with 4-year-old children.

A. Transcript (English) of the group reflection meeting on 10/15/90 about the teaching/learning episode. Participating were Loris Malaguzzi (director), Tiziana Filippini (*pedagogista*, translating), teachers Laura Rubizzi, Giulia Notari, Paola Strozzi, Marina Castagnetti, and Magda Bondavalli, Vea Vecchi (*atelierista*), Carolyn Edwards and John Nimmo, and two visitors from Norway. (Note: The transcript of the video under discussion is found in Part I.C.1 of this volume).

B. Charts (Italian) prepared by Laura Rubizzi to summarize children's interaction, which she presented during the meeting on 10/15/90.

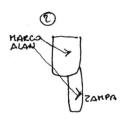

27

A. English transcript of the group reflection meeting on 10/15/90 about the teaching/learning episode

Children 4-Years-Old Build Animals of Clay

Setting: October 15, 1990, at 4: 00 p.m. Present at the discussion are Loris Malaguzzi, Tiziana Filippini (translating), Laura Rubizzi, Giulia Notari, Paola Strozzi, Marina Castagnetti., Magda Bondavalli, Vea Vecchi, Carolyn Edwards, John Nimmo, and two visitors from Norway. Alberta Basaglia from Venice translated this tape with Carolyn Edwards.

Laura presents a summary of the video, utilizing a chart of the coded behavior.

Carolyn: [Tiziana translates into Italian throughout]. Let's begin by my expressing for everyone the great interest there is in the United States concerning the meetings we have been having, and the great appreciation of many people for this work that you have been doing with us, and our desire to hear the ideas of all the teachers who have been participating in this valuable project. We have listened with great interest to the interviews that Laura, Paola, and Magda and Marina Mori did with Lella Gandini, and we have used those ideas in thinking about what we wanted to ask today with regard to the videotape, and so although we have only seen this videotape briefly, much of what we are asking is drawn from those excellent interviews. We see the videotape as not the reality of your teaching but rather an opportunity for you to tell us more about your teaching and how you think about your teaching.. So we want to go through the videotape slowly and give the teachers an opportunity to say what they thought was happening and why, and also we have a few specific questions that we would like to include in the interview today. In responding, we would like to hear first from the teacher who was involved in the teaching, and second, from all of the other teachers. The first question we have is a general one. We know that this videotape with the boys is a piece of videotape that you felt very good about

giving to us. We wanted to know *why* you found this videotape so valuable [*valido e significante*] to explain children's cooperative learning.

Tiziana: Do you want an answer to this question? One at a time?

Carolyn: Yes, let's answer this one and then go on.

Laura: It was decided that I have to introduce the material.

Vea: No, Carolyn just said that we have to answer the questions.

Laura: [nervous laughter] No, but I was going to answer.

Loris: Oh, I thought....

Tiziana: We didn't understand what was going on. So, we don't look at the video, we just answer your question?

Carolyn: This question does not refer to any particular part of the video, so we can't look at the video yet.

Tiziana: So we will just answer to this question.

Laura: The cooperative learning [*l'apprendimento cooperativo*] is a very important subject in our experience. And perhaps also thanks to the relationship we have with you. And so it will also help us with our research. Since last year we made six pieces of video. And with the moments of discussion that we had with other teachers, they [the videos] have continued to be things we have worked on and studied. Because we have thought that this was a good video.

We began videotaping the situation of a small group—three children playing with clay [*creta*]—because as you saw also this morning during the visit, frequently in our organization, having two teachers working at the same time, one teacher works with a small group, and the second one instead has a kind of work that is coordinating many different groups of children [facilitating the other children] that in the same time work in several different ways. We tried to understand what happens inside one of these small groups of children—three boys—to whom for the first time it was proposed to make together a prehistoric animal in clay. This is what we asked of this group, and after this they began their work. We wanted to understand—it was our interest in understanding—what was going to happen within this group [of three children]. There was an adult—that was I—available to children to come to. But I wasn't available only to this group of children; I was available also to another group that was doing another work. So I wasn't a figure always present. We thought that this way could be good, thinking that it is a thing that happens every day. Because it looks to us important to understanding what happens inside these small groups. This is our way of organization, this is in a few words what has been our work.

Tiziana states how they started thinking about this topic since you asked us to collaborate with you in this research, and the fact that they made six videos on this topic, that it is not only important for the research that you are doing, but also we get excited about this topic, and so we get very much involved, and then she tried to explain what happens normally when they start working with the children. The fact that there are different groups working, that one teacher may coordinate different small groups that are working, and this kind of video that we are going to see, is good because, just because we are going to see what normally happens. The teacher is taking care of this group and also another group at the same time. That is a normal situation that happens every day. They just wanted to understand as adults how the children can work together making the same thing. In this case they asked the children if they wanted to make together an animal. So it is quite an everyday situation.

Carolyn: Good, that is very helpful.

Laura: I wanted to say one more thing. The first time we saw the video, we liked it very much because the first impression we had was of children very polite [*civile*], that were able to have a kind, or polite, relationship [*rapporto civile*]. The moments in which they could be listening—the attentive moments—were very long. This activity has gone on for more than an hour. And it looked to us that they also liked staying together. This was the very first impression we had. Then came the second one. It was this. I asked myself, what did these children get: not just their staying together, but beyond their just staying together? Is it possible to

understand something more about this way of staying together? So it was possible to get to understand better what were the dynamics in the relationship between the children. And so many questions arose, and the need of getting into it much more for understanding more.

Tiziana: [translates in English] The first time Laura saw this video, she liked the way the children were staying together. They were having a very good and fair relationship among themselves, and also they paid very much attention to what was going on. They spent about one hour in doing this. And also there was a lot of joy and happiness in what they were doing.

But the second impression was, well, have those children realized more than what I just saw the first time? I mean, is there something more than the fact that they are enjoying staying together? Have they realized something or learned something more? What kind of dynamics, really, happen among them?

Carolyn: All right. Does Laura want to begin looking at the video now?

Laura: I don't know if you want to see it, but we already saw it ourselves. I thought I could [first] speak about some points I took from it. I will tell you the more important moments of the video. Then, in case we can eventually see it [the video], for example, I can say. . .

Tiziana: Can't you say it while we are watching the video?

Laura: It's not so easy. Also because the video goes on for 15 minutes. There is a problem. The activity has gone on for an hour. We have two video recordings: one that cuts the hour down to half an hour; and another that cuts the half an hour down to a quarter of an hour. So I have been able to put together a structure through the analysis of the [complete] audiotape of the dialogue of the children.

Tiziana: [in English]: Laura has written down some key words for better understanding the video. The video lasts only 15 minutes, but the whole [original] situation lasted one hour. So she probably recuperated from the tape recorder a lot of things that are not on the video. If she gives us some of the key notes, then we may better understand what comes out of the dialogue.

Carolyn: Let's do that. I don't think you need to translate all of that for me, rather let's not take the time to do that, but instead record it and Lella will explain it to me later. [Tiziana translates this and the work proceeds].

Laura: Perhaps it is better that I explain to you something about the groups. Well, then. This videotaping has been done in the classroom where there were children 4-years-old. There were three children, and the question was the one we said before. The children are in the central part of the classroom. Also it was easier to videotape them there. They had a big piece of red clay, a thread of wire for cutting the clay [*tagliaterra*]. In addition, on top of the table near there, there were some books in case children needed them, and some animals that children individually had previously made were on shelves that the children could reach. On a second table there were materials that usually children use for making structural foundations. When they have to make animals, it usually doesn't work without something that holds the animals up, for example, pieces of wire, pieces of wet cloth. There were three of us there, and yet another teacher was present to watch the other children. Marina was the cameraman, and at the beginning she also had to make a photo record [*foto reportage*] parallel to the video record. Then, there was the audio recorder turned on, for trying to get all the dynamics coming through children.

The three protagonists were three boys: Alan, 4: 9; Marco, just turning 5; and Filippo, 4: 11. Why three boys? Because I was interested in going on with a study of the strategies in the masculine groups. The same thing has been done with a group of girls.

Why these three boys, given all the ones we had? Because they aren't a close threesome. Two of them play frequently together, and the third one usually has other partners in his games. Alan and Marco, the two of them that you know, usually go on with their activities by themselves in a very autonomous way and prefer having as a referent an adult, either me or Marina. The third one, Filippo, tends to work as little as possible, forgetting work done in the end. And only sometimes does he work harder. They all use the clay in more or less the same way. And also they have ways of staying together. Filippo and Marco have the same way of staying together, while instead Alan is a child more reserved, much more careful in the things he chooses.

We must first consider the kind of videotaping we have done, because I found myself in a big difficulty. I had a big problem in putting together the edited videotaping with the audiotaping. And another thing has provided a complication; there has been a reduction of the time. Because very frequently 15 minutes of videotaping aren't enough for understanding which are the *knots*[1] through which the thing goes. So ideally I think it would be better to have a continual videotaping, and then you work on the material that comes on that. Also because the parts that are only audiotaped, compared to what are the children's expressions, the children's dynamics, the dynamics that the images provide, are two important facts. And sometimes reading it only in one way, looking at that situation, it seems you can see also other situations.

Marina C: And also because the visual language, there are moments that aren't held up [kept up] by different modalities of communication. You can get the importance of a sentence that in the whole text can be "neutral"[meaningless] and when you

---

1. The idea of "knots" is explained in Carolyn Edwards' chapter on the Role of the Teacher in the edited book by Edwards, Gandini, and Forman, *The Hundred Languages of Children* (all 3 editions). In project work with children, not only must the larger investigation contain meaty problems, but even a daily work session should ideally contain sticking-points, or "knots." Just as a knot (whorl) in wood grain impedes a saw cutting through, and just as a knot (tangle) in thread stops the action of a needle sewing, just so any problem that stops the children and blocks their action is a kind of cognitive knot. It might be caused by a conflict of wills or lack of information or skills to proceed. Such "knots" should be thought of as more than negative moments of confusion and frustration, however. Rather, they are moments of cognitive disequilibrium, containing positive possibilities for re-grouping, hypothesis-testing, and intellectual comparison of ideas. They can produce interactions that are constructive not only for socializing but also for constructing new knowledge. The teachers' task is to notice those knots and help bring them to center stage for further attention—launching points for next activities.

see it again with the text it gives you a different meaning, fitting better with the situation.

Laura: Well, then, to get to the structure I'm speaking of, I have been working on the audiorecording—on the transcription of the recording of the children's language. So that means on the whole complex material [*materiale complessivo*].

Tiziana: [translates] She is going to give us the structure based on listening to the verbal language of the children.

Laura: First thing, the children were very happy about my proposal. It was the first time that they found themselves together, to make an animal together. But they didn't take up problems, and it looked as if it were a usual thing for them. They were happy. I think that also on this we could make some hypotheses. Immediately afterwards they began consulting the books they had there, but this kind of consulting is very superficial [approximate]. And Alan and Marco are the protagonists of this consulting. The books and the images shall be left there and picked up again only when the animal will have a real structure and needs to be completed.

Each one of the children chooses the part of the animal he wants to make, and declares which part he will do. One says, "I shall do the head." Another: "I do the body." Another: "I do the limbs." Nearly immediately, one of these three children, Marco, who was the one who had chosen to do the body, takes over as leader. Because he is the child who gets the parts done by the other two children and puts them all together. The first parts that were made are—now I can't give every one of you the diagram—I am sorry if they aren't clear but they are notes that can help you understand the evolution. [She hands out diagrams].The first image on the top is a body. The body is a big piece of clay. It's a kind of block. Alan chooses to make the leg. So when the leg is ready, Alan gives it to Marco. And Marco does the first assembling. Filippo had to make the head. Filippo makes his head, and tries to put it on top of this construction. But Marco stops him, and tells him, "No, it's not right. This is the back of the animal."

So I don't know how to explain it, but Marco is making this animal with two blocks—one is the front and one is the back. Here will be stuck a leg, and here another leg. So Filippo is imperfect. Marco sticks the second part of the body, the back part, and in this moment Filippo thinks that he understood. And he's ready to put his head just in the middle. And for the second time, Marco says, "No, it's not right. It doesn't go there." It looks like Filippo has a frontal perspective. But it's not Marco's idea. And there is never an accord between these children. So Marco says, "No, move it over a bit. You have to turn it around." Because he is looking at the animal [mumble].

There is another problem, too, that is not anymore in the drawing. The children have decided to make a prehistoric animal with a long neck. And so Marco says, "Look, the head only isn't enough. We decided on a long neck, and you have to make a long neck." At this point, there is the first moment of crisis for Alan. He had already made two legs and he doesn't know how to go on. First [he did the] block. But now what do we have to do? The arms? This is the image that he has of an animal. So in this case, Marco, who became the temporary leader, says, "We had chosen at the beginning those feet [*pinne*] like flippers [fins]." So Marco remembers for himself and for Alan the initial project they had, and in this way Alan can find again his new way of getting in [inside the process of co-constructing with the others], so he goes to setting up the flippers. And not only that, he also wants to stick some wheels on, and this is accepted by the other boys.

Then comes another very difficult moment for Filippo. He should have prepared the long neck, but he didn't know how to make a long neck. He doesn't know how long it has to be. He had made a little strip, but it wasn't long enough. So Marco suggests to him to get ready three little snakes of clay in order to hold up the head. Because he had already seen that the head had big proportions, so that the neck had to be not only very long but also very thick. In the meantime, the other kid in the group, Alan, was very impatient and kept saying, "Is this head ready?" Now Marco comes in on Filippo's head. He takes it and looks at it and said, "Hey, this isn't a man. It has to be an animal. So also the head is not all right, because it has the eyes, nose, and mouth of a human being. It is supposed to be an animal's face." So Marco takes this head from Filippo and begins to change it into an animal face.

At this point, Alan has another strong perception. Alan looks at the work they are doing and understands that it doesn't look like what they had decided in the beginning it had to be. And he says, "Oh, we didn't say we were going to do this!" and he has a moment in which he doesn't recognize the animal. But the other boys don't give up what they were doing. But from now on, they will go back to the pictures much more than they had been doing up to this moment. So as they had already gone far away from the initial image of the animal, there is now a "moment of going away" that I call "transgressive." And Alan says, "Why don't we make this animal so it is also a rowboat animal? So we can put many moving-parts [ingranaggi] on it." So he pushes all the children towards an animal that is very different from their initial idea.

Someone: Was it Marco?

Laura: [with other voices] No, it was Alan. Filippo doesn't understand well this idea of the rowboat-animal. And also perhaps the idea of putting the pieces together makes the work harder for Filippo. And so from that moment Filippo moves his attention onto a kind of pieces he knows better how to make, those that compose roundabouts [like in a park]. When he speaks of roundabouts [carnival rides], he speaks of those called "Death Circles." This is a moment in which Filippo speaks about his experience on this kind of roundabout. Then he stops speaking and stays within the group. In fact he doesn't know what to do because Marco has the head, Alan has the flippers and the legs, and he doesn't have anything else to do. And so he proposes the rain. A situation in which this situation could be and [the animal] could live. At this time, while this animal can be seen to take shape and hold an image between the children, Marco proposes that after they finish this animal, they could do other animals. So as to go on with this work together.

At this moment, one or two children leave the table while the other stays there. One or two stay near the animal that has to be finished, while the other goes to look at the book. He would like to begin the construction of another animal at this

same time. Here comes a moment of [estraniamento] estrangement. Now comes a moment that I think is very important: when Filippo decides to straighten up the animal, in order to put it at last in the right way. But in fact they are not able to make it stand up.

And so there comes a direct question: Will I help? Alan asks me [if I will help]. I return to Alan the opportunity of finding the way out. And he finds the way by putting by wire mesh under the trunk. They become very excited because they think they have come to the end of their work. So Alan comes back and positions the piece of mesh under the animal, while Filippo puts the animal on top of it. But in the meantime, Marco also sticks the head on, and so the animal falls down. There are too many shoves [pushes]. So let's see, is this net too small? Perhaps we need a bigger one for holding up the whole animal? Alan goes to look for another piece of mesh. Filippo—with my help because he was very upset—gets the animal again to stand up. Putting the legs on, the animal stands up. And he sticks onto it a fifth leg, without anyone noticing it. I myself saw it only later, watching the video. So that the equilibrium could be definite.

In the final animal, there will be no neck. And this is a thing that the children don't care about, that they don't mind. I asked myself some questions about the meaning of this. The animal was very attractive [elegant], now that it was standing up. How nice it is! [Come è bello] So there comes the desire to finish it. There is a moment of admiration. So now comes the wish to complete the animal, to stick the parts on that are missing. So now they go back to consulting the book. The children decorate the body with stripes and markings and scales on the tail. The teeth and the pupils of the eyes. The final touch—the pupils—is Filippo's. Then at the end the animal is abandoned.

Loris: Where is this animal now?

Laura: It's a pity, but it broke to pieces [sad voice]. It dried up and then fell apart. We kept the pieces for a while, but when clay dries up, it disintegrates.

Carolyn: Too bad.

Laura: I'm very sorry. So, this animal was abandoned,

and it is just as if we put a cross on top of it to indicate it was all done. And then they immediately begin another animal. It is a prehistorical bird, and they begin putting together all the parts. They reproduce the structure they made before. Marco is again the leader. He will put together all the parts. The other two, Alan and Filippo, have the wings, but this time they are much more capable. The impression you get is that they know much better how to do it.

Someone: Did they look more interested in the construction process instead of the final product?

Laura: I think they were very interested in being together as a group. The pleasure of staying together was really very strong. This animal was important, but it seems to me that much more important for them was the staying together.

Loris asks an inaudible question, and **Laura** replies: Yes, we shall see this later on. Two children who in the meantime were outside, now come in, and display admiration and offer to come into the group. So in this case, the other boys accept. But Filippo shows them what for me can be the end of the work as a finished animal [the first one],saying, "Look how nice it is! Look what we have made!" And Filippo shows them the finished animal. And then Marco explains to one of them the project. Marco says, "If you want, you can help us make another pre-historical animal. If you are able to, and if you want to." The scene finishes, because it was lunchtime, with this intrusion of Tommaso and Alessandro into the group of children who wanted to go on with this activity.

Just before you watch the video, I want to tell you some things that I asked myself after we have made that structure. So one of them is this. Marco, on this occasion, seemed to have in his head the total project of this animal. Also, he knew the prospective from which it had to get done—this one [She shows the drawing]. But his

> *The pleasure of staying together was really very strong. This animal was important, but it seems to me that much more important for them was the staying together.*
>
> *—Laura Rubizzi*

knowledge wasn't communicated or discussed with the other children. During the first phase of the work, the other two children move as if they were blind. And he is the only one who knows what to do. So I ask myself, if it is a correct thing to leave the children to look for the way out, or if it wouldn't be better to get them to discuss the project together? For example, when a child has a project, should one ask him to communicate it, discuss it? And try to make sure there is one first moment where they all communicate and have a moment of contact?

And another thing that left me disappointed is that I didn't notice the neck problem that seems a very important component of the animal. Perhaps because it was too difficult to make the neck. Marco tried for a while but was unable. And they let go of that problem. Instead, it seems to me that it could have been an element to stick with. Another thing was getting children used to thinking and finding structures—different kinds of structures—because it appeared to me that their knowledge wasn't sufficient for projecting three-dimensional structures with their own stability [equilibrium]. These are the first thoughts I have had. Now I think we can watch. And then I can go on with my analysis, for getting into an understanding of what we are seeing.

Carolyn: Okay, let's watch the video now. [The group watches the video.] We wanted to ask, when the children are looking through the books to make their plan, we wanted to know, without the books and photos, could they have made this plan? [Tiziana translates].

Laura: I think so. Also because this interest in prehistorical animals is very strong. And the information that children have on them is so extensive that they would have been able to do it even without the books and photos.

Tiziana: Perhaps Carolyn wanted to know something more. If they would have been able to get along together without having images as mediators for the project. Because a thing [the photo?] is saying, "This is a thing we all want to make and we see it and we know what it is." Instead it is different to reach an accord.

Laura: Perhaps they would have discussed more about the kind of animal [if they hadn't had the books]. As we have already seen in other situations, when children employ only words, frequently there are moments of incomprehension. And very frequently children use different kinds of languages, for example, drawings, and the showing of drawings. Perhaps if we hadn't had the books, the child who had the whole plan of the animal in his mind would have communicated much better to the other kids what was his idea.

Loris: We should try to understand whether the image in the book has been respected [followed closely in their construction], or whether it has just been a point of departure for the work. So that the children leave it behind. Also probably because there is salient agreement [*patteggiamento*] among the children: "All right, we will look at it, but we won't be able to do it like that. We can do one that looks like it."

> *It is important that they have detailed photographs and not reproductions like the kind that are usually made for children*
>
> *—Vea Vecchi*

Vea: I think that in this moment, the images provide a moment of importance to the [children's] community [NOTE from translator: She uses the term, *momento aggregante,* "unifying moment," an Italian expression that educators like to use—an expression remnant of Italian politically leftist thinking]. It seems they don't care to go check and see if it looks like the picture.

Laura: No, no, they go and look at it and see that it is not the same thing, as I told you before, when they are putting together the pieces, Alan says, "Now we are making a different animal than the one we decided to do in the beginning." They understand, and they return to the picture when they feel like it. Also because they admire and love this animal. and they want to make it in the best way they can. And they have to understand better about the skin, how the scales of the tail are, and the nails. They need other elements. And so they use the book in a different way.   In the first phase, they chose this animal because it was a good animal. So they excluded the carnivores. They chose a non-violent animal.

Tiziana: Probably, Carolyn with this question wanted to anticipate the American audience who could ask questions regarding the use of the book, asking themselves whether the use of the book would limit the imagination of the children.

Vea: I wanted to say something concerning the image [picture] the children are looking at. The image [as experienced] in a group is always an important referent, whether they use it or they just look at it. It consolidates in part. I think it is important that it is there. And I wanted to say another thing that we usually say when we go around speaking of our experience. This is that the children need to have realistic images—in this case it is not easy to have realistic images of dinosaurs. *Realistic* images. It is important that they have detailed photographs and not reproductions like the kind that are usually made for children that are very schematic [sketchy]. Frequently the images are ugly. Saying this, I don't want to say that the nicer image is always the more realistic. For giving extensive reference, it is important that there is a reproduction that lets the work happen. It can't be too schematic [sketchy]. When children consult animal images, we watch out [to see] these images don't represent only one perspective [visually]. For example, a horse painted by Paola Uccello is different from a horse that we can find in children's books where there is the sketchy little horse, that doesn't provide much [information]. So when we speak of images, we can't generalize. I think that the picture is a consolidated agent. It's very consolidated. [Editors' note: Perhaps she means: dense, packed, or well-defined.] Normally when we go to buy books—very often children's book are very lacking in this kind of picture. They contain oversimplified images.

Marina C: The important thing is to not only have one book.

Tiziana: No, they had more than one.

Loris: If your work began from the book, it is clear that this will influence all the work of the children. "You are together, and together you will make an animal." And I would say that what brings them together immediately is the admiration they have for this kind of animals. Now there is a big boom of prehistorical animals, and these are animals are very much inside children's way of life. The second point is that perhaps only the prehistorical animal has these virtues because it is so different compared to the animals familiar to children, so that it helps children not only to remember the picture but also to notice the distinctions instead of similarities. And so this kind of proposal you did to the children is the right one, using this kind of animal. Because you use this image that is so different and so full of pathos for small children.

We could also make some other choices. We could not show any books to the children and ask them to try to remember a prehistorical animal. But what would it have meant? It would have meant that the mediation between individuals—before we could gotten to the problem—would have required much work of consultation for arriving at an animal [plan] agreed upon by everyone—by the three children. This would have meant to go in a different direction. But it isn't necessarily true that this would have been a wrong direction. There are several alternative directions that could have been explored.

> We have to believe more in children, instead of less.
> — Loris Malaguzzi

Vea: We have never to forget the moment. When Laura said we tried to videotape normal situations in which you have different groups of children and you give them different occasions and you also give them strategies and tools [*strumenti*] that they can take charge of. So in the case of these children, the choice was motivated also by the fact that they were alone with the teacher who was coming and going. And so they had available all the strategies that they needed.

Tiziana: What I think Carolyn was saying about the fantasy image [*imaginario*] can turn this situation inside out. You keep inside yourself all what the fantasy means. You have to think how much distance there is between an imagination that is fantasizing and one creating realistic images, not fantastic and new.

Loris: If we start to think what imaginations, whether imagination stays stuck to earth or is loosened from earth. We think imagination is stuck to earth. The three requisites are there [in the situation with the boys]. They are: animals that children like; animals children know probably from books at school and at home; and animals extremely different, that neither father nor grandfather ever saw. So this will be a discovery that is positioned between legend and reality [and partakes of both]. Someone will say that these animals have actually lived. But inside the children will remain the thought that probably they have never lived. Because the first question they pose is, "Daddy, have you ever seen them?" And for the grandfather, "Grandfather, have you ever seen them?" "No." More than that, they can't get more than those testimonials. I never know if children put these kinds of images historically behind their shoulders or in front of them, as if they were animals that could come up. And in this case, there is the wish for a thriller that would give some excitement if they would come back. But if they really could come back, it would be so nice.

Tiziana: Carolyn wants to know whether we think that the work that these three children did could have been done with younger children, 2- or 3-year-olds?

Vea: I am experimenting with very small children, 3-years-old, who are doing very nice things.

Loris: Perhaps small children would not be able. Perhaps we are not yet able to say definitively what children are really able to do.

Voices: Yes!

Loris: So we have always to try to do too much instead of too little. We have to believe more in children, instead of less.

Vea: I don't know how long the activity would last [with younger children]. But I am sure that they could do it.

Loris: They would certainly do it with a different rhythm [order or timing or pace]. [Burst of interjecting voices talking all at once]. I don't know if they would accept so easily to work all together on the same thing.

Vea: I think there are very many different things. The problem isn't the finished product. Rather there is the problem of different strategies that reveal the difference of one year. The friendships of this year, and so on, change very much the strategies. It is really another thing. I am working with 3- and-a-half-year-old children who make these things that are extraordinary, but the strategies, the way in which they work, are very different.

Tiziana: All right. Let us leave aside the finished product. Let's address whether they could really reach the end, but we have to ask whether they would accept to make together one single product.

Vea: Yes, certainly there would be battles. [Voices at once]

Tiziana: At the end of the year, perhaps, when they are 3-years-old. At the beginning of the year, when the children are 2 [in the *nido*] and they change from the classroom of the small ones to the classroom of the big ones, they still they can't do it. When the year passes, and they are 3-years-old, and in the classroom of the big ones, perhaps they can do it. [Voices at once]

Laura: Those three children who were working with clay were able to do it because it was May, the end of the school year.

Tiziana: Yes, yes.

Voices: Children who stay all day long together are probably able to do this. … I think that they certainly would accept to do that. Then we should have to try and see how long the game goes on. But I think they wouldn't have difficulties in doing it.

Carolyn: Shall we go on? [The group watches the video]

Tiziana: Carolyn's question was: How do the teachers respond when children evaluate each others' work? [Voices ask for more explanation of question]

Vea: When a child says something about the work of another one, how do you react?

Voice: We listen to children.

Tiziana: Well, that is a form of reaction. If you listen without becoming involved, you certainly give a message to the children.

Voice: There are very many variables.

Tiziana: [in English] In this particular situation, when one called the other, "Stupid," we don't think it was a real judgment [negative feedback].

Marina C: Watching our way of staying with children, in the situations we are always living, [oftentimes] our adult solicits the child, because what we say and what we do becomes a judgment [evaluation]. Perhaps judgment is too strong a word. It can be the expression of what we do and what we see.

Tiziana: I think that behind this question we have again to read another question. Perhaps Carolyn, with this question like with the other one, wants to anticipate other questions [of North Americans]. For example, you remember when we discussed about me going around [in the US]. I don't remember any more with which American, I was saying that I liked it [what I was seeing] so much. And this one asked me why I was commenting on all these things. [Smiles] Because I am alive! The question was that if you give a positive judgment [feedback], this means that you are reinforcing a kind of behavior or kind of product; you are giving direction [evaluation]. So the question was, is it right? It is a question that you live with as an adult. If it is a problem, it will be much worse if we send it to children, as a behavior between children. There are moments when children ask you for this [praise]. They need reassurance.

Voice: Which is the way in which you can be together without communicating—it would be an autistic world. We have to question ourselves on the kind of judgment.

Vea: We have frequently said that the evaluation children give of themselves is very important. [Many voices]

Laura: So many times, the evaluation of another child

helps a child to understand a problem. There is a need for making new things together. As when children begin to talk about their theories, when children say, "I think you've said this thing wrong, I'm not in agreement with you, because I think in a different way from you."

Vea: Sometimes they are or they appear to us very eager. The judgments are not always good judgments. [Sometimes] they are quite severe. It isn't always a calm thing. Once more there is a conflict. So I think that evaluation and self-evaluation are very important. Certainly it's not a thing that we could take away.

Tiziana: The second problem is: what if the child gets wounded by the judgment of another child, and how much can you as an adult get into it? I'm thinking about that day when my daughter came home very sad because her friends at school described her as always wanting to be boss, and said of her only negative judgments. Instead, she wanted them to say that she was kind and helpful with everyone. So these are things that you have to discuss with her. Because if a person chooses to be the leader, he has to know that he will be unpopular. Or if he doesn't want that, he has to realize he must change himself. So you certainly get into these kinds of concerns as an adult, because you understand that these are very big, important things. [watching video]

Laura: It's not right. And then he goes on. And asks him, "On the back?" as if saying "I didn't understand well."

Tiziana: But later, while he's saying "I'll do also the mouth," he says, "Well, will you do it for me?" Somebody could say that he has been repressed.

Laura: No, that's not true. If somebody watches it all through, they will see that is not so. There are moments in which one is frustrated and moments in which one gets back his strength. If you see at the end Filippo is very uninvolved, and this is a big conquest. [watching video]

> **What if the child gets wounded by the judgment of another child, and how much can you as an adult get into it?**
>
> **— Tiziana Filippini**

Laura: If you watch, the construction is now being done between Marco and Filippo. And Alan is out of it. He is cut out from it, and everything is between Marco and Filippo. [watching video]

Carolyn: We have noticed that the children are very precise with their work. They take elaborate care. We wanted you to comment on that. [Tiziana translates].

Someone: They are used to it. [Much laughter].

Tiziana: This is the typical way of working of our children. They are very concentrated.

Laura: They know their work. They are familiar with the instruments. They are used to doing this kind of work. They don't have the concepts for some techniques; for example, they weren't able to make a 3-dimensional structure. Or giving particular positions to something that they make. They aren't perfect.

Tiziana: [in English] As we were saying this morning, walking around, we could realize that when they are doing something they are really getting involved and so the detail, everything...

Vea: Can I say something here? Many things are passing in front of us. But I am anxious to speak about one of them. The way in which children use irony [humor] while they are working, because it comes in nearly always, first of all for giving niceness to their situation. They also use it when they have to reduce the drama [heaviness] of a situation. They use it very often.

Laura: Also in the moments of waiting. We will later see Filippo, when he has nothing to do, he comes in with his song. [Many voices all at once].

Vea: In this way he helps the other children, for example, Marco. Now Carolyn has another question that came out when Marco said, "Okay, boss, here is another foot ready." So she says that there is formal communication —

Someone: And with humor.

Vea: So we can wait to speak about it.

Laura: No, as it has come up now, we can speak about it now.

Tiziana: She wanted to know what we think about it.

Vea: You are speaking about the way of using humor.

Tiziana: No, because Carolyn didn't give an importance to the fact that the thing the child was saying was in irony. Her question concerned the use of grammar. She just saw that something in their way of speaking had changed. And asked how we saw this change?

Carolyn: Why do you think that using irony is an interesting thing [directed to Vea]?

Vea: It strikes me always when I see, even in children very small as in those of this year who are 3-and-a-half, seeing that they make real jokes. Sometimes they use adult jokes, but sometimes the jokes come from them. It seems to me a very intelligent way of using verbal language. It is a very sophisticated way to communicate. So I think it is a very intelligent way of communicating. That's why it interests me so much.

Tiziana: We agree with that.

Vea: And then, it is a nice thing.

Tiziana: Are we agreeing? [Voices, yes yes, including Loris]

Loris: [whispering] That wasn't a good way to videotape, because it is better to be nearer the children. But it is not a big problem. There is always this respect for the child's image, as if we go nearer we would ruin it. The camera gives value to children without our doing anything.

Tiziana: [to whoever did the filming—Marina C?] We are speaking about the way in which you made the video. We are saying you should have gotten nearer the children. It was a technical comment. [watching video, mumbling and laughing as they watch; now they understand that the boys have finished the first animal and are making the second; Tiziana explains this fact in English to Carolyn and John].

Carolyn: Just briefly, could you explain why it is important for you the moment in which the other children arrive?

Laura: It is a kind of [*collaudo,* test or trial, like when you try out a new car to see if it works] on the kind of work of these three kids who have worked together. So Filippo shows the finished product, which is a very nice animal, and it is as if he is saying, "You also can get to this goal which is nice and interesting." But then you need to be on the same wavelength concerning the project. Marco says, "If you want, you can help us. We want to do this." It is like saying, "If you want to enter the group, you must do this." And then remarks, "If you are able." This means that he already has a story in it and already knows what are the difficult moments, some of which are easy to pass and some of which are not.

Loris: To whom? To Marco?

Laura: Yes. Filippo is the child who shows the finished goal. Between the three of them he was the one who depends most on Marco's leadership. Many times he seeks help. Instead, here there is a kind of victory [*conquesta*]. Instead, Marco has another attitude, that is as he says, "I am the one who has the situation, and I know that for working together we have to have a project." Alan goes after the other child, Alessandro, and the other children who were near there. It seems to me that this is an important *knot.* Because the children would have gone on working together. But some of the things were very clear for them. And Filippo comes in with another item, saying, "Be quick. Or we'll get tired." This comes from the tiredness of having worked one hour together. "I won't have much energy to give. Let's hurry up so that we can finish our work."

> It strikes me always when I see, even in children very small as in those of this year who are 3-and-a-half, seeing that they make real jokes. Sometimes they use adult jokes, but sometimes the jokes come from them. It seems to me a very intelligent way of using verbal language.
>
> — Vea Vecchi

Carolyn: Let's go on to the end of this video. We don't have any more questions on this segment. [Tiziana translates]. [watching video] We could go ahead to the setting of the table. But maybe there is something more that you want to say about this. [Tiziana translates].

Vea: Yes, because we would like to discuss some things. If we can't offer some explanations, they [the videos] shall all look the same. I think we should discuss. [Tiziana translates].

John: Do you want to see it again? Or shall I queue up the next one? [Many voices all at once]

Vea: If we said that we were going to speak!

Tiziana: Yes, but while we are talking, he is getting ready the next video. So when we finish, we will have ready the next scene. So he was asking which we wanted to see next. So they have now agreed that we will all decide what to see next when we are finished.

> We thought that having three of them could generate an interference, that could provide vitality, or that could change the dyad— perhaps thinking incorrectly because now we see that the matter is much more complicated.
>
> — Vea Vecchi

Laura: I was in charge of getting inside this video, but I don't have any conclusions today. I have to propose to you and then seek your comments on the method I am using. Well, then. One of the ways I chose was watching the video, making the matrix that I gave you. [She is referring to the diagrams in Part II, B, that follow Part II, A.] No, it's the one I've got here. Speaking about the kind of verbal language, it wasn't a very long speech [script]. I needed to understand what really these children are saying. I have transcribed the verbal communication in this way. On the left hand side, here is Alan. And I gave him a green route. In the middle, Marco, with a blue route. Then Filippo, with a red route. And then there is me with a possible [inaudible, but perhaps she refers to the dotted lines]. So I have transcribed everything the children were saying. In this way I have visualized in which direction goes the communication. It was quite a lengthy work! In this way we can see in which direction the communication has taken, as

well as the braids [like braided hair] that there are in this communication. Which are the interactive moments between children? For example, the relationship between three children is quite complex. It's not like a dyadic relationship. It seems to me that when there is a dyadic relationship, considering the dialogic level, the moment of communication, a long time isn't accepted [for each speech], so that when there is coming in of the third one, and this changes all the dynamics. Between Filippo and Marco there are many moments of interchange. This has been the first pass of my analysis. And here I have exactly what the children tell me.

Vea: Could you answer a question? As we are also discussing the relationship of two versus three children, you said that frequently the dyad is interrupted by the other one. Do you think that the third element has always a role of the disturber, or do you think he can also have a positive role? Do you remember when we decided that there were to be three, how much we talked about whether to have three or four in the group? We thought that having three of them could generate an interference, that could provide vitality, or that could change the dyad—perhaps thinking incorrectly because now we see that the matter is much more complicated.

Laura: So I wanted to know your first impressions. Most of the time it is a seductive mode of intervening [being pleasing in a special kind of way, knowing what will be appealing to the other]. It's like tiptoeing into this dyad. Or getting in with a question [drawing attention] on what the third child is doing. "I am here also, and I am doing something also." For trying to understand better the nature of this way of speaking by the children, later I tried to analyze this language. And so for understanding when a child enters in, just by making a declaration, just for saying a thing, when he intervenes by being seductive, when he intervenes by introducing a conflict when the other child—

Vea: Modes of communication—

Laura: Yes. When, for example, he intervenes by dominating, or by describing, or by putting a question to one or to both, or by negotiating. So I tried to read again the children's affirmations. And giving to every one of these my interpretation, coding the communication. I have some copies of it. [She passes the handout to the group]. Roberta made them for me this morning.

Vea: How many categories did you find?

Laura: There are quite a lot. There are all these. [She shows] Let me explain this. This is a reproduction of the dialogue. But this is only my interpretation of the verbal language of the children. There isn't the language. There is only the kind of communication that I think the child is doing.

Vea: The communicative categories.

Laura: Yes. After I did this work, I needed to understand in which ways Alan had communicated, and likewise Marco and Filippo. And so I have retranscribed—on this diagram you can see—all the communicative categories I thought I had found. Perhaps this is my incapacity—that I wasn't able to reduce it further into a schema. [Many voices as people try to explain this table to each other. Voices ask if the graph shows real time. Laura says yes]

Tiziana: So using the real time, you have synthesized the different types of communication.

Vea: She took the real time—

Tiziana: The route with the numbers shows the time, the evolution of the events in real time. [Many voices, as people inspect charts.]

Vea: Perhaps we should explain, for those who weren't there, that we chose two videos. One is the clay segment, and one is the computer segment we shall see tomorrow. Because that one is completely different. Because there it was a dyad, and a dyad involves a completely different communicative route. Also the children's ages are dif-

> When they are finishing the animal, that should be a moment of happiness for the group, instead, no, it's a moment of great mobilization. For getting immediately on to the next project.
>
> —Laura Rubizzi

ferent. It is really a different thing. We chose these two different videos because we wanted to see if it were possible to see the way of communication [in each case]. Laura began this work in the way she has just showed us, that we discussed together. We also tried in a different way. Now we shall see which way works better. We shall see, for example, if it is the same in the dyad as in the triad. Or which kind of analysis works better. We really have to find out. This work is done so that we can discuss it. So that we can find more meanings—because watching the video by itself isn't enough.

Laura: I have to go on, and see on this general diagram, which are the *knots* which arise. For example, just after transgressive proposals, there is a movement in the communication that jumps from one child to the other. It is a very strong moment. Or when they are finishing the animal, that should be a moment of happiness for the group, instead, no, it's a moment of great mobilization. For getting immediately on to the next project. This makes me think that they had much more the sense [motivation] of staying together than of making the animal.

Vea: As we all have a copy of this, I suggest we take it up again [later]. We should have some time for studying it. We could also try watching the different situations.

Voice: There is a kind of communication that is very difficult to categorize. For example, a gaze between two children.

Vea: Perhaps in this case the video can help you. When the voices you hear aren't only verbal communications but they also show another kind of language that is the visual one. So that in a communication, you use different modalities.

Tiziana: You have to give much more place to the non-verbal communication.

Vea: Yes, I think they are shown in the same way, but the voices change.

Tiziana: Yes.

Carolyn: I was thinking that sometimes children can't say what they mean. Or their body language says the opposite of what they are trying to say. (This is true of adults also). So in order to understand a communication, you have to pay attention to the whole person, not only the words. What do you all think about that? [Tiziana translates].

Vea: I deal with the 3-year-olds, and I know this kind of communication. So I have to be careful to watch for all those kinds of nuances that have to do with body language. That means staying near or far away, or watching a game or a friend who can be far away. That conditions all the relationships. I was also wondering how to do it so that these important elements wouldn't be lost. I think Laura said it at the beginning that she worked on the level of the verbal language. But she found out how important was working at the same time with the video [image]. I think that for her work, she didn't use only the tape-recording. And this is the same work that Marina has done, which we shall see tomorrow.

Laura: Yes, this happens also in the relationship with adults. For example, when Marco says he wants to make the body [of the animal], he looks at me. As if he wants to ask me, "What do you think about that? Is it all right if I do this? What do you think about it?" Or during the video, some glances—questioning glances—if I don't answer to them, the sense is that what they have decided is okay.

Marina C: When children look at each other, you understand what they are telling each other. I remember that from watching Laura's and my video, we saw that with this kind of work we could see different kinds of communication. Usually we work with audio-recordings, and we have the voices and noises. It's a different kind of transfer. Instead with the video you can re-live the whole situation.

Vea: We forgot to put inside our diagram the real time. I want to know which kinds of categories

emerged in the first five minutes. We have also to keep the empty spaces as we chose only a quarter of an hour out of the whole one hour and fifteen minutes. So that we can know what has happened during the first five or ten minutes, then there is a black-out—it doesn't matter how long—and then something else happened later. Because when we will discuss it, the time will be very important to know.

Marina C: In this video there is a relation between three children. Instead, we shall see tomorrow in the computer video that the time is a very important factor. Sometimes children have very many quick communications within a small period of time, and then [other times] they can stay without having any for a long time.

Vea: We have to be careful not to over generalize situations. For example, several times it happened to us to give different kinds of interpretations of the same communication that a child has with another. For example, it begins with a mediated argument [argument where each child knows he has the other there before him, careful of what they are saying] and finishes with one that involves a kind of direct command or conflict moment. In the same period, there can be at the same time different kinds of communication, so you have to give different interpretations.

Loris: I think that the permanent rule of these children who play in this way is a rule that maintains the game. This is the fundamental rule for children. Every one of them feels that he has to keep going the game they are playing. This means that on this feeling, probably many kinds of communications and of continuities that aren't really understood by the other one, can break down the "horse's trot." So I would say that their interventions are always very short. Very short. They are always small segments that guarantee the continuation of the interaction that the pleasantness of staying together can continue. And that the game can go on until the end, getting to [the point of] having the animal done. What I want to say is that the language that the

> It is very important to know that every child produces something. Every child reflects himself uniquely, in the final work.
>
> —Loris Malaguzzi

children use has to be categorized with consciousness of the situation, and of the feelings to which children give priority. So I would say that children are much more able to express a priority for the game in which they are involved. This is very nice. The atmosphere is very nice. It is an atmosphere that keeps an even tone, without fervent ups and downs. This is the conjunction of all the things that the children produce—because it is very important to know that every child produces something. Every child reflects himself uniquely, in the final work. And this is a very important function.

Look. I think I should say something about the methodology. It is very important that we look at these interpersonal moments. First of all, because now we have children who are much more sociocentric than the children of years past. There is a culture that brings children to have different experiences that aren't only the repetitive ones that they have at home. Children today have many mothers and many fathers. Okay? That is why they are extremely sociocentric. And this means that every child thinks that he can converse with everyone. And if possible he can work with anyone. I think that this is a situation that is much more diffused than [it was] ten or fifteen years ago. Children hope to stay with other children. This kind of hoping to stay with other children means that they are able to create behaviors and conversations. This means that there is a scheme for waiting, they are already able to anticipate what will happen later. So we can say that the behavior of the child has been already planned before. The kind of planning is already inside the children as germs. It's like the pod that has the peas inside it.

The third point, as I was saying this morning, is that these games are very ambiguous. We can't either call them wonderful or throw them away as worthless. What didn't come out through to-

day's discussion, what we didn't speak about, are the traumatic events.[1] There are children who can play with other children without producing anything. They can produce loving declarations of submission, or submissive declarations. But nothing happens. If nothing happens, this means that nothing happens, really. It is an unproductive operation [occasion]. If I don't see traumatic events, I can think that there is only a sentimental [Editors' note: pleasant, amiable] game going on [passing between children]. So that the whole game resides in [the exchange of sentiments]. This isn't something to throw away, but it is not even something on which we can construct a theory about staying together. So a kind of way of thinking about ways to stay together. So I think we can presume that children have learned something.

The second point [about that] understands the importance that the language has in the determination of attitudes or of the events. You can see immediately the difference when even one child has different linguistic maturity. I am very happy seeing that you have worked very much on the conversation, because the conversation isn't only what the children have said, but why they said it.

So you can understand that history can become drama or tragedy that you may not recognize because it doesn't show all the signs of tragedy. But it would be wrong to misunderstand all the kinds of vibrations children have in this conversation, that sometimes we underestimate. This demonstrates that their egos are emerging. If we had three children with the same level of linguistic maturity, we could think that these three children would also have the same kind of thoughts.

The problem is knowing whether the thought comes before the words—this is an old discussion. So we have also to decide at the theoretical level whether the dialogue comes before the monologue. So we say, at the beginning there is the Di-

> *The problem is knowing whether the thought comes before the words—this is an old argument. So we have also to decide at the theoretical level whether the dialogue comes before the monologue. So we say, at the beginning there is the Dialogue.*
>
> *—Loris Malaguzzi*

---

1. Editors' note: "moments of crisis," times of intellectual conflict in which learners experience consierable disequilibrium that unsettles and creates a sense of uneasiness about how to proceed, but also creates conditions for new learning.

alogue. Thus, all that comes after is a direct line [from that]. Dialogue means interaction. Interaction means active capacity coming from the three participants in the interaction. But if I speak of interaction, I certainly get into a conflict with the theoretical interpretation of the Piagetian egocentrism. So we negate the egocentrism of Piaget, and we also negate from this theory the idea that every child has the property of self-construction of the thought and of the word. [Burst of speech by others.] If you say that at the beginning there is the Dialogue, it seems clear that the word construction and all the behavior of construction come from the interaction. There can be moments in which the child can interact with himself. Yes, there can be. There can be children with a certain kind of behavior, because they are tied up to different theories [they have]. During the children's games, the theories are often jeopardized. When the child goes back home, he thinks through what he has done and can change them [the theories] spontaneously. This is an aspect that we can't see. This means that there can be also inter-individual communications and not only intra-individual communications.

> Everything depends on how the adult reacts.
> If he gives too much value or too little, [then] certainly he breaks up the construction that the child is making inside himself.
>
> –Loris Malaguzzi

So we could go on seeing the things that still connect us to Piaget. Above all, if we think of the social psychologists' books, so we have to take the Piagetian child, who would die or would be a kind of medieval ascetic, who decides to go live on a mountain and be a hermit. So we have to bring this hermit into a normal condition that is living with others. If it were possible, we should use small hierarchies that there always are—the conflictual moments—Certainly there are different typologies in different situations—we have to revisit the conflictual moments that are the moments of trauma, that wait to be reconfirmed as traumatic by what will follow. If not, I can't be sure that something is traumatic. I know that I need conflict to dis-equilibrate and then to re-equilibrate again. Here we have to understand whether chil-

dren perceive the disequilibrium. And if children who find themselves in front of a disappointing moment. The child accepts such moments, takes them inside, and then gets them moving, and so can accept a movement from an old equilibrium to a new one. Perhaps not a new one but certainly a different one.

So in this case [the video we are watching], we can certainly begin to think that this happened because there is a change in the thinking of the child, to a more advanced structure. There is a moment in which there is a kind of negotiation because the animal's face was given as a human face. There is an immediate repulsion because it cannot be real that way. It can't be possible that an animal like that could have a human face. So he says, "No, we have to give him back an animal face." What has happened inside the child? Inside the child who made the human face instead of the animal one? We have to see if the child is able to choose if he is right. But he can also still go on if he wants to. But we have to say that he is right. The point which no one is discussing leaves in him the liberty still to make dinosaurs with the human face, with the mouth, the nose and everything else.

Everything depends on how the adult reacts. If he gives too much value or too little, [then] certainly he breaks up the construction that the child is making inside himself. So we have to be very careful. When, for example, Alan asks something that for me is surreal, when he comes up and speaking to himself, says, "It's enough with these animals, they are false, they are made out of clay, let's put inside them mechanical parts," certainly it is a surreal inspiration. In reality it's just a transposition of the games he has with transformers. And he puts in these mechanisms into an animal that would surely support them if they would help him to live and to move. King Kong. This is another point that seems to me to be slipping away. It is too surreal. Too far away to be captured. Also because it seems too difficult—

Tiziana: On the plane of reality—

Loris: Another trauma that comes up but is hidden, and I'm not sure that the children understood is this fifth leg stuck on by someone. It's a bit like the assassination of [Italian prime minister] Aldo Moro or the unsolved murder of a woman. But what does this fifth leg say? On one side this shows that children are able to find a solution even without the help of an adult, using a behavior that probably an adult wouldn't accept, and perhaps it is just for this reason that it has been done sneakily. Because probably if the adult would have been there at that moment of the fifth leg—the stupid adults that we are—he would have entered saying, "What are you doing? Five legs? Don't you know that he has four legs?" Instead, the fifth leg was much more important than the other four because the four of them live only because of the fifth one. [Burst of voices]

Vea: [to Marina] This is something we found out.

Loris: In this situation I would be very careful to see all those things that Americans I think call "petting,"[in English this word] the lovers "petting."

Vea: I would call them seducing.

Loris: Yes, but seducing means that you are trying to seduce someone else. But there is a kind of "petting" that is a trying of different treatments that you think can give a kind of pleasure. The other thing that we have to look at is what place the children give in the space to the instruments they need to use. Because all of them—two are on this side, and the other on this side—they have to produce a decentered space. I have to sit in Marina's space in order to understand what she sees. I have to get up and come over to your space in order to see what you see. So the spatial dislocations aren't only perceptual difficulties that require a big movement, we have to be very careful because they are also changes in value. There is a hierarchy of values. That's why we always put grandfather at the head of the table. [Laughter] Head of the family at the head of the table. And that is why we have terrible ceremonies for a marriage, with all the name cards on the table. The first part of doing this involves thinking about how to do it. This provides much clarity. I want to say that spatial disloca-tion is a very heavy thing. So we said before that in this game the children were three [in number]. If each of them had an individual way of moving, the game would stop. So if we think that the children are inside a *piroga* [boat, like a shell], that the first, the second, and the third of them, all are forced to go in it. So that is a function they have to respect. The first one has a hold of the rudder, and the other two have to row. It's not possible that this situation doesn't exist in every social triangle. So the leader is indispensable; if there is not one, they will create one. We could see—if we take Marco and watch Marco, and we ask Alan, "Who put all the pieces together?" "Marco." "Good. Now let's do it again with you putting together all the parts. Would it be all right?" "Yes." So we will experiment with a changing of the roles so that we can see where the subordination that we expected doesn't exist anymore, or if there is a difference in the children's behavior.

Laura: There is a very nice moment of trying—Alan's moment—in which he says, "Let's make another animal, and you will have to make the body, the wings," just like at the end with Filippo. There is already natural need.

Loris: Yes, yes. From a technical standpoint, we were talking about it on previous days. It's not possible to work well on such a long video. If it would be possible, we should divide it into two, three, four, five acts, knowing that every act has significance. Another possibility, instead, is to videotape situations that can be undone [broken into parts]. Because we really want to see what has happened in the first five or six minutes. It is the moment in which there are different behavioral rules that can be explicated or not, that will be utilized later.

Marina C: Watching again the video, you lose all the explanations that for example Laura gave before about it. It is quite difficult to find out inside the video the things that were important for her that she told us of. Perhaps if it were made by putting together many pieces that could convey the intensity of the situation—

Loris: I think I would try and do it as we were saying the other day. The first five minutes, in which there is a sort of presentation as with the credit card or the identity card, that can be quite disorderly, and that tries to synchronize three different radios that aren't synchronized naturally, that have instead to find the same "chord" unless for understanding each other. And so we could expect that this video exploration could be if necessary stopped. And in that moment could come up the teacher to explain, without waiting, that the video is finished, saying "Until this moment"(probably after seeing all the other parts, and in this way she knows where the scene finishes) "I don't know if you noticed it, but so far the preoccupation is to show their credit cards, their personal credentials, for understanding how they speak, how the other one speaks, how they see, what kind of gestures they use, it is like the players do before a game, that they sort of play before the game starts as if they wanted to know each other." If going on, another trauma comes up, I want to be able to stop again, because this is the work that goes not to me and not to you who made it.

Tiziana: Perhaps it would be better if we returned to these methodological issues, how to do the videotaping, in another moment. Better we get back to our other issues. We will certainly need to go on speaking about the methodological issues, because they are very important for our work.

Carolyn: Let me ask one question. This whole analysis has had to do with the situation of children creating something new, or working together on an artistic project. Do they see anything fundamentally different between this kind of activity and one—as we will see later—of children conducting a routine task, something they do every day, such as setting the table or preparing the beds. [Tiziana translates]

Vea: As Malaguzzi said before, I think that every situation and number of children reveals a kind of language that sticks to that particular situation. According to me, in each case there can be a rule that could also be a general rule.

Tiziana: So let's say it better. If we see differences between the children's abilities with respect to the cooperative way of working, watching the situation on the construction of a new animal, instead of the routine moments.[Many voices] If one of those two situations is an easier one...

Laura: According to me, I think that the traumatic

moments that Malaguzzi was speaking of, this kind of researching of the other person, the use of charm [seduction], there are many ingredients of a situation, just like the one of the clay, but in the same way also in the one in which they set the table, that we shall see.

Vea: Just a moment. Be careful. The situation in which all three of them set the table, they all three know quite well what they have to do. Probably all their strategies change. I think that knowing what they have to do changes a lot their behaviors.

Loris: It changes because they know that it is the repeating of the same things that happened yesterday, and that will happen again in the upcoming days. It is a kind of ritual that certainly loses the "heat" that it had at the beginning, that they have when they begin this kind of operation [activity]. Unless they don't find games in it.

Voices: Yes, yes.

Loris: There are kinds of digressions that confirm the heaviness of routines. And they have to get out of it because every day the same thing goes on repeating itself. Every ten days the child does the same things. But I think we can say that all these things that happen are taken by the child through all his life.

Tiziana: Does anyone else want to say anything on this?

Vea: I don't know if it was one of her questions but he spoke about the communication. But we can't forget that there is also the manual activity when we see a situation such as with the clay.

Loris: I think that one of the most extraordinary things about children is that they are at first univocal, then multivocal [Editor's note: unilingual, then multilingual].

Many voices: Mmmm-mmm. Lovely!

Loris: They feel that they are owners of different languages. The ironical [humorous] language is a second kind of language. And being ironic [humorous] is a bearing of or detachment from the normal language. And it is a kind of behavior that is sneaky, and that can also be jovial. It shows a great vitality. So irony isn't a way of detaching from reality, it's not a way of saying, "I go to be a hermit." So wit [humor] is a way of keeping contact using another code. Using another code, another language, a symbolic language [*linguagio symbolico*]. This symbolic language is important because it is one more language of the child. When we say that the child uses a hundred languages, it's because we think children have many languages. He chooses the one that fits that situation. So he certainly has a kind of wardrobe [closet] in which he catalogues all the types of his languages. I'm not sure but if you look well [at the video], there is the child in the middle who repeats the game the mothers use with children. Such as getting smaller the noises of the voice, so that the voice sounds like a child's [falsetto]. Always the child in the middle—at the beginning of the scene has a kind of squeaky voice that children usually have when they intentionally regress, for becoming more interesting, in front of the grandfather or the mother. And I should say that in this case he is doing it as a plea. Also adults change their voice. Adults use different kinds of voices.

> And so children are very careful not to produce silent moments. And so they keep filling up the holes in the conversation, because they feel that the silence is an enemy of the relationship.
>
> — Loris Malaguzzi

Tiziana: Yes, yes, yes, yes, yes. [All laugh].

Loris: The last point—[All laugh] —in a game of this kind the worst enemy is the silence. That is a kind of laceration. The communication is a kind of outpouring that usually goes on and on, and so there aren't silent moments in the middle. There is a common saying that when there is silence, a priest is born. [Voices laugh and say, no, the saying is that it's the Pope who is born. Now quarrelling, and laughing, whether it is the Pope or the priest. Voices sound restless] What I mean to say is, also between grown up people, when there is a silent moment; you feel there is a chasm that breaks open that vitality that was running along before. And so children are very careful not to produce silent moments. And so they keep filling up the holes in the conversation, because they feel that the silence is an enemy of the relationship. That is why there are never big

[samples of] reasoning—there are always very short thoughts expressed, and I also think that this is a very important thing. There is instead a kind of ping-pong game: "I said 10,""no, 20," "no, 30," "40." What I want to say is that nearly always between the children there isn't reasoning. So we can say that there is a kind of language that is used for communicating and that is used for sustaining the communication. Communication can be held up [sustained] with banalities, or on satin threads.

Tiziana: Oh, children are very clever in doing this!

Loris: So there is a kind of communication that is called reasoning. That means speaking, and you immediately hear that the other one stays silent, while you are speaking they understand that you are doing a very difficult work and they have to listen so that your words can get into the running of the speech. So there are few children who reason [in conversation]. There are also didactical strategies that seek to simulate children's hypotheses that sometimes can be used.

Someone: On what occasion?

Loris: For example, in the situation of the human and animal face, I can go near the child who is making the face as an animal face, and I can tell him, "Do you know that yesterday Arturo was telling me that everyone has to make animals with human faces. What do you think about that?" So when the problem or the situation isn't there, I can simulate it, pretending that someone before him or after him or away from him has given a different interpretation; and try to see how he answers. So that's how I take him into the way of reasoning. [Voices say, I do that. I do that].

Someone: When does reasoning appear with children?

Loris: What is the risk? Every time we setup a cooperative situation, or a situation that we presume to be cooperative because we want the cooperative values of the game to get into the children. It can also happen that if we aren't clever, nothing will happen. If not, effusive [*effusivo*, i.e. outgoing, expansive, affectionate] language that retains the dignity of the situation but doesn't really get into the changing of thoughts, and so at the submission of the child to the verification of what he already had before. All the times that we live a situation, in which we know a new thing, there is a kind of revolution on the back of us. A part of it rolls off, and we take it in, and the reconstruction is different from the one we had before. So we have new bricks and old bricks, or it can destroy all the old bricks and give a different kind of bricks. This happens spontaneously in children's lives, this happens even when we don't want it in all the spontaneous situations in children's lives at home with their family—

Vea: Yes! This is just what I wanted to say.

Loris: On our side, there is a major intention: we do everything in order that certain things can happen with the engagement of trying to understand what is coming up, knowing that we are not frightened of children's words. But parents are. Teachers are frightened of children's words. Children's words frighten teachers. [Rumbling of voices]

Vea: No, what frightens me is the trauma. Perhaps there is an excess of evaluation that the teachers do. And I am one, also. The effusive aspect, and the civil aspect that is very important and very little appreciated in the cooperative learning—

Loris: Yes, yes, certainly—

Vea: And the fact that there is conflictuality, something that stops the engagement—

Loris: When we speak about conflictuality here—

Someone: I was asking myself, if this kind of effusive way of staying together, could be more typical of the little girls—

Voice: Not always—

> The cooperative feeling is composed of a sweet conflictuality and a hard conflictuality. But they all have legitimacy and can lead to positive actions going through different paths.
>
> — Loris Malaguzzi

Tiziana: This is a much wider moment—

Loris: A thing that I wanted to say and then I am finished, [it's about] conflictuality. The cooperative feeling is composed of a sweet conflictuality and a hard conflictuality. But they all have legitimacy and can lead to positive actions going through different paths. [Many voices: yes, yes, certainly]. Yet, the literature here [on this topic] is all about conflictuality as negating. Instead, there is a kind of conflict that is sweet in which they use different strategies. These are all conflict moments that change the child's intelligence through always sweet [soft] ways, "soft" [He uses the English] or there can be the explosion of the strong conflict, the harder one can come for example when children are playing and it is not necessary that the conflict is a positive one. It's in some way coming up as a means not an end. Like an immediate solution but it hasn't got intentionality and we have to work to make the conflicts come out. If conflicts don't arise, if there are no confrontations, if there aren't moments in which there is a losing of equilibrium, if the certainty doesn't leave room for the uncertainty, if a child doesn't accept the flux of insecure moments, the climbing up stops. So this means that we have to keep the child in a situation of permanent uncertainty, and this is the maximum of security he can have.

Vea: I am going on thinking of situations where every day you see these groups of children with two teachers—one stays with the group and the other one goes around—and all this we already saw is quite difficult to [arrange] to be done with a small group of children. In the normal situation, instead, we have many children. So the coming in of the adult who can determine the disequilibrium is very important because it can be in a certain way for three of them a disequilibrium, and for others not.

Loris: Yes, but the thing is, you have to set up as many situations as the number of the children, affirmative situations, if we would be able to do all of this.

Vea: I don't want to speak about ideal things. I'm only thinking we can use these concepts we have been speaking about for finding meanings for our work.

Loris: We have certainly been speaking about problems that weren't necessarily inside the situations we saw in the video, but that we use in occasions of an alert. All this can get into the behavior of children at the *asilo nido*, being sure that some of the things will turn back inside the child whether the child is six months old or two years old. I would never put the child of six years old with the back [facing the other child]—if we put them face to face we give them the possibility to appreciate their relationship, the possibility of a relationship not only physical but also human. You have to know, to keep present, that all of Piagetian theory is in a way very limited because it is all on the relationship between the child and the object. But not between the child, the object, and the individual. So I can think we can put two children not necessarily one in front of the other. Such as all the games they have around can be tried out, looking from the vantage point they are in, "You can see it this way," the way you use for watching changes, the act changes, the directions change, if we have two very small children and we put in between them the treasure chest, what kind of situation are we trying to set up? A situation in which the children can take when they want from the same chest the things they want, being able not to relate themselves with the other one but also with the things.

So to arrive to connect things that otherwise wouldn't be connectible, so that they discover relations, so we have to make an important analysis of the objects that we shall put inside. They have to be common objects and also objects that are very far away from the everyday. One child is here, and the other one is there. I don't know if you are still doing it? Do you remember when I said,

> *If conflicts don't arise, if there are no confrontations, if there aren't moments in which there is a losing of equilibrium, if the certainty doesn't leave room for the uncertainty, if a child doesn't accept the flux of insecure moments, the climbing up stops.*
>
> *— Loris Malaguzzi*

you have to do things with two children at a time. Why two children? Because two children are two children, and because we have two hands and two arms. We take one on the right and one on the left. And we go around—going around means going out, going on the road, going on the bus. This means the more you move the children away from the situation, and the more you tie them up to a relationship that puts together the children and the adult, so this grownup has to walk around in the street with the children. He has to go when there is the moon, he has to go again on the bus, on the bicycle with one in the front and one in the back, so what I want to say is that it is possible to think like this— [Everyone laughs]

When we brought the kitchen inside the schools, it was because we wanted to reproduce a relationship that wasn't there. So you have to think that every one of these moments is a system. I want you really to understand this. If I go to Paola's house, I am sure that you have a kitchen that is different from the bedroom and the dining room. [Laughter] So I am creating a system in which I have the most possible relations that I can have, when I put there everything that I need, the plates, forks and knives, I am creating a system of relations that is the most economical for me and at the same time is the one which accomplishes the most.

When she [Laura] was speaking of the initial scene and said that with the clay there could have been the knife and the clay knife, I want to say that she is getting ready a scene in which there can be a big possibility of relations, of different relations, and also of relations that can build. So we can say that also the *atelier* is a system where the relations between things are of the *atelier*. And at the function of who is inside it, of the children who are working in it. This creation of places that can be talked about until you feel boredom, or you get breaking action inside, being careful of what you do inside them. Your mother would never cook if she hadn't the instruments that get her cooking in 35 minutes instead of an hour and a half. So if the napkins were in the bedroom and the pasta hidden in the basement, and so on. [Much laughter]

Tiziana: Yes, because he tells you it is open and it is closed, and so for opening it you have to close it— and you open only when you want to— [Laughter] In this way I feel like in three hours a day—I can give back—taking care of all this is too much. Or I can't stand it, or I don't understand it. No, I am not tired. She and I, probably someone else, feel a little sorry because we have spoken, let's say we have lost some time to address some questions that are not so close, not so related to what you [Carolyn, John, and Lella] were looking for. But that is the way it is and how we work.

Carolyn: No [I didn't feel that it was unrelated], most of it I found to be related.

Tiziana: Everything is related. I hope you find it is worthwhile, you can use all this material. That is just the way we are.

Vea: Did you understand anything, since you don't even have the translator near you?

Carolyn: Sometimes, yes.

Tiziana: And then she goes to the dictionary, and then she has something more.

Voice: [in English] Well, I think it is very interesting to see how we work together, because I think that you forget that we are foreigners...

Tiziana: For today we can just close it here. And then start it again tomorrow. Do you have any more questions to ask now, or can they wait until tomorrow?

Carolyn: This is more of a provocation than a question. In Bologna, children also do many group projects in art, when children enter the final year of the *scuola materna* [preschool for children aged 3-6 years]; they do more individual projects to prepare the children for elementary school, what do you all think about that? [Tiziana translates].

Marina C: Projects in art?

Carolyn: Yes, like making a work in clay together, or a mural together, in Bologna [I am told] they would do those things more when the children are three or four years old than when they are five years old. When they are five, they think the child should work more individually [than together] to get ready for the elementary school.

Tiziana: Oh I misunderstood! [She corrects the translation, adding that she is a bit tired and that is why she translated it wrong]

Loris: I don't know, perhaps this happens in Bologna or it happens in some schools. But there is an ancient tradition that would like to see a relation between the last year in the *scuola materna* and the first year of elementary.

Tiziana: But we don't agree [with that]. And I can tell you in my observation for my daughter that was not true. She was not ready to work by herself [in the final year of preschool] …

B. Charts for Animals in Clay

PAG. 1.   Laura's VR

ALAN	MARCO	FILIPPO	INS.	TOMMASO

1 COMUNICAZ. DICHIARATIVA

2 _ COMUNICAZ. DICHIARATIVA

3 _ COMUNICAZ. DICHIARATIVA

4 _ COMUNICAZ. SEDUTTIVA

5 _ SCELTA NON CONDIVISA

6 _ COMUNICAZ. CONFLITTUALE

7 _ COMUNICAZ. DIRETTIVA _ DESCRITT.

8 _ COMUNICAZ. DICHIARAT.

9 _ COMUNICAZ. DIRETTIVA DESCRITTIVA

10 _ COMUNICAZ. SEDUTTIVA

11 _ COMUNICAZ. DICHIARATIVA

12 _ ARGOMENT. CONFLITTUALE (NON COND.)

13 _ COMUNICAZ. DIRETTIVA

14 _ COMUNIC. DICHIARATIVA

15 _ COMUNIC. DIRETTIVA (DESCR.)

16 _ VALUTAZIONE SEDUTTIVA

17 _ ARGOMENTAZ. SEDUTTIVA

18 _ COMUNIC. SEDUTTIVA

19 _ COMUNIC. COLLABORATIVA

20 _ COMUNICAZ. DIRETTIVA

21 _ COMUNIC. COLLABORATIVA

22 _ ESORTAZ. COLLABORATIVA

23 _ COMUNICAZ. DIRETTIVA

24 _ AZIONE (ASSEMBL. TESTA)

25 _ SCELTA NON CONDIVISA ESORTAZ. DIRETTIVA

26 _ RIFLESSIONE AUTOCRITICA

27 _ RIFLESSIONE COLLABORATIVA AUTOCRITICA

28 _ COMUNIC. INTERROGATIVA AUTOCRITICA.

29 _ COMUNICAZ. DIRETTIVA

30 _ COMUNICAZ. INTERROGATIVA COLLABORATIVA

. PAG.-2 .

ALAN	MARCO	FILIPPO	INS.	TOMMAS.
	31_ COMUNICAZ. NEGOZIALE			
		32_ COMUNIC. DICHIARATIVA 33		
	34_ COMUNICAZ. DIRETTIVA			
		35_ COMUNIC. IRONICO / SEDUT.		
36_ COMUNICAZ. COLLABORATIVA (IRONICA)				
	37_ COMUNIC. DIRETTIVA SEDUTTIVA			
38_ COLLAB. SEDUTTIVA (IRONICA)				
	39_ ESCLAMAZIONE COLLAB. /SEDUTTIVA			
		40_ COMUNICAZ. INTERR. COLLABORATIVA		
	41_ COMUNICAZ. DIRETTIVA			
		42_ COMUNICAZ. INTERROG. COLLABORATIVA		
	43_ COMUNIC. DIRETTIVA			
		44_ RIFLESS. AUTOCRITICA INDIVID.		
45_ COMUNIC. COLLA- BORATIVA				
	46_ COMUNICAZ. DICHIARAT. OPERATIVA			
		47_ COMUNIC. OPERATIVA COLLABORATIVA		
	48_ COMUNIC. DIRETTIVA			
		49_ COMUNIC. OPERATIVA INTERROGATIVA		
	50_ COMUNICAZ. DIRETTIVA			
		51_ COMUNIC. IRONICO-SE- DUTTIVA - ARGOM. TRASGRESSIVA		
52_ COMUNIC. NEGOZIALE				
	53_ CONDIVISIONE			
		54_ CONDIVISIONE TRASGRES. COMUNICAZ. DICHIARATIVA		
	55_ RIFLESSIONE COLLA- BORATIVA AUTOCRI- TICA.			
56_ COMUNICAZ. NEGOZIA LE -VERBALE				
		57_ CONDIVISIONE SEDUTTIVA	INTERROGATIVA	
58_ COMUNICAZ. INTER- ROGATIVA				
		59_ COMUNICAZ. DICHIARAT.		
		60 2_ COMUNICAZ. INTERR. ESORTATIVA		
	61_ COMUNIC. DICHIARATIVA COLLABORATIVA			

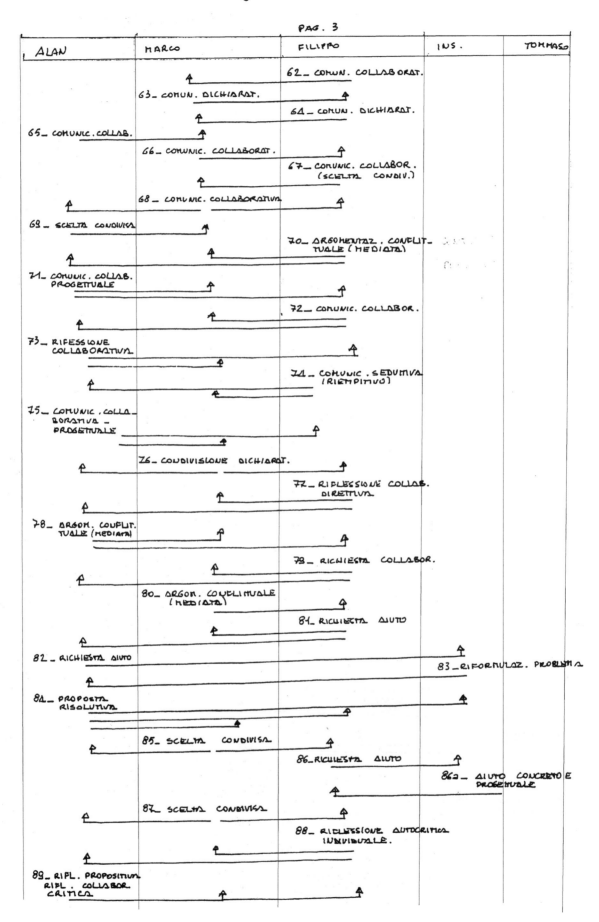

PAG. 4

ALAN	MARCO	FILIPPO	INS.	TOMMASO
	90. ARGOM. NEGOZIALE (OPERATIVA)			
91_ RIFLESS. COLLAB.				
	92_ ARGOM. NEGOZIALE			
		93_ ARGOM. DIRETTIVA SEDUTIVA		
94_ COMUNIC. COLLAB. DIRETTIVA				
	95_ COMUNIC. DIRETTIVA			
		96 (COMUN. DIRETTIVA) RIFL. COLLABORATIVA AUTOCRITICA		
	97_ RIFLESS. COLLABOR. AUTOCRITICA (SCARAMANTICA)			
		98_ COMUNIC. SEDUTIVA		
99_ INTERROGATIVO COLLABORATIVO				
	100_ COMUNICAZ. DIRETTIVA			
		101_ COMUNIC. COLLABOR. AUTOCRITICA _PROPOSTA COLLAB.		
	102_ SCELTA CONDIVISA COMUNIC. DIRETTIVA			
103_ RICHIESTA COLLABORATIVA.				
		104_ COMUNICAZ. DIRETTIVA (DIMOSTRATIVA)		
	105_ COMUNICAZ. DIRETTIVA			
		106_ COMUNIC. DIMOSTR. (ESP. PROGETTUALE)		
				107_ PROPOSTA COLLABOR.
	108_ RICHIESTA CONDIVIS. PROGETTO			
		109_ COMUNICAZ. DIRETTIVA ESORTATIVA		
110_ RICHIESTA CONDIVISA				
	111_ INCLUSIONE NEL NUOVO PROGETTO (CON CAUTELE)			

	ALAN □	MARCO O	FILIPPO △
COMUNICAZIONE DICHIARATIVA	□ ( )	o o o o	△△△△△△
COM. DICHIARATIVA - OPERATIVA		o o	
COM. SEDUTTIVA			△
COM. IRONICO- SEDUTTIVA (:)			△ △ △ (2)
COM. CONFLITTUALE (NON COND.)	□		△
COM. CONFLITTUALE - MEDIATA	□	o	△
COM. DIRETTIVA	□	o o o o o o o o o o o o	△△
COM. DIRETTIVA - DESCRITTIVA	□	o o	
COM. DIRETTIVA - SEDUTTIVA ②	□ □ □	o o (③)	△ △ (2)
COM. COLLABORATIVA	□ □□□□ (IR.)	o o	△ △ △△
COM. COLLABORATIVA - PROGETTUALE	□ □		
COM. INTERROGATIVA	□		△ (OPERAT)
COM. INTERR. - AUTOCRITICA			△
COM. INTERR. - ESORTATIVA			△
COM. INTERR. - COLLABORATIVA			△ △
COM. NEGOZIALE	□ □	o o o	
COM. OPERATIVA			△
COM. RISOLUTIVA			
COM. DIMOSTRATIVA (ESP. PROGET.)			△
SCELTA CONDIVISA	□	o o o	
SCELTA NON CONDIVISA		o	
ESORTAZIONE COLLABORATIVA			△
ESORTAZIONE SEDUTTIVA			
ESCLAMAZIONE COLLABORATIVA		o	
ESCLAMAZIONE SEDUTTIVA			
RICHIESTA COLLABORATIVA	□		△
RICHIESTA DI AIUTO	□		△
RICHIESTA CONDIVISIONE	□	o PROG.	
VALUTAZIONE		o	
RIFLESSIONE COLLABOR.	□ □ □	o o o	△ △
RIFLESSIONE AUTOCRITICA			△ △ △
CONDIVISIONE		o o	
CONDIVISIONE TRASGRESSIVA			
CONDIVISIONE DICHIARATIVA			
PROPOSTA RISOLUTIVA	□		
INTERROGATIVO COLLABORATIVO	□		
AZIONE			△
ARGOMENTAZ. TRASGRESSIVA			△ △
CONDIVISIONE SEDUTTIVA			△

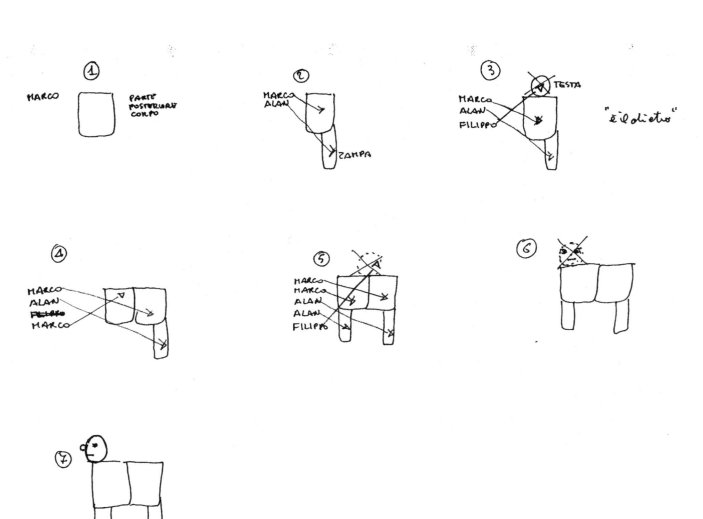

① MARCO   PARTE POSTERIORE CORPO

② MARCO ALAN   ZAMPA

③ MARCO ALAN FILIPPO   TESTA   "è il dietro"

④ MARCO ALAN ~~FILIPPO~~ MARCO

⑤ MARCO MARCO ALAN ALAN FILIPPO

⑥

⑦

Part III. "Drawing a Castle with a Logo Turtle"

A learning encounter led by teacher Marina Castagnetti with 5 year old children.

A. Transcript (English) of the episode, involving two boys and a Logo Turtle, transcribed and translated by Flavia Pelligrini and Carolyn Edwards.

B. Transcript (English) of the large group reflection on 10/16/90 about the teaching/learning episode. (Translated by Flavia Pellegrini, Silvia Betta Cole, and Carolyn Edwards). Participating were Loris Malaguzzi, Lella Gandini (translating), Marina Castagnetti, Vea Vecchi, Carolyn Edwards, and John Nimmo.

C. Charts (Italian) prepared by Marina Castagnetti to summarize children's interaction, which she presented during the meeting on 10/16/90.

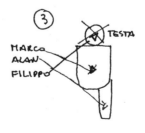

A. Transcript (English) of the episode, involving two boys and a Logo Turtle, transcribed and translated by Flavia Pelligrini and Carolyn Edwards.

Transcript of two boys playing with Logo turtle at Diana Preschool. Translated by Flavia Pellegrini and Carolyn Pope Edwards on March 8, 1991. This episode was not part of the original set provided to the UMass team and thus they had not seen it before the videoreflection discussion.

Tape begins with Marina Castagnetti stooping down and talking to two boys.

Marina Castagnetti: And we can make a castle just like you wanted.

Alessandro: [to friend, Tommaso] No! Let's make a house.

Tommaso: No, let's make a castle with a lake, and here is the grass.

Alessandro: [runs over to show on huge paper]. Let's do this. Let's make here the castle, and here the lake, and here the grass.

Marina C.: Even the grass? Even the lake? [Looking at Tommaso]. *Bravissimo!*

Alessandro: We can even make a bridge.

Marina C.: Even a bridge! [Pointing to computer] Do you want to start now? Come on! If you have anything to ask me, I am right here.

[She stands up, boys cluster around computer].

Tommasso: Let's go straight [pointing] A A. [*Avanti, avanti;* Straight, straight.]

Alessandro: No [as Tommaso punches key].

Tommaso: You can even make a meter. No, let's do 10, no, 11. [spins around to see what happens with LOGO turtle].

Tommaso: Now 10.

Alessandro: Now 20. [Alessandro takes over keys].

Tommaso: 2 0. No, wait, Ahead 2 space 0, and now Enter. [Alessandro does].

Both boys: Look, look! [They look at turtle]

Tommaso: Let's make only the castle.

[Tomasso goes to computer].

Alessandro: Now make it go 3 meters to the right.

Tommaso: [To Marina] To turn? How does it go this way [gesturing with right hand, so does Alessandro].

Marina C.: Which is the right hand? *[Both boys stick out right hands].*

Editors' note: This episode with the children and the videoreflection discussion that follows are notable because already in 1990 the Reggio Emilia educators were looking for more interactive and innovative uses of new technology at a time when computers were typically absent or a passive presence in early childhood programs.

Left: Developer Seymour Papert of MIT, with a Logo turtle robot, which moved a pen across the floor and was controlled from a computer using a visual programming language (VPL).

Both boys: This one!

Marina Castagnetti: That one?

Alessandro: Yeah, Giovanni told me this is the one.

[Tommaso steps up to computer]

Alessandro: Press D [*Destra;* Right] space. How many meters?

Marina C.: Three.

Tommaso: Yes! [Looking at turtle]. Now make it go ahead 10 meters.

[Alessandro presses keys. Turtle moves to the right.]

Marina C.: 10 meters!

Tommaso: What if I go across that way? [Speaking to Marina, and pointing]

Alessandro: [Excited] No! Do you know what we will do? We'll go up, and then we will make a roof.

Tommaso: [At computer] And now, we'll come down.

Alessandro: Oh, no, now we have to turn 3 meters. [Crouching on paper. Alessandro comes near and holds arms straight out, maybe in answer to Marina's question].

Tommaso: Look, this is the left!

Alessandro: [Crouching on paper]. No, Tommi. Tommi. We'll make it turn this way, and then this way [pointing]. We'll do this, make a roof, and then come down.

Tommaso: No, see, look. Let's make a house. This is the door [pointing to paper].

Alessandro: No, no.

Tommaso: Well, come on, let's make a house.

[Skip in tape]

Both boys: [Standing close together, arms straight out]. Let's make it turn this way.

Alessandro: Straight! Two or three meters! At a certain point it will curve this way [pointing], then it goes down, and then it goes...

Tommaso: [runs to computer] Which one?

Alessandro: Left.

Tommaso: [Shrugs] How many? 40 meters.

[Alessandro gives him dubious look]

Tommaso: So, 30 meters.

Alessandro: 30.

Tommaso: [Punching] Oops, two zeros.

Alessandro: Well, try it.

Tommaso: 300, no way! 300 is too much. [Fixes it] Okay, here we go, 30! [Turns to look as turtle goes round and round].

Tommaso: Left and right are three? [to Marina]

Marina C.: No, it's not only 3, before you had written numbers like 3 and 10, now you wrote 30.

Alessandro: So? So now?

Tommaso: [To Marina] Make it turn that way [pointing to right].

Alessandro: 3 meters.

Marina C.: [At paper] It's still turning. [She is holding the wire up so it doesn't twist].

Tommaso: [to Alessandro] 200!

Alessandro: [At computer] No, what do you mean, 200? So, I have to press, Right, that way.

[Skip in tape]

Tommaso: A. [at computer, pressing]

Alessandro: 12 meters.

Tommaso: Let's make it 30.

Alessandro: No, come on, 12.

Tommaso: No, 19.

Alessandro: Let's make it, then, 11.

Tommaso: Aaah! [Pressing wrong key]

Alessandro: 11

Tommaso: [Making gesture of shaking hand] There! Enter. [looking at turtle] He received it! [Both hop over to look, Tommaso holding wire up].

Alessandro: OH! How much? [As turtle goes off paper].

Tommaso: It's going to come down now.

Alessandro: [Runs to computer] Now A 3.

Tommaso: [Runs to paper, holding arms straight out]

Both boys: Down.

Alessandro: No, it's the other way. [Tommaso turns around]. The head is that way. Now, let's turn it 3 down. Is there a G [*Giro;* Turn]?

Tommaso: [Running to computer] Yes. There is a G. No, you can't G. [Pointing to paper]. It's going off, the pen.

Marina C.: G is a different command, Alessandro. Let Tommaso explain it to you.

Tommaso: Let's try I. Backwards! [To Alessandro] You want to go backwards, down?

Alessandro: Let's turn it 3 meters [Punches keys].

Tommaso: [Pushes Alessandro aside] No, you made a mistake! Okay... You do...You want to go down? How much? Three?

Alessandro: No, two.

Tommaso: No, more. You can even do 30 or 40 to go down.

Alessandro: 8.

[Skip in tape]

Tommaso: No, you do it. Because I just did 18.

Alessandro: Okay, I have to turn.

Tommaso: How much?

Alessandro: Three.

Tommaso: No, go forward.

Alessandro: Yes, but first I have to turn [gesturing] so when it comes down, it will make a type of house. [Turning to computer] First I have to press Ahead.

Tommaso: [Comes to show, pushing Alessandro aside] No. It has to go Backwards [gesturing behind head. Alessandro presses keys].

Alessandro: Yes. Now I'll press Behind [turns to look]. How much? 8 meters.

Tommaso: It's too much. You have to do up to seven.

[Alessandro does something. They look]

Tommaso: Now, it's going!

Alessandro: Now, press 4

[Tommaso at computer]

Alessandro: Now press 5.

[Skip in tape]

Tommaso: Press the I!

Alessandro: No, it has to go down. [They struggle]

Tommaso: Try making it go Backwards. Then the house will be prettier. [Goes over to point at turtle] Then there will be a chimney here. You can make it go backwards, and here there will be the chimney. Come on, let's make the chimney, too.

Alessandro: [At computer] I'm going this way. And then, I'll go that way.

Tommaso: Come here! Come here! [Runs to computer] But look, you can press this and make it go backwards!

Alessandro: [At computer] Ahead, yes. *Bo!* I'll press it. I didn't do anything! [Laughing] I pressed first the 0, then the 3. I didn't do anything! Okay, one second and I'll try again.

Tommaso: [Runs over] You have to do a space, then 1, then 0.

Alessandro: I didn't press the space bar!

Tommaso: Good! [Runs to paper] And next I'll go back 20.

[Skip in tape]

Alessandro: [To Tommaso, next to him, at computer] 1000 meters.

Tommaso: [Presses] 20 meters! Weee! [Jumping up and down] I cheated! I tricked you! Now it'll get ahead and it can do the chimney!

Alessandro: [At computer] Now, I'll do it, okay?

Tommaso: Ahead, 3 meters.

Alessandro: Well...

Tommaso: Please, please, please [Makes a praying gesture].

Alessandro: [Hands to face] Mmm, no. [touches Tommaso's shoulder].

Tommaso: Well, no, then I'll go ahead 3 meters. [Both run to paper]

Alessandro: But I want to turn it this way.

Tommaso: We can make it go backwards, so there's a chimney. [Stands] And then later we'll go ahead.

Alessandro: But we have to make the tower. If you want to go ahead, then we'll go diagonal. But now we have to go back down.

Tommaso: [Running over] But now, down 2 meters. Then we'll go up, then we'll go down.

[Skip in tape]

Tommaso: I want to make the chimney.

Alessandro: But if we go that way, then we'll make a door, and then we'll make a chimney.

Tommaso: [At computer] Uffa! [Oh!]

Alessandro:[Runs over to computer] Tommi, I'm not going to do this with you any more. You tricked me.

Tommaso:[Pesses keys] Now, we'll make a tower. Then we'll come down [pointing], and then we'll make the chimney. Let's do it that way. [Goes to keys]

Alessandro: A A A.

Tommaso: 100 meters.

Alessandro: No, wait.

Tommaso: No, 10 meters is too much. Let's try 100. [Turtle goes off paper]

[Skip in tape]

[Boys are seen trying to wipe ink off floor, after turtle has gone off paper]

Alessandro: [Laughing] Good heavens!

Tommaso: Let's erase it [tries] Now, it has to go backwards! Go backwards!

Alessandro: [Gets up to go to computer. Tommaso lifts turtle, but it continues to move]

Tommaso: It's going ahead! Now I'll show you how much 100 is.

Alessandro: Do 100 meters again. No, do 1000!

Tommaso: [Runs over to turtle, stuck against wall] I'll move it a little, like this.

Alessandro: The machine is coming! It's squishing! [Turtle runs onto white tile.] Ahhh, there, it's on the paper.

Alessandro: [Jumping up and down with glee] To the right! 200 meters! [Tommaso at computer]

Tommaso:[Jumping also] Yes, 200!

[Skip in tape]

Tommaso: Now, 0. [looks at Marina] How many zeros?

Alessandro: You forgot the space bar!

Tommaso: 200 meters. [Presses keys] And Marina . . . [Tape cut off]

[Skip in tape]

Alessandro: [Turtle is off paper again] It did 200! [Laughter]

Tommaso: Let's make it go ahead. We made a mess. We have to do it over.

[Skip in tape]

Marina C.: Up to now you've made many tries.

Tommaso: But we made 1,300 chimneys. One, two, three, four, five, six [pointing] eight.

Marina C.: Well, you could have made just one. If you want, now that you have made these attempts, and you have gone off the paper, and you have tried all of these numbers, but you still have to make the castle. We could always change [the paper]. As you want.

Alessandro: No, a house! A house is easier.

Tommaso: A bridge?

Alessandro: [Shakes head, no]

[Skip in tape]

Marina C.: Earlier you gave us a series of numbers that were always different, and for that reason perhaps the forms that came out on the paper were always different. So if you like you can try and make a drawing yourself, then using this drawing, give the turtle commands.

Tommaso: Shall we make the roof first?

Alessandro: No, the chimney.

[Skip in tape]

Marina C.: This [holding paper] is the thing that can help you very much. If you want to draw the chimney, you can try to draw it on this paper as you like it. And then do it with the turtle. Following the commands here on the paper.

Tommaso: [Holding turtle] But we get to write the numbers in. We don't even have to write the numbers on the paper, or else we'll make a mess.

Marina C.: As you like.

Alessandro: [To Tommaso, about turtle] Put it in the position for the chimney.

[Skip in tape]

Tommaso: No, after we finish the chimney, then we can continue the drawing. [Plan of chimney is seen]

Alessandro: Okay, you do it. Be careful. Ahead.

Tommaso: [Smiling] And the chimney. How do we do the chimney? It's really difficult, can we do it without the chimney?

Marina C.: First, why don't you find the right position for the turtle. [She bends down at paper]. To begin.

Tommaso: Oh, it's like that [Stepping over paper].

Marina C.: Which way does the roof go?

Tommaso: Like this, diagonally [*di traverso*]. It's straight but not really straight [Gesturing].

Marina C.: This part right here, how long will you make this piece?

Tommaso: Four meters.

[They watch turtle go]

Tommaso: A little more.

Alessandro: Hit 10.

Tommaso: What if we make a mistake? [Turtle goes]

Alessandro: [At computer] Down. Now it has to turn. [Goes over to turtle, Tommaso joins him] We have to turn it.

Tommaso: We have to turn it like this. [He turns it manually]

Marina C.: Tommaso, maybe there is a command that will make it turn by itself.

Tommaso: No, it doesn't exist.

[They crouch over their diagram]

Tommaso: No, not on the roof, over here.

Alessandro: [Draws] Not the roof too. Let's say this is the back of the house. [Draws 3 sides of a square]. Let's do the back.

Tommaso: Okay...No, we have to do the front. [To teacher] Is it true?

Marina C.: You can do either one.

Tommaso: No, no, the back. [He draws, turns the paper over and starts again, draws house with door].

Marina C.: What is this, the back or the front?

Tommaso: The back. [To computer] How much do we want to go ahead?

Alessandro: [Gets up] No, 23.

Tommaso: No, more, 30. [He does it]

[Skip in tape]

Tommaso: [Adjusts turtle] Shall we make a cube?

Alessandro: No, we'll close it down here. [Tommaso. adjusts turtle]. Ahead 10!

Marina C.: [Comes to computer] This one is Du D.

Tommaso: *Destra* [Right]

Marina C.: Up to now, what commands have you used? Let's look at the printout.

Tommaso: A.

Marina C.: See how many times you wrote A. A. A. A. A. Before, when you wanted to make the turtle turn, there were these other commands as well. Try and use them. You can try them if you want.

Alessandro: Ahead.

Marina C.: You remember, Alessandro?

Alessandro: A space four. [Turtle goes ahead. They scream because it's going the wrong way].

[Skip in tape]

Marina C.: If you want it to go that way, which way does it turn?

Tommaso: [Gestures] *Su su* [*Sinistra*, left].

Marina C.: If you don't make it go left, it will go over there. But where do you want it to go? [She turns turtle] Before it was turned this way and it was going ahead. Now if you want it to go this way, which command should you give it? [Gestures to her right]

Alessandro: *Destra* [right]

Tommaso: S — left.

Marina C.: [Takes Tommaso by right arm he has outstretched] Which arm is this?

[Skip in tape]

Alessandro: We're doing it, it's working. [They are both very excited]

Tommaso: It's still too small.

Alessandro: Put in 9 again. [Tommaso is at computer]

Tommaso: No, less. [Turns around clapping. They both laugh and run over to turtle].

Both boys: It's doing it!

Tommaso: And it's also making the chimney!

Alessandro: We should have gone...

Tommaso: Yeah, we should have gone more up.

Alessandro: [Leaping in air] We should have gone 3 or 4.

Tommaso: Now it's this way!

Alessandro: Left! Left! [They rush to computer. Tommaso steps on Alessandro's foot. They issue the S command]. No, no, right, right. [Runs to paper].

[Skip in tape]

Alessandro: What did you push?

[Skip in tape]

Alessandro: Still one more. [They laugh, standing at computer]

Tommaso: No, that's enough.

Alessandro: No, one more still. [Issues command]

[Skip in tape]

Tommaso: [Grabs turtle] The door! The door!

Alessandro: No, it's on top of the cord [Removes cord from under turtle].

[Skip in tape]

Tommaso: [To Alessandro] You are stupid[?].

Alessandro: Four.

Tommaso: [Runs to paper, back to computer] No, more, more. No, that's enough.

Alessandro: [At computer] Now *Vu*.

Tommaso: It's put like this [holds arms out straight].

Alessandro: We have to make it rotate to the right. [Returns to computer]

Tommaso: How much? Three.

Alessandro: It's done!

Tommaso: It's too low. [At paper, near turtle] Okay, put the S.

Alessandro: [At computer] No, I want to use A. [They are fighting and pushing.] Tommi, I want A.

Tommaso: Stupid. [Playfully punches Alessandro].

[Skip in tape]

[They are rolling on paper. Alessandro points to diagram].

Alessandro: It has to go here.

Tommaso: [Moves turtle] And now we're going to make the door bigger. Here.

Alessandro: Ahead, four.

Tommaso: [Moves turtle] No, excuse me, over me.

Alessandro: I'm going to push A.

Tommaso: [Both boys are at computer]. 5 or 6. This looks like a real door.

Alessandro: 4.

Tommaso: 3. [Punches it in] In fact! It's right! [Raises arm in cheer].

Alessandro: A.

Tommaso: How much? Four? [They turn to look and cheer]. Two more now. [Tommaso does it].

Alessandro: No, 1. [He is down on paper near turtle].

Tommaso: See, it's one meter. [Gives command, Alessandro raises arm in cheer].

Both boys: We did it! [To another child who has just come into room]. Look how good we are!

Alessandro: Why don't we make a window now?

[Tommaso returns with other children he has brought. He jumps up and down.]

Tommaso: Now we have to do the window. It's like this [gestures] We have to go to the right. [To other children] Look now.

Alessandro: We did it! We did it! [To Tommaso] How far do we have to go down?

Tommaso: [To other child] You don't know how to make such a beautiful house. Now, S, let's try it, 3. [Jumping and leaping]

Alessandro: That's right, now go ahead. [Tommaso gives the commands]

[Skip in tape]

Child: It went out.

Tommaso: We just did the double window. [Picks up turtle.]

Child: Completed! Completed!

Alessandro: Let's make a garden too.

Tommaso: [To teacher] Let's change the color.

[Skip in tape]

.

Alessandro: [Returns turtle] Now we want to move it down. [They go to computer]

Tommaso: 30. [Other boy gives the command]. No, that's too little. [He points to keys and hits one] D. No, that's too much. [They look at paper]

Alessandro: Right! Right! [they look] Left!

[All the children come in]

Tommaso: Squeeze my leg [all children squeeze it]

Marina Castagnetti: Why are they touching your leg?

Tommaso: I just finished this hard job! We did two papers! We covered two papers.

Alessandro: Look, first we went here [pointing] then we went here [pointing].

Laura Rubizzi: Show me everything you did.

Tommaso: Door, window, window, roof, chimney.

Laura Rubizzi: Did you draw it? [All stand and admire]

[Skip in tape]

Alessandro: Look there's a magic marker.

Laura Rubizzi: Where?

Alessandro: [picks up turtle] Here! [shows where magic marker is under turtle.

Vea Vecchi: How do you do it? Does it go by itself or do you move it?

Tommaso: No! With the keys! [pointing to computer] [to children] You can put it wherever you want. [Punches a command. Turtle moves.]

End of tape.

B. Discussion: "Drawing a Castle"

English transcript of the large group reflection on 10/16/90 about the teaching/learning episode (Part III, A).

Participating were Loris Malaguzzi, Lella Gandini (translating), Marina Castagnetti, Laura Rubizzi, Vea Vecchi, Carolyn Edwards, and John Nimmo.

(Translated by Flavia Pellegrini, Silvia Betta Cole, and Carolyn Edwards.)

Marina Castagnetti begins preliminary description.

Marina C.: Children had already learned commands on the computer, and had ended their first encounter with the computer with the wish to build a castle. Before, they had not encountered problems of coordination, orientation (therefore right and left), and also last time they had had fewer chances to try. They had just drawn and given commands—very free commands—

Loris: I have some doubt. You have to give children problems that they are able to resolve themselves, even when there are difficulties, and here I am afraid that the children have been put into a situation that they can't get out of on their own.

Lella: They did arrive at a solution.

Loris: The conclusions that they arrived at were pretty uncertain, pretty insecure. They still have not arrived at the fundamental executive acts to be able to foresee how to measure a certain intended distance. And perhaps they remembered that RIGHT 3 creates a right angle.

Lella: As Marina was saying, the first encounter was an experimentation in learning right and left, forwards and backwards. This second one—

> **You have to give children problems that they are able to resolve themselves, even when there are difficulties, and here I am afraid that the children have been put into a situation that they can't get out of on their own.**
>
> **— Loris Malaguzzi**

Loris: [to Marina] They had done right and left?

Marina C.: Yes, they had encountered it, but—

Loris: Had they encountered the right angle?

Marina C.: No, no, no, no, no, this is the first time that they find themselves in front of a concrete problem [an *operativo*], and they had the choice whether to move it or not.

Lella: This seems to be a second level in comparison to what happened the first time. They move the turtle when they find it in front of themselves.

Loris: They do, with their hands.

Lella: But this time we are at the second level. The next time they try this experimentation, they will have these other things to show (or prove, *mostrare*).

Loris: I don't know if they will remember that to make a right angle, they have to press 3, and this is only a part of the problem. Because if they can't foresee the measuring of the distance, of the height of the house for example, they keep making little attempts, bit by bit, but they don't know if the last bit will be exactly what they wanted.

Lella: So they could skip this step that they did here?

Loris: I would have given the children more information beforehand. [I would have] given the velocity of the turtle, and the space that the turtle can go across, I would also have given the possibility of three different angles in order to let them have a right angle, an oblique angle, and a third one absolutely improper.

Lella: So I can ask myself if, without having done these imitations—it's very interesting when they find themselves seeing the turtle go around and around—and that is when the problem poses itself. If they hadn't arrived at that point, would they have assimilated these pieces of information? It's a question.

Loris: Well, I don't know...

Marina C.: They found themselves in front of moments of need to clarify some things and that probably giving them this piece of paper right away—and it was ... I would like to know what does that mean, "We burned some moments"?

Loris: What I meant was that the distance for the children, they have to get from A to B, I'd like to see if they have the potential means (methods) and levels of reasoning, leaving room for error, too. But to see if they have the force of reasoning to tackle all the problems that will lead them to point B. We have found some very tenacious (stubborn) children, and also distracted ones, who continued but continued through trials and errors. Now trial and error is fine for a certain period of time, but after a while the error should be wiped out, because they should be assimilating the knowledge.

Lella: According to me, on seeing this video, this method of trial and error already from the beginning to the end [of the video] is very different. They adjust their aim tremendously. At first they are going everywhere on this sheet. They are also playing. Afterwards, when they effectively want to build this house, their attempts are a lot more measured or careful [*misurati*]. They start to have an idea of distances—that's when you should give them—

Loris: [to Marina] You intervened when the turtle started going around in circles.

Lella: Because they asked for help.

Loris: If she hadn't intervened, they would have been in a mess up to here. But the intervention that you can do is very ambiguous. You have to tell them RIGHT 3, so you give the children the solution.

Lella: She reminds the children what they had done earlier.

Loris: How do they go from 30 to 3? It's not a real passage (step) for the children.

Vea: I have the feeling that at the base of this discussion—

Loris: It's okay as an experience—

Vea: We are always like the children—

Loris: Yes, yes, yes—

Vea: We feel the need to—we tell the children, "We are here for you. You can call us." It's clear that if I'm closer, he will call me more, and if I'm farther, he will call me less. But we also have the need to see how the self-initiated learning [*auto-apprendimento*] of the kids goes, what rhythms it has, also to understand when we give them this type of information [pointing to paper] if we anticipate the children too much [give them the answer too soon], or if we give them the right information, I feel that it is a need of ours—

Loris: It's not that we are ___?—

Vea: No, no. Well, you are probably right. It is true that we are not *nato ieri* [born yesterday]. When you teach, you know it. But we always have to adjust ourselves in respect to the children. We have to listen to them more. At least once or twice a year (these are precious moments for us) maybe we are wrong, but we feel the need to—

Lella: Carolyn wanted to make a little observation on this. I had explained to her that we were talking about intervening and giving information.

Carolyn: In regards to this issue, in watching the video, I was paying particular attention to the emotional highs and lows among the children. I thought it was an episode where they began with what Loris said yesterday was, a main goal was to work together through to completion. [Lella translates into Italian.] And as we watch the video, we see that there are certain moments where they go from their usual mode, which is discussion and collab-

> Now trial and error is fine for a certain period of time, but after a while the error should be wiped out, because they should be assimilating the knowledge.
>
> — Loris Malaguzzi

oration, into a high gear. And there are several times when that happens. One of them is when the turtle goes off the paper, for example. I think that these represent "teachable moments," and in fact, they are moments when Marina does intervene with some help to them, and so as they occur, they lead to the children gradually iterating to the final knowledge that was very appropriate. [Lella translates.]

Loris: Yes. Yes, only she [Marina] can't offer it to them.

Lella: In what sense can she not offer it to them?

Loris: Because she can't offer it to them. [To Marina]—When the turtle went off the paper, what did you tell them?

Marina C.: No, no, I didn't intervene—

Loris: So you didn't intervene? So what did the children do?

Marina C.: They thought about what command to press to get it back on the paper.

Vea: And from that moment on, they re-dimensioned all their numbers [so they would fit on the paper]—

Loris: Yes, yes, yes, yes—I'm not saying our children are stupid, they are intelligent, but there are some "knots" [problems] that they can't overcome.

All: [Talk at once.]

Lella: Carolyn is saying, isn't it shortly after that that Marina suggested making a plan or sketch on the paper?

Vea: [Nods "yes."]

Carolyn: I thought she waited, she let them get it back on the paper—it was excellent—

Marina C.: But even when I intervened, there was a tendency that before it could have been a game [*gioco*, game or play], and there was the temptation to let this turtle go wild, and I asked them which were the commands to move the turtle— which commands they had succeeded in using— because they always use the command A [*avanti*, advance] to move the turtle, and it seemed they had forgotten the existence of LEFT and RIGHT.

Laura: And also the mother [of one boy] was telling me that they have been in the middle of moving house. And so he had arrived with a drawing, a plan of how his new room was arranged. And he says that since at home the only thing discussed was the plan of their new house, they started measuring their furniture, and he's always measuring, and I have tried, even here in my classroom, some problems of measurement. And in effect, she knows what he is doing. Obviously he is using the method that the workmen use, and he can orient himself pretty well.

Loris: He's discovered the red numbers and the black numbers [on the ruler].

Laura: He knows that 100 is the end of the meter, and 200 is the second meter, and so for Tommaso the ruler has become an instrument he knows.

Loris: I want to say that for a kid, the ruler can be used as a glass. The little kid knows what to do with a glass. And he knows that a ruler is for measuring. But it is a very rough or simplistic association, unless you tell me that he has learned that by adding the red numbers and the black numbers you get a meter 45.

Laura: A meter is a hundred centimeters. He can find the end of one meter at the 100 mark, so he can count one centimeter, two centimeters, three centimeters, four centimeters...

Loris: So he can measure one meter 53?

Laura: Yes.

Loris: And what does he write?

Laura: 153.

Loris: So what does this mean?

Laura: It means that, according to me, when they first operate with centimeters, so he understands the hundreds, and even though nevertheless he makes wrong measurements, they have arrived at operating within the tens—not 300 but 30. And according to me, even though he hasn't completely mastered it, still it doesn't seem completely casual this passage that they undertake.

Loris: This is still an operation that has nothing to do with what is going on here [in the video]. That a child can understand there are measurements inferior to the meter, it's a discovery; but if he doesn't know that to make 50—he knows that 50 is half of the meter, it's less than the meter—he doesn't know how to hit the button that will make the turtle go half of the meter. In other words, here is an extra machine- -which isn't there in your case—which if you don't know how to use, you can't go ahead.

All: talk at once.

Loris: [Pats Marina]

Lella: [to Carolyn] Laura said, He is like a German to the kids. [To the group of adults]—These are different problems, because the meter doesn't correspond to the measurement on the computer. So how do you make this extra—

Marina C.: One step of the turtle is 10 centimeters.

Loris: If they had had next to them a 10-centimeter ruler that looks like a normal ruler, then they would have put this object next to the line they were drawing on thre computer. [He demonstrates on the paper.]

Marina C.: [Mumbles something.]

Lella: It should be the next thing to try.

Marina C.: It is right that this is the first time you use the ruler, yes?

Lella: Carolyn says that is a very interesting question.

Loris: It's not that I give them the ruler, saying it's a ruler. I just place it there.

Laura: Well, the children will understand that it's a ruler if you put it there, because they are intelligent. You just tell the child, "You can use this."

Loris: That is what I want [to happen]. I want them to see this relationship, because this game on the computer is nothing other than a game of relations. It's a dry, straightforward relation between the paper, the turtle with the magic marker, and the button on the computer, which is an indication of moving ahead. It indicates whether to go ahead or backwards. The child can do nothing but straight highways. They are in no condition to do anything else. A house is in the distance—when we asked them to do a house with a castle and a chimney, they give you exactly the distance in light-years. Between the objective possibility of the action, that the child or children can presume together, in respect to the house as a dream, there is too much distance. There are light years in between.

Carolyn: Did the children ask for a ruler?

Loris: No, no, they don't talk about a ruler.

Carolyn: In other cases do they ask for rulers? [Lella translates.]

Vea: When they have more information about its use.

Carolyn: If they know how to ask, then the fact they didn't ask is significant.

Loris: The ruler is a didactic tool that is absolutely necessary. Until we find that there is something wrong with the ruler didactically, we will always find children who know that it is a ruler, because the ruler is a word or image, but it is nothing more.[1] Until the child is four years old, he must not see the ruler. The best thing would be to have one carpenter's rule, a tape measure, and a 10-centimeter ruler, or a normal ruler that has the divided lines, because the relationships will be found by the children later. Objectively there are tools to make this relationship and to redo this journey, and thus, the perception of the ruler [coming to understand it].

Marina C.: We began with some evidence, and there were certain situations created in respect to the children, the trial, the ruler, orientation. We should have been able to foresee this situation.

Loris: We have to know how that works. If you told me how to work that thing [pointing to the computer] if nobody tells me I can't find it [figure it out].

Marina C.: This is a method in respect to these children, by using the word "to try," it's a key word in respect to the computer, for fear of surpassing the machine—

---

1. Editors' note: We think he means the child does not understand how to use this tool until he is about four years old.

Loris: I can't give the children the conjugation [*coniugazione*, logical map] of trying. The child tries and explores, there is no doubt that the child tries, fixes it, tries again, and fixes it, and tries again. This is a capability of learning that the child has already after four days of life. The problem is to try, in view of that we have to take a hypothetical approach that lets us, on the basis of intuition, and with the experience of a child—for example, I give the children this assignment, where they don't have the means right now, but there are means that the child could grasp by himself, the children can take them, and in that way they can arrive or understand the assignment. It's a very tiring game. There is a fun side to it, because of the turtle, but if there were no turtle but only the computer, the game [playful interactiomn] would stop.

Lella: That is obvious.

Loris: The great vitality of the game is given by the turtle, which leaves a tangible sign for the children. It is the energetic support.

> The child tries and explores, there is no doubt that the child tries, fixes it, tries again, and fixes it, and tries again. This is a capability of learning that the child has already after four days of life.
>
> — Loris Malaguzzi

Marina C.: For example, in comparison with the games that the children do with the turtle on the floor, and that of confronting a labyrinth (maze), because with the labyrinth, you know the exact distance that you want to cover, in that way you measure and you give the computer a command, for example, 50 centimeters.

Loris: With the labyrinth the child is forced to study a dimension. While here with the turtle, the limit is infinite.

Vea: I don't know about you, but he has convinced me! I agree, because like I was saying before, if the teacher wants to see, he must foresee as well. In that way the teacher should use some instruments that are relative to this process. In that way you give the child extra routes [*percorsi*, pathways].

Loris: The experiment *per se* is interesting. [Everyone interjects.] It is interesting as it is. In fact, everything that we do that is different and is not attainable, we do not for the child but for ourselves, to understand more. We need this, not only to make some subtractions, but to make transformations of proposals, and this proposal can be added on a hypothetical basis, in a way that comes spontaneously from the child himself, without the adult having to intervene. Because if there is an adult, one must understand what is the role that the adult plays, and see whether he is an observer who interacts at key moments, or is a detached observer who supports but does not interfere. If he doesn't interfere, it is clear that I would have to lower [*abbassare*] the project. In a correct didactic situation, we should always have the ruler at hand. And if you discover with marvel that the child is measuring all the furniture in the house with a ruler, you can't understand why.

Marina C.: Because he didn't ask me.

Loris: By measuring all the furniture in the house, and having fun, why can't he have fun inside [himself] as well?

Lella: There is another point of view. The idea of motion is different. Carolyn said that one of the things that is hardest for children is to turn around and get a sense of direction. But that's another discussion.

Loris: The two difficulties are, first, that the child makes this movement ahead, but at the same time he can't govern or control this movement ahead. And the second thing is that I find that there is no solution to this. It's unsolvable because of the mistakes they make. For example, if they go 10 instead of 2, and then if they go 3 more, and then 5 more, and then 4. There are two ways of moving ahead. There is a real progression, the children make adjustments with this attempt to re-establish the right to control this—the important thing is not to take away the right of controlling that the children have—and the right of being put in front of a knot is more the right of the child than that of the adult.

Marina C.: I think it is also a more prolific situation in respect to the numbers. Because we are in this situation that there is this ping-pong using the numbers, and there are many other situations where the child is put in this situation of having to choose and make decisions concerning a quantity. So which situations are these?

Loris: In terms of quantity, I don't know.

Laura: There are many complicated solutions.

Loris: For example, there are Legos, and wooden blocks—they find adequacy in these situations, and the rule [of quantities] becomes contained in the objects. All the child has to do is perceive that one piece is the same size as another one. So then putting one here and putting one there, he sees that he has two of the same height.

> *In fact, everything that we do that is different and is not attainable, we do not for the child but for ourselves, to understand more.*
>
> *— Loris Malaguzzi*

Laura: But he also encounters a problem with the length [of the object]. The objects can be many times of different lengths. Sometimes there is something on it to indicate its length, but the little child doesn't notice it.

Loris: You have this instrument that I gave you, that I've never seen anywhere else, where there are all these indicators for the comprehension of numbers. Where all these objects are inside the box. It has nothing to do with the ruler. It's an experiment from the School Piace Diana [?], that I brought back from Switzerland.

Laura: We want to try it first.

Loris: The maximum that can be done with the computer, the computer will help us spit out all the didactic inventions that we can make with poor materials that have nothing to do with the computer. I can assimilate the computer by playing. We have to take the computer and shoot at it and make it disappear. So now you play without the computer as if you were the computer—this is the di-

dactic. Look at these things [papers on table]; this is a game that you do all the time, you do it like a robot because you do it so many times, isn't that what a computer does? This isn't the game of the 90-degree angle. These are the things we do that the computer spit out at us. The only thing that came out of the computer are those things [papers], which are very ingenious, but that is the only thing that the computer produced. That is like the "basket of miracles." It regenerates all the miracles that you put into it, and it reproduces other ones. I know that I am in front of a problem that the children cannot resolve, this problem of the right angle or the determination of the angle. And then I intervene, and I teach them while they are doing it. This is a method that could be considered good. Because when the children find themselves in front of a problem that they can't get out of, the adult intervenes and helps them get out of it. When the turtle started turning on itself, this created a problem. At the point when the turtle was turning around and around, her intervention was necessary, so it is justifiable because it was necessary.

Lella: Carolyn is asking, how much it is necessary for the children to know beforehand? Because this is the key—

Loris: As much as is necessary. If I put you there and we start playing robot, you do exactly what I want you to, and I'm telling you that you have to go straight. And you obey and go straight. These are the conditions which the children started off with. And then it seems that they have no further capacities. But instead, children can say, "Now turn to the right. Now this way," and you turn this way. "Go the other way! Go the other way" and you go that way. If instead of a small angle, I want you to make an angle with 30 and 60 degrees, in other words, playing with your whole body, this is what should have preceded that first part. But someone says there is a big leap between this game and that one, and I know this, but that's where I want afterwards the more complicated relationship [referring to the first game]. I am teaching them the computer. But I am teaching them the underlying rules of the computer, and these are the rules the kids will find out for themselves later on, so the determination of the right angle, or greater than 90 degrees, with that game there [pointing to papers] they can make one very well. That game there in reality gives you the variations of the angle and also the dimensions of the angle. Now I don't remember whether they were two or three, and what was the command.

Marina C.: It doesn't make a difference. But in regards to the video, you are just talking about right angles and such. For instance, what if Tommaso says, "Let's put this diagonally [*di traverso*]" because he wants to make the roof of the house. There's a diagonal, and maybe a right angle—

> At this point, as a teacher, what am I supposed to do that I didn't do?
> — Marina Castagnetti

Loris: But there is, according to ..[points to video]

Marina C.: Yes, there is, but for instance, here he moved it with his hands, because he still wasn't fully in control of how to operate the computer, and he puts it diagonally [*di traverso*]. At this point, as a teacher, what am I supposed to do that I didn't do?

Loris: According to me, I think you did fine. You just should have pointed out to the child that lifting up the turtle was outside the rules of the game.

Marina C.: And in fact, later I did, reminding him what the commands were.

Loris: I have to say, this is a solution that exists, but they don't know how to find it even though they know it is there. The solution exists—so now they know the solution exists and they have to find it, but they don't know how—they can't. Because it's the machine that has conventional keys. If you know what these keys mean and one says, "Indianapolis," and you push it and get 30. But until you know that Indianapolis equals 30—

Marina C.: It's a possibility you can have, of course.

Vea: [Mumbles.]

Loris: The relationship was, trying to discover if they could go from the pinks and the greens [pointing to papers], if they could come to an understanding of the computer. And I would have told them, "Watch out, because the computer contains those elements [pointing to coding on the documentation papers]" The turtle is made so that it will obey all the commands that are in it. At one point they ask you, "What is the rule? Will you find it for me?" Marina at that point would have taught them to press right 3, left 3—that's the correct point for her to intervene. This is the great discovery of Vygotsky [Lella nods "yes"], when you see that the child is taking the first steps on this road then it is logical and right to give him the keys that will allow him to walk further.

Lella: Yes, but this is the delicate part we were talking about. When you hand him this [key]...

Loris: Yes, but Lella, try and imagine the difference. If she had told the children right away, that to make a right angle you need Right-3, it would have been all within a cold moment. At a certain point the situation becomes "hot," because the children put all their work into it. They use both their lungs and then even find a third lung—we don't have them but children have a third lung—

Vea: We have one too! [laughs]

Loris: Well, you are teachers. [smiles] But the children had undoubtedly used all their capabilities. They had offered up their heart and their spleen onto the alter of the country [*Altero della Pace*, in Rome].

Laura: In that moment, you have the choice of telling them how to do with the computer what they had done with their hands...

Loris: Because they need a right angle at this point, I

would have taught them how to make a right angle. I won't teach them yet what is beyond the 90 degrees. I won't tell them yet, the 95 or the 85. When they pick up the turtle and put it on the diagonal [*in traverso*], that's the right point to teach them about the 95.

Lella: But Loris, it seems to me that what you were saying now is a little bit different from what you are saying before. Because here we have a hot moment. Right? which suggests itself as a moment in which to teach. But before when you talked about information to give them, you were talking about "cold" information, you were saying, "Let's close the ruler."

Loris: No, I always leave the ruler—if they had used the ruler beforehand—the problem is, would the children have remembered that in a case like this the ruler is necessary and important?

Lella: So you were saying, in another preceding hot moment, the children arrived at the ruler.

Loris: If they had used the ruler beforehand and had been here alone, they might at some point have remembered that they have a ruler at their disposal, and that to understand how to finish their path, maybe they could have used a ruler. They would have discovered many things which here they didn't discover. In other words that the turtle precedes at a certain velocity and this velocity equals, I'm not sure, three centimeters [someone interjects, 10 centimeters] okay, ten centimeters, if they had had a ruler nearby, they would have discovered that if the turtle goes 10 centimeters, they look at it—they discover something! So I take the ruler and I put it here, so I discover that I have to do this command twice. In other words, the problem for the children is finding the relationships. If they find the relationship, and here the most important relationship is concrete, and there are some moments in which you have to

provide the objects, because they are products of human culture and they don't just happen to be there, and this falling back on the objects allows the child to find hidden relationships and to come into possession of an extra mental structure. Here there is a jump in the mental structure, in other words, what you add is an improvement to what you had before, but the learning, in order for it to take place, needs these structural passageways. The procedures in themselves do not guarantee that they will come to understand the structure.

Lella: No, no.

> This is the great discovery of Vygotsky, when you see that the child is taking the first steps on this road then it is logical and right to give him the keys that will allow him to walk further.
>
> —Loris Malaguzzi

Loris: You need some sort of *spark* [*scintilla*], the one that will make you come into possession of the knowledge that you didn't have before.

Lella: So the delicate moments are, when using objects like the ruler that have become familiar and can provoke a spark, and also the intervention of the teacher, who can provide a support [*stampella*] which helps them to arrive at the new level. So we are at a completely different level, because the problem of the angle is much more complex, also because it involves the computer.

Vea: Even though in a simpler way, it would have been enough, even if they had not intervened. In other words, if you foresee all the objects that could possibly set off a spark and provide them, almost certainly the children would have understood and used them. So I think the children would have used them.

Loris: You could have done it even without using the ruler, maybe. If pressing the key makes the turtle go 10 centimeters, they still haven't been able to master this measurement. If they had mastered it, they would have used it to go on. But if I see that the children cannot discover on their own that the turtle is going to go 10 centimeters, we take a piece of paper and we cut it and make it as long as this...[gets up and walks off].

Lella: [To the others] Carolyn had a question. The first time you noticed the children picking up the turtle with their hands, the children seemed to ignore your intervention for a couple of incidences, as if they enjoyed this act of...it was easier for them.

Marina C.: But this is a situation of challenge in a way, as well as of transgression. On the one hand, it is also easier, so we have the economy side of it, and it is also a challenge to the teacher. It's also the numbers, they are having such a good time and no one was stopping them, they made their turtle go all the way to the window. And afterwards they waited for it to come back— even there they could have picked it up with their hands. It had gone off the paper, so it would have been more time saving to pick it up with their hands, but they waited for it to take all its little steps on the rubber [linoleum], which also takes longer, while the solutions of the computer were more convenient. I can't say to what degree we can establish this. [Lella translates into English.]

Carolyn: I was surprised when they shifted from lifting it by hands to using the computer. It seemed satisfying to their need to do it quickly. Then they could go back to moving it by the computer. [Lella translates into Italian.]

Lella: Even because they seemed to have forgotten their right and left for a while, but then they remember it again. And they are very happy about remembering it. And they are very satisfied.

Carolyn: I think it was wise, in fact, that you let them satisfy that need to act and then that was followed by a need to think about, like they almost had to recover themselves. [Loris returns.]

Vea: I just want to say one thing in regards to what Carolyn is saying. Whenever a child does something—and maybe we do this wrong, there is always a doubt—we wait a moment, because we notice that the next time they can resolve it on

> *But you are always afraid that you are going to lose the hot moment. It's really a balancing act.*
>
> *— Vea Vecchi*

their own. But you are always afraid that you are going to lose the hot moment. It's really a balancing act. And I believe in intervention, but personally I tend to wait because I realize I have the tendency to hurry to intervene. I have noticed that the child often resolves the problem on their own and not always in the way that I would have told him to. They often find solutions that surprise you and, among other things, they teach you something. But sometimes waiting means losing the moment. So it's always a decision that is in part conflictual.

Loris: They continue to pick up the turtle. If she [Marina] is absent, they are authorized to think of themselves as in a desert, and they don't even have a water bottle—[Vea and Marina seem to shake their heads, no]—no, no, because they legitimize this up until the point that they are disturbed by the intervention of the teacher, who says, "Look, there is also this written rule." The children, who were looking for the solution, would have gone over to the computer and realized that Right-3 was the solution they were looking for. The more you indicate or persevere with a mistake, the more the child legitimizes it. He puts his roots into it. And they are pretty desperate roots in this case because there are no saints that can be invoked to help them. But if you say, "No, look, there is a possibility here, if we are in the desert, and I have a radio, we can transmit with it." If someone tells the child that they have this object they can use, they can call home with, at this point the object becomes Jesus Christ with all his Apostles. [Everyone laughs.]

Lella: Let's see some of the video, because all of these interesting points have come up. Do you have any particular observations?

Marina C.: Well, in regard to the analysis of the language of this possibility to group, in situations that are collaborative or conflictual, for instance, in reading the language, the word "Let's do"[*facciamo*] appears 17 times, and not only this but also if we can do it, let's try, let's see, we must, let's do, let's turn around [*riusciuamo, proviamo, vediamo, dobbiamo, andiamo, rivolgiamo, torniamo, retorniamo*] they are all action verbs in the plural that always refer to [moves hand back and forth to signify teamwork] especially Tommaso, who 13 times in a quarter of an hour [Loris interrupts, Vea touches his shoulder to try to restrain him] it's to help the other boy—

Loris: The plural form is a compensatory plural of help …

Vea: That is just one opinion—[refers to Marina as holding another]—

Marina C.: No, it means that we are here together—

Lella: No, it's not true [smiling]

Marina C.: What he is saying?

Vea: [Shakes head.]

Loris: Verbs.

Marina C.: They are all knots in which there is *faccio* [I do].

Loris: They are all verbs that any individual when in the Amazon jungle would say—"*Andiamo, tentiamo, proviamo,* [let's go, let's try, let's test] maybe we're making a mistake." [All speak at once.]

Lella: No I think it's the fact that there are two of them. They are used to working more than one.

Loris: Yes, that's a possible interpretation, but—

Lella: But it's the two of them discussing together—

Loris: Yes, but I think it's a very reasonable response, very logical, very intelligent. They realize that they have two, to get more effort than just one of them can put in. So they get together, and in that moment they strengthen each other. And they tell each other that they are tied together to the same destiny.

Lella: But the question is, *facciamo,* meaning "let's agree on this course of action."

Marina C.: Yes, and always in the language, in the knots of the choices, the fact that they start off with a proposition that is not yet mutually agreed upon—

Loris: [leans over to study chart] They say *facciamo* [let's do it] 17 times, it's because they are two of them—

Marina C.: Yes, in fact there are two of them. But the tenacity of which she [Carolyn] spoke before, in regards to the choices before them, yes they have to take into account their number [the two of them] but there is also the capacity to be able to follow a project that they want to do, with all these problems—one wants a castle and the other wants a house—and there are moments in which one gives into the other, and sometimes they come together, and sometimes they don't, whether to make a castle or whether to make a house. They need to give themselves a goal, something they can do together—

Loris: Whether they make a house or a castle, the distance varies, and so they need different instruments—

Vea: But what if it were as Marina is saying, they understood that collaboration and mediation were the two forms of communication that they had achieved—and I had added in my notes, it seems as if the children were using it a lot. But there is the presence of other forms of communication, from the non-mediation to mediation; the conflicts; the conflictual argumentation. These move away from moments of need and survival, and this underlines a need to build—

Loris: Yes, but what does this mean, to build?—

Vea: But it is not only a negative form, as in trying simply to survive. Otherwise there would be only these two forms of communication. The others accentuate thought that is progressing.

Loris: [Mumbles, deep in thought.]

Vea: [pointing to graph] In that case we would have a very flat graph. Not a graph like the one we have.

Loris: In a situation of this kind, if you evaluate everything, you realize that the moments of conflict are few—

Vea: No, no, that is only in the first 10 minutes, afterwards there are more conflicts.

Marina C.: For instance, in a moment of conflict,

when Alessandro says, "Tommi, I'm not going to do it with you anymore, because you trick me..."

Lella: Could you explain that again, because that is very interesting?

Marina C.: They are moving in 2 different roads [*strade*]. Tommaso wants to include ... he wants to add a chimney to the house at all costs; even before he had expressed this desire. So Tommaso says, "Let's go up and let's come down, I want to make a chimney," and Alessandro says, "Come on, let's send it ahead, look if we put it here, we can make a little door. And then from the door we'll turn and go up," and Tommaso says, "*Uffa!* I've already put it here." And they were arguing about the commands. Tommaso wanted it to go backwards and Alessandro wanted it to go forwards, and this was a moment in which neither one gave in, because one was always sending it forwards and one was always sending it backwards. Alessandro feels tricked, and then he turns his shoulders and says, "I'm not going to play with you anymore"—

Lella: Because the other one is pressing the other key—

Marina C.: Yes, and the other one had already done this once before, this was the second time. There was already one time when Tommaso had said, "I've fooled you, I've fooled you," because he had given one command unbeknownst to the other.

Loris: Yes, there is a traumatic moment, but it was not a generative conflict—the movement ahead. It's simply a moment of different choices. It doesn't touch any problem, because it is only a dispute between one who wants to make a chimney and one who doesn't.[1]

Vea: Because when they were here [pointing to the graph] one of them thought it would be a lot less time consuming to make the chimney and then continue on instead of how the other one wanted to do it—draw the door, then draw this [pointing to her drawing], then draw the chimney. So

one thought one choice would be a lot less time consuming.

Marina C.: But it's also a choice, because later the conflict is resolved by Tommaso who says, "Okay, let's make the door, too," because he is not only going back, not only to the less time consuming idea, but also to the original idea of Alessandro.

Vea: But going back to the conflict, which you [Loris] were saying had to be qualified as a hard or a soft conflict, so we can't look only at the conflict, we also have to look at the voices, for instance, non-mediated argument [a teacher doesn't intervene], a choice that's not agreed upon, and so there seem to be different phases of the conflict. If we look at the quality of the argumentation of this conflict, we should analyze the entire process. I continue to believe that it is important to mark the time, because in the first 10 minutes, there is an initial stage of communication, and in the last 10 minutes, for instance, they modify the stages a lot. I also have to look to see if there hasn't been a productive progression in the communication.

Loris: There is a difference between assimilation and accommodation, an *equilibria maggiormente* [a balance leading to growth]. You can understand what could happen in the moment that the child gets a new stimulus. When the child assimilates, he is simply assimilating a food; he just puts it inside himself. But in the case he doesn't only assimilate it, but he breaks it down and rebuilds it in new terms, so he has understood something. So the equilibrium that causes increase is when this passage from here to there enlarges his capabilities. So we have to ask ourselves whether in this case if it was a line of reasoning that led him to a higher plane of reasoning, which would have occurred if the child had said, "It's better to go from here to here" [pointing to the drawing] but if this has not happened, it is simply a choice of your mood ...

Vea: Certainly, certainly, that's right, that's right, I agree. I think that this happened maybe not with the quality that it would have had we—in this I agree with you [Loris]—

---

1. Editors' note: See earlier discussions about "trauma." We think he is saying here that the minor conflict does not concern a meaningful problem and therefore is not serious enough to be engaging and productive.

Loris: I want to explain this to you, because there are no conflicts of this type here. Because there is an invitation for both of them to be significantly ahead in his thought, so both of them are together in these oscillations that are contained, because neither one of them has the possibility to discover what they can't discover [Vea nods, she agrees]. So the conflictuality of this type cannot exist. There is a conflict of options [choices] only. The quality of the proposal has within it the possibility of generative conflicts, or of conflictuality that is in some way lasting. The reflection that you have to make right away, and if we had done it earlier, we might have resolved similar problems. What you need is to understand right away that if you give them an unresolvable problem, you can't have conflictuality, because no one can arrive at ideas that are more elevated than the others. So this is a situation where, lacking conflictuality, inevitably I have to come across some large quotas of collaboration, which is an anxious collaboration—sometimes fun [*divertita*] and sometimes not. And there is schizophrenia, highs and lows and mood swings in here that transpires through the words. The words are the words even in the dark. But even in the desert the words are the same. So there is a repetition of terms used, which is hard for the children to escape from. So it plays with itself. It bites its own tail. So what I want to say is that every hypothesis can be preventative with a lot of caution, calm, and patience. After a work of this kind has been done, we have to explain to ourselves, maybe the titles of collaboration and the cooperative thought of learning can exist only when the situation of the children has at its availability the possibility of some advancements in respect to, therefore, of more advanced intuitions in respect to the other, and of more courageous hy-

> *... in those moments where we let children go for a really long period of time, united together, the fact that accepting the theories of the children is like that of accepting a proof—a proof that was inside and also outside.*
>
> **— Vea Vecchi**

potheses, and so in that case, there is a conflict. If there are only two of us, there can be collaboration, if there is no third party, then maybe the passage is a lot more sincere, open, and pleasant, and if there is an adult, we have to see what kind of relationship the children have with the adult. Because the adult can sometimes bring out the conflictuality.

Vea: [to Loris] I would like to stop on this a moment. This is the type of analysis that is tied in general terms. But we used the computer and the shadow, so that the computer has certain rules so that it can make its movements right away. But the shadow always has rules in the action of space that are very different. This type of letting go makes the idea of the shadow stronger. Even though I gave them a series of instruments, like the flashlight in their hand, the streetlamp, and in fact, we gave them a lot of instruments. For example, in those moments where we let children go for a really long period of time, united together, the fact that accepting the theories of the children is like that of accepting a proof—a proof that was inside and also outside. The ruler in respect to the children is also like a recipe [set of directions]. It is also in part a game in respect to the modifications and making the activity flexible.

Loris: I think they are kinetic things, and the kinetic aspect should not exist. Confronted with the shadow, the multiplicity (*casistica*) of the reasoning for the children has its limits, but these limits can be surpassed. If I am going from A to Z, and I arrive at M, I have already done everything that I have wanted to do, and this is a lot.

Vea: —the [educational] objectives in-between—

Loris: The situation is pretty analogous, because the children don't have the key of the physics—the shadow in their hands. There is no solution in both cases. When George Forman came here, he showed us some machines. The objective contained in these machines was that of redoing and comprehension, that was contained in the rules of the machines themselves. The point is, to see the objective.

If I want to go up Mont Blanc, I know that it is over 4,000 meters, I know there is ice, I know there is danger, I know there are needed pitons to climb it—one thing is ascending the mountain itself, and the other thing is just knowing that the mountain is there.

In this situation [with the Logo turtle] it is not like that. It is all depending on Divine Providence. This is like the insertion of a *siepe* [hedge], and beyond the hedge, who knows? [He gestures.] It could even look nice. In reality, the barrier the child confronts is like "the Infinite" [*L'infinito*] of [Giacomo] Leopardi [19th-century Italian poet]. This doesn't take anything away from the worth of the activity. But these values are tied in contingently to the intent. This could not allow more than what did happen. We could have had some limited actions on the part of the children, the loss of reticence and of concentration and exploration, I continue to insist that the turtle was essentially or substantially the motor of their Formula One Racing, in effect there is in this design a sort of unbalance. Because one of the elements acts more strongly in respect to the other. If I gave the turtle to a one-year-old child, and this turtle starts making lines, it would be magic for the children.

Lella: It's too fascinating [for the one- year-old]. I just wanted to ask you about something that Carolyn wrote. If you wanted to pinpoint the purpose of the situation—because one of the questions that should be asked in regards to an activity with children, is whether during this activity a moment of

> ... one of the questions that should be asked in regards to an activity with children, is whether during this activity a moment of optimal learning occurred, that included the solution of the problem.
>
> — Lella Gandini

optimal learning occurred, that included the solution of the problem. This could be considered a fundamental and important [pivotal] moment. But are there other pivotal moments that you can underline?

Loris: This is the maximum ambition. And we don't ever know if such a moment will happen, but we must predict that they might happen. In the design of the whole project, the situation to explore, I can increase or decrease the probability that such events may or may not happen, but I do not have any certainty.

Lella: [translating for Carolyn] In planning, I should take into account and make it probable or possible for this to happen—as likely as possible—to do the best for it to happen. It's like an optimum condition for teachers. I cannot guarantee it, but I should make it the goal.

Carolyn: And there are no other equally fundamental goals than that?

Lella: What do you see as the most important goal? And do you see other ones that are just as important?

Loris: There is the possibility of prediction. I see this topic as an exploration. If I am here and I am planning, I can predict an encompassing [*reticulare,* linear] situation that can be different, because this is the optimal form. But there are some intermediate stopping-points [objectives] that can start moving the children ahead. Should I expect everyone to reach the maximum point? No. That solution is not there. You cannot bring all the children to the maximum. I can only bring them to this point by using a type of symmetry like this one [I'm drawing here, with uneven outcomes, all have moved some ahead]. These partial routes [journeys] are extremely important because they induce the children to move forward. When children are in this situation, they create a situation where they step on each other's feet and fall one on top of each other. [He breaks into song from Verdi's opera *Il Trovatore*, *"An-diem', andiem', andiem'."* Vea bursts into laughter.] The children stop, and make a mess [*pastiche*] and stay there … always. If they discover that they can move even a small amount that will allow them to proceed even more. It's very important, one child sees another moving ahead even more, and then that one gets going. They all see the maximum possibility. We come back to the invention of fire [rubbing two stones together]. If I put one stone here and another here, we have to see if we can get them close enough together to make a "spark." There is sometimes a cognitive conflict. We must help these ones [pointing to picture] to enter into the area of the conflict. It might happen that this conflict is resolved independently by the children, but it is probable that they need the help of the adult. The important thing from the standpoint of research is that we see that there must not be excessive distances between the children. So the optimal situation is to have differences, but not excessively large ones. These differences lie in the different levels of the maturity of thought. Also differences of social competence [*padro-nanza sociale*]. Because there can be some very intelligent children that are scared and ashamed to show their intelligence. That's why we start when they are very little, we put them in a pair, it's still a private competition. With three children, it is still a private competition, but with the possibility of an inferiority of one of the three. With four children, it's another type of thing altogether. In theory, it offers the possibility of many different dynamics. There can be one leader, or two can get together as leaders, or if A protects B, then C and D need to make an alliance. So that there devel-

> The important thing from the standpoint of research is that we see that there must not be excessive distances between the children. So the optimal situation is to have differences, but not excessively large ones. These differences lie in the different levels of the maturity of thought. Also differences of social competence.
>
> — Loris Malaguzzi

ops a division or partition in the group. Or B can ally himself with C and D against A. This creates a dynamic possibility that is superior to groups of two or three.

Lella: Do you think this grouping is connected to the age of the children and with how well they know each other?

Loris: Yes, there are the factors physiological and of social-cultural providence [family background], of language capability, and also the capability of having control of your body in respect to the others. If we must choose the organization of groups, I would insist on two or three, or four. With more children, I do not know what would happen. I could even get six children together, but then the game would have to be adapted. We can even play Bingo with 12—

Lella: Everyone has their own card—

Loris: But the maximum productivity comes out of three or four children, from the point of view of research. But whatever the results that are obtained, there are always results with great positivity. As if the results were not only dependent on the behavior of the children but also the behavior of the adult.

Lella: The important thing is that the adults have certain behavior among themselves and there is a different way in which they treat children.

Loris: That is one of the fundamental questions. If operations of this type can be done, where the children can recall models or examples that are ambiguous, [in terms] of dialogue, of problematic, compared to where children live [at home?] without models of problems of socialization, of discussion, in the level of the adult world...

Lella: In one of the interviews, someone talked about

the civil attitude of children, and I thought that this was their [adult] attitude. This is reflected in the parents. It all becomes like a reflection, where through their behavior with the children, and also with their attitudes toward the teachers, the children and at school...

Loris: What do you think would happen if the parents saw all of this stuff? They would find themselves in front of a new world. Christopher Columbus is not here yet. The children are still in an America that has not been discovered. If you showed them that the children are doing this, and you introduced them to this, and you let them in, they would encounter a new child. The usual reaction for a parent is to run away! Because they feel incapable of governing this machine. Because they can't govern this with respect to the times they are in, their culture, and its unfamiliarity.

Lella: We are returning to the point of where the child returns home after school ...

Loris: The poor person is like the rich person. In a moment of opulence or comfort. A child who is poor ... The more the time of the parents' relationship to the children is shortened, the more they need to qualify it to the maximum, the quality of their intervention. The child needs confirmation in the morning, in the afternoon, at night, all the time.

Lella: The doubts the parents have, they are even bigger.

Vea: The question is the relationship. But also for the teachers. Sometimes when I go around, the way to work it's *labile* [unsteady] because you see the teachers become pale. Because this represents certain models of communication.

Loris: We see that these are extraordinary things. But paradoxically, they should be kept almost secret. [to Lella] Do you understand? Even if another instructor or teacher sees it.

Lella: These are the kind of things that take a lot of energy out of the teachers. Nobody wants a child who is going to get in the way.

Vea: No, no.

Loris: The child who gets in the way [*ingombrante*], nobody wants him. It is not only the child who is difficult for his behavior, it's also a question of sensitivity, or the level of "why." He is the child of no one. Nobody wants to be the mother or father of Mozart. At this point we can consider theories of social representation.

Vea: Yes, yes.

Loris: Those social representations are not prejudices [stereotypes]. They are theories that are divulged and sometimes manipulated. Sometimes because they inevitably play their game, but that they are inside our dialogues, our words, when we talk in the bars, like the woman who screams from the fifth floor down, and chatter in the cafe, and discourses in the academy.

> What do you think would happen if the parents saw all of this stuff? They would find themselves in front of a new world.
> — Loris Malaguzzi

Social representations are like a type of rules, brain clots, they are intrinsic to our way of thinking, working, acting, even our imagination is not completely free. So we have inside ourselves a certain amount of social representations which are cultural representations, which in a certain sense are a parody of the real culture. They are everyday things that take on [are possessed by] bigger problems. Other times they are theories that are made to seem irreversible, precise, and many times these theories are dumber than common sense. So many times these social representations that are even in our behavior .... The big theme here is that many times these "isms" such as behaviorism or realism [take over]. Moscovici [social psychologist] says very clearly, we are today in a civilization that is behavioristic, and so we see ourselves as in a behavioral way. This is the way things are. If this is the reality, we have to start looking for more things within ourselves. We have to pull more things out.

Lella: Speaking of social expectations, and behavior that comes from theories that are half-absorbed, because in the United States they have different social expectations. We are not speaking about very big differences, because our cultures have been shaped by similar influences. And because they are subtle differences, if you look at it in comparison to the education that they receive in Africa or the East, it is a lot easier to see the differences. And it is these subtle differences that make it interesting, coming to see what they do here, or going to Amherst, because you have to dig out what the expectations are.

Loris: Now I understand why the Piagetian discovery in the United States was so strong. Because one Piaget—not the Piaget—but one Piaget coincides perfectly with—

Lella: But Piaget, who always spoke of the "American question," the questions Americans always asked Piaget was why can't we accelerate these stages, and he couldn't stand this.

Vea: [Laughs heartily.]

Loris: It is the auto-construction of the child that they accept. The things that Carolyn is saying are much more advanced. She voids the vision of—

Lella: She [pointing] has a more anthropological viewpoint.

Loris: It's fuller, it's more correct. I don't want to say more progressive, but more correct.

Lella: It's a different viewpoint.

Loris: I think that in the more advanced places [pointing at Carolyn], they are recuperating critically Piaget. They are coming to understand that the child of Piaget is a child without reality. He is a formal and fictitious child. And there is also another very important criticism in respect to egocentrism. When Piaget tells a child, "You are egocentric," it's because the real egocentric one is Piaget himself. Because in the first place, he is thinking as an adult and looking at the child and

comparing the child to his mental capacities. And so it is a capacity of decentration. The second thing is that Piaget values only the logic of the child.

Carolyn: But the child's real difficulty is not egocentrism. We know now that the child's difficulty is information processing—how many dimensions of information the child can coordinate at one time—how many facts or dimensions can the child deal with cognitively at one time? We know that the brain is somewhat limited, and that is why we have to simplify problems. The problem is not egocentrism as Piaget said. Egocentrism arises when the child is in too difficult a situation and there are too many dimensions to coordinate at one time, so they focus on only one. [Lella translates.] And already the infant—the first words they are learning are a whole dialogue. They are incorporating a whole social situation at the same time they are learning a phrase. A good example of that is my baby Rebecca. When she was only one-and-a-half, she wanted to tell me that she had spilled something, and she didn't know how to say that, so she looked at me and said, "Oh, Becca," which is what I might say when I saw the spill. She had learned that "Oh, Becca" was an envelope that she could put around the situation of having spilled something. [Lella translates.]

Loris: Yes, yes, they are extraordinary things [these phrases].

Carolyn: It is true that dialogue precedes monologue.

Loris: Without dialogue there would be immediate death. You can pretend to use psychology on the child, but in reality you are using psychology on a dead person. Like that character [the Headless Horseman] who was riding a horse and he knew he was dead...

Lella: Carolyn, did you think this session was fantastic?

Carolyn: Yes! I am still interested to know what you see are the important features of a situation, and

> ... the child of Piaget is a child without reality. He is a formal and fictitious child.
> — Loris Malaguzzi

how you go about thinking about the questions. Again I see this very detailed way that you take on a problem and then talk about it until it seems evident what might be a solution. It's also very sharply critical, and at the same time, maybe not so critical that people can't stand it. [Lella translates.]

Loris: [reaches over and hugs Marina]. We always have to have two pockets: one pocket for satisfaction; one pocket for dissatisfaction.

Marina: [Smiles with pleasure.]

Carolyn: Aha! That takes care of that.

Vea: This visualization [pointing to Marina's chart] is very interesting. I was just saying to Michele who called me on the phone for something else, I just gave him one example, for instance, mediation and collaboration. You can see them in a very positive way, but if you change your point of view, they can be seen as just group survival where the lack of conflict ....

Loris: If I want to be very graphic and give some typical examples ....

Tape ends.

> We always have to have two pockets: one pocket for satisfaction; one pocket for dissatisfaction.
>
> — Loris Malaguzzi

C. Charts for "Drawing a Castle"

Charts (in Italian) prepared by Marina Castagnetti to summarize children's interaction, which she presented during the meeting on 10/16/90.

Marina C.'s VR

SUL PENSIERO COOPERATIVO "DUE BAMBINI AL COMPUTER CON LA TARTARUGA ROBOT"

MARINA, INSEGNANTE A.28	TOMMASO, A.5;6	ALESSANDRO, A.5;5	
OGGI SE VOLETE... POTETE COSTRUIRE IL CASTELLO CHE VOLEVATE FARE INSIEME...	...E QUI NELLO SPAZIO FACCIAMO UN LAGO... NO FACCIAMO UN CASTELLO, UN LAGO E L'ERBETTA	...NO FACCIAMO UNA CASA.	SCELTA NON CONDIVISA
		...FACCIAMO QUA UN CASTELLO, QUANDO FINISCE QUESTA RIGA UN LAGO E QUA L'ERBETTA E FORSE RIUSCIAMO A FARE ANCHE IL PONTE.	RIFLESSIONE COLLABORATIVA
SE AVETE DELLE COSE DA CHIEDERMI, IO SONO QUI...	SI, DAI. SI, QUESTO, METRI... NON 1 SI PUO' FARE ANCHE 20.	ANDIAMO DRITTO, A - AVANTI.	ARGOMENTAZ. NEGOZIALE MEDIATA
	NO FACCIAMO 10,... NO FACCIAMO 11, 1-1	FACCIAMO 20...	
CI SIETE RIUSCITI!		COMANDO	
	ADESSO 10	NO ADESSO 20	
	2- O ADESSO COMANDO	GUARDA VA FORTISSIMO.	
	SUPER, DAI FACCIAMO SOLO UN CASTELLO DAI.	SI	RIFLESSIONE COLLABORATIVA
	SI E' PIU' BELLO.	ADESSO FALLA VOLTARE DI 3 METRI	ENUNCIAZIONE DIRETTIVA
	VOLTARE? COME E' LA D? LA D E' DI QUA?		RIFLESSIONE COLLABORATIVA
QUALE E' LA DESTRA PER VOI? PROVATE	QUESTA?	QUESTA SI, GIOVANNI ME L'HA DETTO.	
		D - SPAZIO, POI QUANTI METRI VUOI?	
	3	COMANDO	
	AVANTI 10 METRI	AVANTI - SPAZIO - 10	SCELTA CONDIVISA
	SI, DOPO 10 DO ANCORA 10 METRI DI TRAVERSO COSI' (DIAGONALE)		ARG. NON MEDIATA
		NO, SAI COME FACCIAMO...	
	FACCIAMO UNA CASA...		ARG. NEGOZIALE MEDIATA
		ANDIAMO SU E POI FACCIAMO UN TETTO E DOPO RITORNIAMO	
	...FACCIAMO UNA CASA E ADESSO ANDIAMO GIU', VA BENE?	NO ADESSO VOLTIAMO DI 3 METRI COSI' VA GIU	ARG. NEGOZIALE NON MEDIATA
	QUALE E' LA DESTRA MARINA? E' LA DESTRA GIU'.		RIFLESSIONE COLLABORATIVA
		NO TOMMI, LA VOLTIAMO DI COSI', SI FERMA QUA, POI FACCIAMO COSI', IL TETTO, POI VENIAMO GIU'.	SCELTA NON CONDIVISA
	NO FACCIAMO UNA CASA... QUESTA E' LA PORTA.	NO	
	BE' DAI... FACCIAMO UN CASTELLO...		ARGOMENTAZ. NEG. MEDIATA
		ECCO LA DOBBIAMO FARE VOLTARE DI COSI', DRITTO,	

③

POI VA SU DI 2 O TRE METRI
POI A UN CERTO PUNTO
CURVA DI UN PO' POI VA
SU UN PO' E DOPO COSÌ...

QUALE ?		RIFLESSIONE COLLABORATIVA
	SINISTRA	
QUANTO ?	40 METRI	
ALLORA NO 30	30 ?	
(CREDE DI AVER SBAGLIATO A SCRIVERE) NO 2 ZERI, NO 300	PROVA DAI PROVA	RIFLESSIONE AUTOCRITICA IND
300 E' TROPPO	SI, DAI	RIFLESSIONE COLLABORATIVA
ECCO 30 COSÌ COMANDO		
MA SCUSA, GIRA SEMPRE... AH SÌ PERCHE' DESTRA E SINISTRA SONO 3		AUTOCRITICA INDIVIDUALE
ADESSO FALLA GIRARE...	DI 3 METRI	RIFLESSIONE COLLABORATIVA
	ADESSO DI 4 METRO	ARGOMENTAZIONE NEG. MEDIATA
200		
	MACCHE' 200... ALLORA..	ARGOMENTAZIONE NEG. NON MEDIATA
	DEVO SCHIACCIARE, UN ATIMO DESTRA..	ARGOMENTAZIONE NEG. MEDIATA
NO A. AVANTI		ARGOMENTAZIONE NEG. NON MEDIATA
	12 METRI	MOMENTAZIONE NEG. MEDIATA
FACCIAMO 30	MACCHE' 30	" " NON MEDIATA
SI DAI 12... ONO 19?	SI	" " MEDIATA
	FACCIAMO ALLORA 11	
NO DAI...	SI 11	ARGOMENTAZIONE NEG. NON MEDIATA
L'HA RICEVUTO, OH QUANTO, ADESSO VA GIÙ		RIFLESSIONE COLLABORATIVA
	ADESSO VOLTALA 3 METRI	
(SI ORIENTA RISPETTO AL ROBOT) IN GIÙ	NO E' DALL'ALTRA PARTE, LA TESTA E' DI QUA, PUOI VOLTARLA DI 3 METRI IN GIÙ, C'E' LA GI?	
SÌ, C'E' LA GI... NO NON PUOI GI VA SU LA PENNA CON LA GI, PROVIAMO A FARE I, INDIETRO VUOI FARE INDIETRO GIÙ?		
	VOLTIAMO DI 3 METRI	
NO MA TE HAI FATTO UN POCCIO! SI FA... VUOI ANDARE GIÙ, QUANTO 3 ?		
	NO 2	
NO DI PIÙ, GUARDA CHE PER ANDARE GIÙ..	4	ARGOMENTAZIONE NEG. MEDIATA
GUARDA CHE DI PIÙ, SI PUÒ FARE ANCHE 30, 40	8	SCELTA CONDIVISA
8		
NO FAI TE PERCHE' IL TUO TE L'HO FATTO IO	ALLORA DEVO VOLTARLO DI..	ARGOMENTAZIONE NEG. MEDIATA
DI QUANTI ?	30...	RIFLESSIONE COLLABORATIVA
NO, AVANTI DI..	E SI MA PRIMA DEVO VOLTARLA COSÌ VIENE GIÙ E FACCIAMO UNA SPECIE DI CASA..	
SI, SI... QUANTO ?	PRIMA COSA DEVO FARE ? AVANTI ?	

(5)

Child A	Child B	Category
NO LA I GUARDA CHE FA ANDARE INDIETRO VERO? VUOI ANDARE INDIETRO? ALLORA I QUANTO?		
	VEDIAMO ... 8 METRI	
AAA... TROPPO	VA BE'...	RIFLESSIONE AUTOCRITICA IND. RIFLESSIONE COLLABORATIVA ENUNCIAZIONE DIRETTIVA
DEVI FARE FINO A 7 PUOI	COMANDO	
HA RICEVUTO, GUARDA, VEDI CHE VA.	ERA 8, ADESSO METTI 4	SCELTA CONDIVISA ENUNCIAZIONE DIRETTIVA
NO VA INDIETRO	NO IN GIÙ VA INDIETRO	ARGOMENTAZIONE NEG. NON M.
PROVA ANDARE INDIETRO, DOPO VIENE PIÙ BELLA LA CASA... CHE POI QUI VIENE IL CAMINO, FAI ANDARE INDIETRO QUESTA QUA E QUI C'È IL CAMINO... DAI... FACCIAMOCI ANCHE IL CAMINO.		ARGOMENTAZ. NEG. CONFLITTUALE
	NO, IO VADO AVANTI ORMAI HO SCHIACCIATO A	
GUARDA CHE PUOI ANDARE ANCHE INDIETRO, PUOI...	AVANTI DI... NON HO FATTO NEANCHE 1 METRO, HO FATTO PRIMA LO O POI 1, NON HO FATTO 10, UN ATTIMO CHE RIPROVO	ARGOMENTAZIONE AUTOCRITICA INDIVIDUALE
A - SPAZIO - 160 - BRAVO QUESTO È 10 E DOPO IO TORNO INDIETRO DI 20 COSÌ IMPARI!		RIFLESSIONE COLLABORATIVA CONFLITTO
	1000 METRI...	CONFLITTO
TI HO IMBROGLIATO... TI HO IMBROGLIATO... 20 METRI IO ADESSO LO SUPERO, E FACCIO IL CAMINO, FACCIO IL CAMINO...		CONFLITTO
	ADESSO IO	ARGOMENTAZIONE NEG. MEDIATA
SI, VAI AVANTI 3 METRI, PER PIACERE LA I, LA I E DOPO VADO AVANTI ANCORA DI 3 METRI		
	E MA IO NON VOGLIO VOLTARLA COSÌ	ARGOMENTAZIONE CONFLITTUALE
NO NON FARLO CON LE MANI SI ROMPE SE NOI LA FACCIAMO ANDARE INDIETRO COSÌ C'È IL CAMINO	MMM.... (DISAPPROVAZIONE)	ARGOMENTAZIONE NEG. MEDIATA SCELTA NON CONDIVISA
SE NO ANDIAMO AVANTI...	MA DOBBIAMO FARE LA TORRE, SE VUOI ANDARE AVANTI 4, FACCIAMO COSÌ DOPO	ARGOMENTAZ. NEG. MEDIATA
ANDIAMO IN GIÙ...		RIFLESSIONE COLLABORATIVA
	SAI ADESSO DOBBIAMO TORNARE IN GIÙ, SAI QUANTI METRI?	CONFLITTO
MA ADESSO GIÙ DI 2 METRI, POI RITORNIAMO SU, POI ANDIAMO GIÙ... VOGLIO FARE IL CAMINO!!	DAI, A-21	ARGOMENTAZ. NEG. MEDIATA
	GUARDA CHE DOPO RIVOLGIAMO LÌ, POI FACCIAMO UNA PORTINA, POI DALLA PORTA VOLTIAMO E ANDIAMO...	ARGOMENTAZ. NEG. MEDIATA
UFFA... HO GIÀ MESSO LA I, BASTA.		CONFLITTO
	TOMMI GUARDA CHE IO NON LO FACCIO PIÙ CON TE! PERCHÉ TU MI IMBROGLI!	CONFLITTO
OH! PERÒ FACCIAMO LA TORRE, POI ANDIAMO GIÙ, POI TORNIAMO SU E FACCIAMO IL CAMINO, FACCIAMO COSÌ, EH! A - 5 METRI		ARGOMENTAZ. NEG. MEDIATA

(7)

A DI 100 METRI, NO DI 100 TROPPO... DAI PROVIAMO 100...	A... NO ASPETTA, FORSE MI SONO SBAGLIATO	RIFLESSIONE AUTOCRITICA INDIVIDUALE
	1 - 0 - 0 , DUE ZERI	RIFLESSIONE COLLABORATIVA
DAI TORNAMOLA, ADESSO DEVE ANDARE INDIETRO, DAI INDIETRO, MA VA AVANTI, MA GIRALE... VA AVANTI QUESTO E' 100? ADESSO TE LO FACCIO VEDERE QUANTO E' 100		ENUNCIAZIONE DIRETTIVA
		RIFLESSIONE COLLABORATIVA
	E' QUESTO 100 DOBBIAMO FARE ANCORA 100 METRI ANCORA	
SI	NO 1000 COSI' FACCIAMO IL CAMINO...	

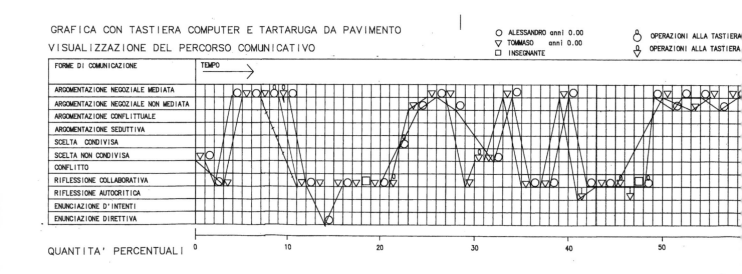

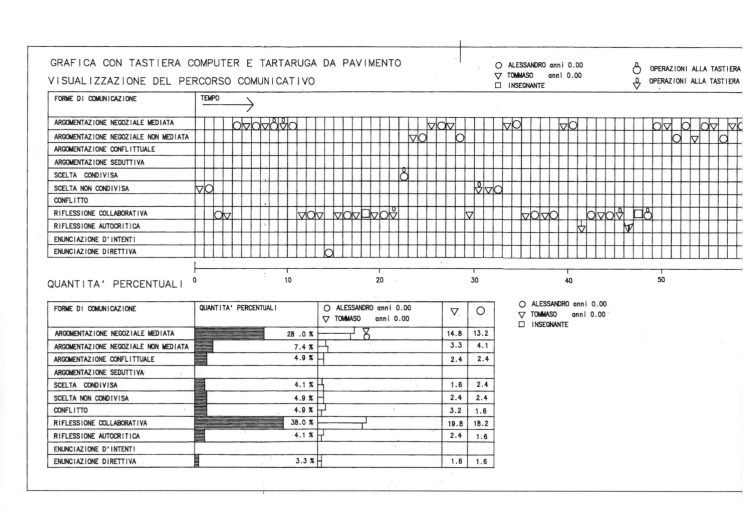

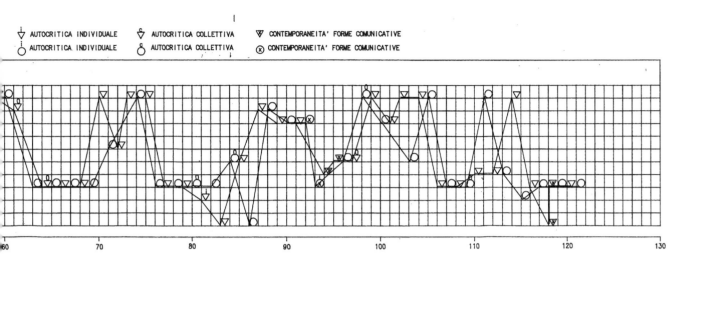

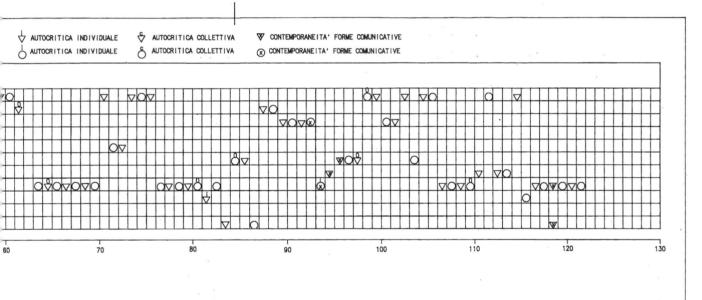

Part IV. "Children Explore Wire"

A learning encounter led by teacher Paola Strozzi
to introduce 3 year old children
to the material of wire.

A. Transcript (English) of the large group reflection on 10/18/90 about the teaching/learning episode. Participating were Loris Malaguzzi, Paola Strozzi, Giulia Notari, Tiziana Filippini, Vea Vecchi, Laura Rubizzi, Marina Castagnetti, Magda Bondavalli, Marina Mori, Lella Gandini (translator), Carolyn Edwards, John Nimmo, and Diana Preschool auxiliary staff. Translated by Flavia Pellegrini and Carolyn Edwards.

B. Transcript (Italian) of children's words during the episode, prepared by Paola Strozzi for the meeting on 10/18/90.

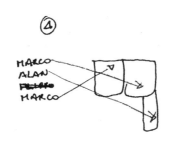

A. English transcript of the large group reflection on 10/18/90 about the teaching/learning episode.

Children 3-Years Old Explore Wire

Setting: October 18, 1990, morning.

Present at the discussion are Loris Malaguzzi, pedagogista Tiziana Filippini, atelierista Vea Vecchi, co-teachers Paola Strozzi and Giulia Notari, co-teachers Laura Rubizzi and Marina Castagnetti, co-teachers Magda Bondavalli and Marina Mori, and Diana auxilliary staff, along with Carolyn Edwards, Lella Gandini,(acting as translator) and John Nimmo.

Video initially translated by Lella Gandini (impromptu) and Carolyn 1/30/91, then by Flavia Pellegrini and Carolyn Edwards 2/15/91.

Carolyn: We have had two excellent meetings so far and are looking forward to this one. We would like to have contribution from anyone in the group about our topic [today].

Paola: The excerpt we are going to see refers to the beginning of the year. There are four children between 3: 6 and 3: 7. One of our objectives was to discover was to discover the different identities of material. Clay, wire, and cardboard. For example, one of the identities of wire is the possibility to be transformed. For instance, a small gesture is enough to change the shape of wire. And very little is needed to go back to the initial shape. It is a material very transformable. This is the second time that these children, 3-year-olds, have experience with the wire. Already in the first encounter the children had communicated to us the characteristics of the material. For example, a child, while working with wire, said to me, "This wire is like a Transformer, because the head can become another head. Therefore, prior to the second meeting we [the teachers] have thought more about these characteristics of the material in order to present it, in order for the teacher to have a more pointed and specific intervention. We thought carefully about how to present the material to the children. We said, "This is a piece of wire" [to Lella: I'm telling you this because I think it is important]

"You can move the wire as you like and you will find many different shapes. Here is a list of things I said. "What has it become [changed into]?" Also you can see [some of my] non-questions, [in] a sort of notation, "It is transformed into .... How is it changed? Before it was... Now it is.. It has returned to be.... What did you discover? How did you transform it from ... to ...?" With intention to give back to the child the sense of process. What we will see is the teacher who will ask questions, the teacher who listens, and the teacher also who experiments herself with wire in a sort of ostentatious way. She is ready to respond to the child's remarks about what she the teacher is doing. You will see the children often turn to the teacher. They say, "Look, I've done this," etc. As they are children at the beginning of the year, they tend to turn to the teacher instead of to the other children, so it is my role as a teacher to return these remarks to the whole group, by saying "Look everybody..." Okay, we can look now. Something more could be noted, analyzing the exchanges between and among children.

The group begins to look at the video. The teacher is seen, saying, "Do you remember this?" Children reply, "Yes, it's a wire."

Lella: I've noticed with interest that on a particular moment, one of the children made an octopus, and the girl next to him said, "It hurts" [it's dangerous] and the two children talked about this without looking at each other but always turning toward the teacher and using Paola as a communication transmitter; and this happened again when they were talking about a whale.

Paola: These children at that point had been in school only one week or ten days. They really don't know one another yet. So they turn to the teacher, who is an intermediary. She is the [searches for word] First Referent.

Someone: Interlocatory?

Lella: Carolyn noticed that Paola is very careful in the way that she presents things to children, and also the words she says, and their economy, as if she had thought a great deal about that. Would you comment on that?

Paola: As I said, many of these remarks had been prepared already, based on the previous encounter with the children. About the economy of words, we always talk about trying to do that, because the risk that the teacher runs is to use too many words. Speaking still of the economy, I think that it could allow the teacher to pay more attention to the children. Even watching this before, we noticed that Marina [one child] was very seldom focused on with the video camera because she spoke very little. Therefore, we think that four children, at this age, at the beginning of the year, are too many.

Vea: One thing I wanted to add is that this experience is part of a wider project which is the comparison of three different materials [wire, clay, cardboard]. Paola said that. One thing that Paola didn't mention yet is "evocation." When you start exploring a material, the teacher should experience it first. What we wanted to see in comparing the three materials with regard to "evocation" was how each medium was producing changes in language and evocation [what images were coming up]. Now we have done several groups—I did some, Giulia did some—and we will be able to see what kinds of images will come up for the three different materials. We will examine that. One thing that I noticed in the video is the action of the children with the wire, and my impression is that with wire more than clay, the lack of action is substituted by evocation by words. [The words supplement their actions, but are not based strictly on them]. Sometimes when the shape that the children are trying to make is not easy, not understandable (definite), they complete the evocation they are labeling with words with gesture. For example, a child took a piece of wire and said, "This is a cape," and made the gesture of swirling it around himself. Making a more complex image that way. Sometimes they work on various small details labeling them as they work on a shape that is not recognizable. We like to extend this playing with evocation, and we have made some plans with Giulia about that. For example, we would work behind the shadow screen, or we would work with the game of "telephone." [Pointing to the video] There, the capacity of the children is increased as they become more skill-

ful with the material, so they acquire skills with wire. They acquire skills in communicating with the teacher and the other children. The same type of evocative game could be done with other objects and media. A dangerous thing one has to watch out for is that the child might think that the teacher always expects for him to evoke something, while it should be clear to the child that the process of exploring is valued itself by the teacher. Here, for example, I don't know how much the child had thought about something, nor was actually responding to Paola's prompting, by saying something. It's a game that children play spontaneously—to create images—even at the infant-toddler center—and we know how important it is, also, in terms of creating metaphors. Therefore it is a game that has to be supported but with the care of leaving the child the possibility to deviate from figurative representation [i.e. not producing verbal images].

Carolyn: Are you very interested in this?

Vea: We are working, comparing various situations.

John: Do you think that rather than responding to the prompting of the teacher, there is a need on the part of these 3-year-olds to be more interested in representation? Because there is a transition at that age from movement as such to the interest in producing something.

Vea: I don't know. Children are so keen and sharply attentive to the requests of the teachers that one has to be very careful about how one poses things to them.

Carolyn: Even at the beginning of the video we see children approach the activity with a great attentiveness and sense of expectation toward this small piece of wire. How does Paola create that or set that up? Like children sitting on the edge of their chair, as if for an opera.

Paola: Regarding how we present things to children—whether a piece of wire or a sheet of paper—there is a great attention on our part. Even the way we

> As they are children at the beginning of the year, they tend to turn to the teacher instead of to the other children, so it is my role as a teacher to return these remarks to the whole group, by saying "Look everybody..."
>
> — Paola Strozzi

position our body is all deliberate. Just the same way as we take care about the environment, so that it creates expectation. It is a matter of *civility* of relationships among people and with materials and the environment. So children feel that, and they respond to it with the same attention.

John: These children feel also the attention that this teacher has put in setting up this kind of choreography for just the four of them. And they respond to it.

Loris: The enthusiasm that is in the adult about trying out something with the children gets communicated to them. I am not considering only this particular situation, but it as if we are starting off together on a trip (voyage). It could be short; it could be long. But it is an eagerness of doing it together. So in this case, we see something very small, almost banal [the wire], but the eagerness of the children is authentic, and the same eagerness is in the adults. So where could this lead us? Here I also see that even though the children do not look at each other, they are listening very carefully to what is said by everyone, and they respond very appropriately to these remarks.

> It is a matter of civility of relationships among people and with materials and the environment.
>
> — Paola Strozzi

Carolyn: What were the specific things that Paola did to help the children enter to one another's thoughts?

Paola: When a child had done something, I would say, "Show it to the others." Except that one of them placed something he was doing right on the nose of the child next to him.

Tiziana: Without taking anything away from Paola, I wanted to note that some of these children might come from the infant-toddler center...

Paola: Yes, all of them.

Tiziana: Therefore, it would be interesting to see when this capacity of the children to communicate first starts. Even with regard to the concentration and attention with which they work, I am referring here when you were looking at the clay activity were noticing how many details kept the children intently occupied. The children's capacity to stay with an activity comes from their previous experience at the infant-toddler center. Their experience there is in tune with our whole project, [ages] zero to six. They work in small groups and they are accustomed to projects and experience. I hope this is heard without taking anything away from the teacher here, and the way she has organized this activity.

Vea: Look at Loris, he is here, we must let him speak!

All: Of course! Of course!

Loris: The first image I have is negative.

Someone: Oh, boy!

Loris: Maybe I should not speak...

All: Speak! Speak!

Loris: In my opinion, it is okay. There is some kind of subtle observation to make. [words or meaning not clear to Lella]. I think you have to decide more clearly what you think that you could obtain. Here, what do you think that you could obtain? Perception of the material? Then you have to think about it. Perception of the flexibility and softness or hardness of the material? Then you have to think very carefully about that. Do you want to extract from the use of the material a word that corresponds to an image evoked? Then you have to think well about it. I am always of the opinion that a game of this kind offers very little, according to me, because it is probable that none of the perceptions that you have forecast are there. There could be a perception which is so volatile [fleeting] that it would escape the child or us who are watching. To see what kind of meaning it has for the child to produce that particular image. I see (feel, sense) that it is difficult to be able to distinguish if we are perceiving the word, the wire, or the movements that the child is making casually, or not, with his hands. I don't know where the image emerges. And I don't know if the image is the result of all this (movement, word, wire). The wire is so thin, the possibility to manipulate it seems so meager that I don't know with this thinness if a hair would not be the same thing.

This is the first question. The second question is, if we stay there, and each of us in turn asks a question, we will receive an answer, a verbal answer, where the child goes from the physicality of manipulation to the sound. Instead, if we start by giving the children a piece of wire, and asking the child to produce an image, they will give you another result. So you have to keep in mind that every result excludes other results. You are blocking one way for the child. The other important point, which is a fundamental requisite, is that we should never, absolutely never, expect that the child will return to us *meanings*. At least for what concerns the first manipulation (for young children experiencing a new material for the first time), the child has to manipulate material to his satisfaction. He has no debt to us. There is no proposal that the child has to make us. He has to savor, to play, to experience the sense and the materiality of the object. Perhaps the more silent he is, the more he is listening to the materiality of the object. And perception is founded in that. You should give [the children' this wire with other types of wire, never one element at a time, never. [Scolding] That way, children discover simultaneously what is different, what is the same. While these wires pass through his hands, the child will feel the differences and with the differences, the child will know [learn] about the identity of the material. Without differences, identity does not emerge. So you can distribute wire which is like a wire, but at the same time you should also give a wire which is thicker and one which is so resistant that it requires a tool to bend it. [NOTE: Lella, translating afterwards, comments that she thinks this would be a mistake]. And I'm not distributing this material as if it were the "host" [the holy bread at Communion] during the morning Mass. This is a very negative image [pretends to give out the host to the congregation]. Well, you take Communion, then you go to Paradise, okay.

All: [giggles.]

Loris: After saying all that, this is a negative image [*nefanda*]. And yet, this game is, for me, okay. But you need to think more about it. I'm convinced that the children cannot even feel that wire. And it seems to me that here that why it produces here so much evocation.

Lella: Because there is so little to manipulate.

Loris: In fact, the children here produce so much evocation because Paola's expectation was toward evocation, in any case. Without leaving the child the time to discover by himself many shapes and to discover by himself the image and the word without our requesting it. That's true also when the child draws. The child has to feel that he has guardian angels who are not constantly sitting on his shoulder. It has to be an angel that flies above, independently. The angel goes to the movies, eats, walks around, and does not hover. I think if we had seen a video where we had placed a pile of different wires, just available, not distributed—because the moment you distribute them, it means that you expect some exact thing that you have in mind. That shows that you don't know how to wait, because what you should expect is a surprise. Maybe a ring will come up, or a duck, who knows. The children try out, explore, mess about, then they try out different kinds of wire, and then maybe they make a ring, who knows. The evocation of what the children do, if they want to say it, and if they say it aloud, and there should not be a precise expectation about it. Unless we do another type of game where from a clue that I give to the child about a shape, I want the child to arrive to that shape itself. But then it's a different activity. Some children go from clues about shape that are more accidental than intentional, and discover the image from something that has practically "exploded" in their hands. And I think that it is a mistake to try to have the child to reconstruct a process that he has never gone through. How could a child do that? It's ab-

> ... the child has to manipulate material to his satisfaction. He has no debt to us. There is no proposal that the child has to make us. He has to savor, to play, to experience the sense and the materiality of the object.
>
> — Loris Malaguzzi

solutely forbidden and impossible. Also because the time to propose or suggest something, assess it and evaluate it, is not given to the children when you call on them to produce an image.

Lella: Would children 3-years-old be able to do that, that is, reflect and then produce an image? Because Paola told us that the children had just arrived.

Loris: It's not that this approach [of Paola] doesn't leave tracks. Anything we do leaves tracks. I think that the right way to proceed is always to let the children define by themselves the meaning of things.

Vea: I think you are right. But something has to be clarified. The children [probably as a whole group] have been allowed the situation—exactly what you are describing—before. With wires of different thickness and color, to explore by themselves. And as a result, the children came up with all the meanings that we have then placed there [probably referring to a poster with many pieces of wire shaped in all sorts of ways, and labeled with the children's own words]. So we had decided, probably mistakenly, to try to extract that meaning, and to try to offer it to the four children that we have seen in the video. Probably making a mistake, in terms of all the things you are pointing out now. Now I'm thinking, taking into account all that you have said, that probably more time we should have given to that. But sometimes we see a meaning that we find interesting and we want to re-propose that specific meaning [*significato*] [NOTE: Lella, translating, suggests: possiblity, example] to the children, as we did here. We like sometimes, following one intuition that we have, to propose something to the children to see what happens [NOTE: Lella: Vea here highlights a researcher attitude on the part of the teacher]. Although I am keeping in mind all your observations about the mistakes, and I think you are right, I have ab-

> The child has to feel that he has guardian angels who are not constantly sitting on his shoulder. It has to be an angel that flies above, independently. The angel goes to the movies, eats, walks around, and does not hover.
>
> — Loris Malaguzzi

stracted meanings from this activity that I didn't have before. So maybe I am always optimistic. [NOTE: Lella: Vea feels responsible for the mistakes of her teachers]. I think you are right about letting the child decide when and how he wants to mention an image.

Loris: I think one has to remember that we learn by comparing differences. Therefore, this idea that some educators have about presenting things piecemeal and sequentially—for example, from the thinnest wire to the thickest, or from the simplest to the most difficult—is absurd. Children need many things in order to understand any one thing. And to understand possible relationships among things.

If you have a smaller [shorter] wire and a bigger [longer] wire, the possible relations are very few. But to have a thicker wire along with a thin one, as the child works on it, he will have more sense of shape and also as he works to make an object, the child will have a chance to absorb at the same time the sense [identity] of the material and a sense of shape. This wire [Paola used] is so thin, if you just move your arm, it bends. The problem, again, is always to play on differences. For example, don't give the child only one glass [to explore]. Give him a bottle also, an empty one and a full one, a spoon—the complexity helps the child to find relationships and meanings, as the game [challenge] is exactly that. Things that are not in relationship are not of interest to us. When the children grow up, they will be able to find relationships also using abstract images. Now they need to find, to discover, variations and changes, using the strength and motion of their hands, the resistance and meaning of objects. If you had given the child a silvery wire, probably the child will construct a piece of jewelry, instead if you give the child a piece of iron wire, the child will come up with something else, and a wire with a red coating, yet something else again. And even a combination of two or three kinds of wire could evoke something else again.

I think you should try it, because it would be a wonderful performance to see children manipulating different wires—how they work with it, how they hold it, what they say—because here [in the video] the children say words to one another, but it would be much more interesting what they would say if they were not responding to a request from the teacher. Evocation emerges spontaneously but it emerges with a sort of double source—it could be coming from the physical manipulation of the wire, or just from an idea in the child's mind. The question is that you never know whether the evocation precedes the working with the wire, or whether it comes out of it. In my opinion, didactic genesis of the use of the material should be the use of material sufficiently homogeneous of the same category, differentiated within the main category as a subset of the system. If the system is the wire, the subsystem consists of the set of qualities of wire. They are a subset but they have the potential of relationship to each other. Children need differences. Children need to know with their hands and their mouth [words], and in this case [the video] they are mostly knowing with their mouth. I don't mean that you should put together clay and wire. The child has to understand that when we say a word such as "wire" it is one word, but it has ten meanings that correspond to ten different materials [copper, silver, etc.] with different properties. The family of wires is like a family of animals. If we say "cat," we intend to cover all of the kinds of cats in the world. Also the word "man" includes all kinds of peoples. This is a very important point to keep in mind, and I think it is important to work that way with children 3-year-olds in spreschool and the infant-toddler center—later you can mix different kinds of material. But I think … .

Vea: In fact, we can only give to the children three kinds of wire, otherwise a fourth kind would end up being too difficult for them to bend. But I want to point out something that is coming to my mind. That is that the "100 languages of children" refer not only to the possible variations that the three kinds of wire suggest, but they are also coming from the various possibilities that the child discovers while working within one category. For example, if I give to the child a board with nails in a grid, plus a piece of wire, then he can make all sorts of shapes. Or if I give to the child, in the way we often do, the same kind of wire in relation to chicken wire, aluminum foil, and other objects, what the child will do again involves many possibilities. I think that to limit the possibilities of the "100 languages of wire" to its thickness only is too constraining. I discovered the many possibilities through a series of different actions. It is true that the video is wrong [pedagogically], but I can extract from the wire, images by making shapes, tying it to other material; therefore, for me, it's not only a question of the one dimension [thickness or color] but a sort of dialogue. [In the same way] she [pointing to Carolyn] changes communication with me according to her gestures, and according to my reaction, and then her reaction to my reaction.

Loris: I think we should respect some kind of genesis of growth, because I don't think at this point it would be correct to give the child too much. Of course you could, but I don't think it would be too good. If you want to complicate things, I'm always the one who complicates things. You could give different wires, okay? Maybe you could add different scissors, sticks, or straws, things the child can relate to the wire, but I think that if you exaggerate with different things, I'm afraid you want end up by impoverishing the material [the wire].

Vea: I agree but... and this is not just for the sake of argument... it is for me a didactic genesis. The identity of material, for example of wire, which has a big or important graphic possibility, and the possibility to be sculpted (in fact, contemporary artists use wire in a cubist fashion, because the sculpture looks two- dimensional and three-dimensional at the same time), so it is fair that the teacher asks the child to explore the material by itself as such for the many possibilities there.

Loris: It depends on what is your objective.

Vea: We had other encounters with different objectives.

Loris: Oh, it's hard to believe that you could have an encounter with the material prior to this one. Because more primitive than this you could not be!

Vea: Yes, there is the possibility for them to experiment freely with the material.

Loris: If the objective is to have the children learn about the substance of wire [materiality]...

Vea: One of the aspects of the substance of wire!

Loris: What do you want to explore?

Vea: The identity of the material.

Loris: Well, if you want to do so, it is clear that the identity of the material is perceived only through a very strong tactile exploration with an extremely varied range of sensations: strong, smooth, pliable, feathery, light, and so on. Then I acquire the sensation of the wire. When I say "a rose," how many roses are there? There are pink ones, perfumed ones, short ones, long- stemmed ones.... You have to assume the didactic and ethical responsibility, because we have not only to clarify our objectives but also our intent. It is a kind of declaration that we have to make every time that we prepare to start something. Keeping in mind that I would always start from complexity rather than simplicity, because complexity has the gift of offering the child an understanding of variations, which is a powerful concept for a child. And that the different qualities of materials make the child aware of the shapes that he is making in manipulating the material. Accidentally is more powerful than intentionality. The more a material needs to be manipulated, played with, made mistakes with, and corrected, the more the material becomes familiar to the child. But these are just a few remarks. The methodology could be pushed to infinity.

If I want to teach music, I don't teach only one note. I teach the child to hit many keys. It doesn't make any sense to teach only "la." Unfortunately, there is this idea that children should be taught only one thing at a time.

Vea: I absolutely agree. But the time is short!

Loris: To teach only "la" does not make any sense. You also have to teach "fa, so, mi, do."

Vea: No, just a minute. If I give the child a blue mark across the page, it's not only like one note, "la." It's more complex than that. But there is not time to discuss any more of this.

Loris: Okay, okay, if you think that any complication is dramatic, then go ahead and just simplify things. [He appears to give up, with a gesture of resignation].

NOTE: The next day, Vea brought together the same group of children and let them explore wire again, with a variation of thicknesses, as Loris had suggested.

> *I would always start from complexity rather than simplicity, because complexity has the gift of offering the child an understanding of variations, which is a powerful concept for a child.*
>
> **— Loris Malaguzzi**

B. Transcript (Italian) of children's words during the episode, prepared by Paola Strozzi for the meeting on 10/18/90.

Paula's
VR

CARTONCINO ONDULATO   (3 anni)

protagonisti : Bobo a.3,7
                Claudio a. 3,9
                Marco a. 3,8

(il linguaggio trascritto si riferisce all'inizio dell'incontro
 dei bambini col materiale)

B. -(con una striscia di cartoncino in mano) METTIAMOLO SOTTO A
    QUESTA STRADA

C. -E QUESTO METTIAMOLO SOTTO A QUESTA! (anche lui con una striscia
    in mano)

B. -METTIAMOLOCOSI' (tenta di chiudere la striscia facendone una
    forma chiusa   ASPETTA MARCO CHE HO UNA BELLA INVENZIONE!!!

M. -HE'!!! SIAMO NOI GLI INVENTORI

B. -MARCO UN PONTE! E' QUESTO (segna il pezzo di cartoncino sollevato)

M. -UN PONTE PER LE MACCHINE

C. -E PER I FURGONI
M. -QUI' GLI UOMINI CI VANNO SOPRA (segna la discesa)
C. -QUELLA E' LA DISCESA CHE FA UUUUUU...BSSSSS

B; -CI VUOLE UNO STOP!

M. -VEDI CHE CI RIMANE ADESSO (probabilmente in piedi come un ponte)

B. -(insiste) SI' MA CIVUOLE UNO STOP!

M. -due... DUE STOP....... (e si allontanano)

Si avvicinano alla rete metallica, la sollevano ed iniziano a riempirla:

    B.- (prende un rotolo di cartoncino ondulato e urla) MISSILEE!!!

    B.- (si mette il tubo davanti agli occhi e guarda C.) CLAUDIO
        EEH!!! MAMMA SE SEI MICROSCOPICO! MICROSCOPICO!!!!

Marco gira con un pezzo di cartoncino legato intorno alla cintura e guarda nel
tubo che tiene in mano Bobo.
Bobo e Claudio fanno una cintura come Marco

    B.- (srotolando il tubo) UNA CINTURONA!

B. e C. si chinano vicino allo specchio con un pezzo (striscia) di cartoncino
arrotolato basso e largo

M. - (con un tubo più alto e stretto) STO ARRIVANDO! STO ARRIVANDO! STO ARRIVA
    e infila il tubo alto nel basso

B. - ECCOLO QUA'!

C; - ECCOLO QUA'!

B. - UNO VA QUI' E ... (segna l'ingresso del tubo)
C. - E CASCA DI QUI' (segna il tubo piu' basso)
B. - EH,EH,EH SI TROVA DENTRO IN UN NASCONDIGLIO
C. - E' UN NASCONDIGLIO QUESTO QUI'! SI' E QUANDO UNO LO CERCA QUI' DENTRO
     FA! : "HOO! AIIUTO!!! C'E' TROPPO BUIO QUI' DENTRO!
B. - NOO! QUI' DOPO METTIAMO UNA LUCE

Marco gira da solo a cercare ltre strisce di cartoncino ondulato

B. e C. scoprono un tubo ancora piu' lungo
C. - OH! CHE GRATTACIELO!
B. - FACCIAMO UN GRATTACIELO, MAMMA MIA! SI' CHE GI METTIAMO ADDOSSO L'altro
     COSI'...
C. - LO METTIAMO SOPRA L'ALTRO COSI' DOVENTA UUU... (mettono un tubo sopra
     l'altro e cadono)
B. - PAFF!
C. allunga a B. il tubo lungo e raccoglieil piu' corto
B. - E' UN CACCIATORE!!!
     (chinando il tubo come un fucile inizia a cantare la canzone dei Gostbust
     TITITITIRI TARATARRA
C. - ANDIAMO FANTASMI!! IN CIELO! CSSSS..CSSSS...
M. entra in gioco e si mette a fare l'acchiappafantasmi
B; - (con il tubo piu' lungo rivolto a C.) NO! METTILO PER TERRA IL PIU'
     PICCOLO!
C. - ECCO QUA'! (appoggia per terra il tubo)
B. - OH! MAMMA SE E' GIGANTE!! GUARDA SE E' GIGANTE (appoggiano i tubi uno
     sull'altro)
C. - STA ARRIVANDO FINO LA' (guarda il soffitto)
M. - QUASI
B. - TOGLIETEVI CHE LO LASCIO!! B. LO LASCIA E CADE e prende il tubo piu'
lungo M. che chiede agli altri due di aiutarlo ad xinserire uno nell'altro
e quindi di aprire il tubo più bàsso

M. - APRITELO UN PO' DI PIU'!!!
B. - EH! COSI? COSI' LO SPACCHIAMO/
M. - EEEEHH
C.-DAI!!!!!
M. - EEEEHH! GIUUUU! MOLTO FACILE! FACILISSIMO!!!

Si riaccostano alla rete metallica ed infilano anche i tubi dentro la rete

B. - E' UN MISSILE!

Iniziano contemporaneamente a cantare un'altra canzone dei cartoni animati
M.B.C. IATTAMAN, IATTAMAN, IATTAMAN ecc...

M. - METTIAMO I MOTORI? EH? DAI!
B. - iniziando ad arrotolare delle strisce AIOTTOLAMOLO!
M. - ARROTTOLIAMOLO!
B. - MA DOPO COME FACCIAMO A RITORNARE INDIETRO?

M. - EH! CI FACCIAMO TUTTO.....
C. - TIRIAMO IL FRENO, FACCIAMO UNA CURVA E POI TORNIAMO INDIETRO!
B. - MA E' TUTTA UN'ASTRONAVE!! SALIAMO DAI SALIAMO!! (fa finta di salire
     le scale)
M.C.B. - PARTIAMO ! (si infilano i caschi e partono)

—

Paula's VR

<u>VIDEO FILO DI FERRO</u> bambini di 3 anni SCUOLA DIANA settembre 1990

3,4
Gruppo: Martina a.✓ Ilaria a. 3,7 Michele a. 3,3   Matteo a. 3,5
insegnante: Paola Strozzi
Ma = MARTINA   IL = ILARIA   MI = MICHELE   MAT = MATTEO.
INS = INSEGNANTE .

Ins.: "Adesso vi do una cosa che abbiamo già visto i giorni scorsi...
      vi ricordate quando i giorni scorsi vi ho dato questo? (mostra
      un pezzo di 30 cm di filo di ferro)
      Cos'è questo?"

Il.: "E' il filo"

Ins. " Un filo ....di ferro....allora io adesoo vi do un filo per
      uno e provate a muoverlo come volete voi e potrete trovare
      tante forme diverse....Proviamo?....Uno per Matteo (vengono
      consegnati i fili di ferro), uno per Michele, uno per Ilaria,
      uno per Martina"

Mi: (guarda Matteo che comincia subito a piegare il suo filo)
      "Non si fa....non si fa così!"

Mat.: "L'edera!"

Ins.: "Cosa? Non ho capito bene, me lo ridici?"

Il.: "Guarda, guarda cosa ho fatto!"

Ins.: (rivolta a Matteo)
      "Fammi vedere bene"

Mat.: "Ho fatto un giro di.....così"

Mi.: "Ma guarda cosa ho fatto...questo.. (è rivolto a se stesso e
      a Matteo)

Il.: "Ma guarda cosa ho fatto" (rivolta all'ins.)

Ins.: "Fallo vedere anche agli altri bimbi"

Il.: (Dondola il suo filo di ferro davanti al viso di Michele)

Mat.: "Guarda, guarda il mio" (spinge il suo filo di ferro arrtolato
      sul tavolo in direzione dell'insegnante)

Ins.: "Bello!....ma cosa è DIVENTATO Matteo? Prova a RACCONTARMELO ~~o~~
      ~~raccoue~~

Mat.: (sillabando) "Un po...un...po..."

Ins.: "Un po....?"

Mat.: "Un pon te"

Ins.: "Un ponte!"

Mat.: "Un ponte che si va su e dopo si ritorna giu'"
(accompagna con due dita i movimenti a ponte del filo di ferro)

Ins.: "E' stupendo Matteo!"

Mi.: "E qui c'è il mio che è una balena....vera!"

Ins.: "Vera?!"

Mar.: (non inquadrata, a sinistra)
"Questo è un pedalò: boing, boing"

Il.: "Un pedalò!"

Mi.: "Adesso questa (balena) si mangia...."

Il.: "Guarda io" (alza il suo filo in aria, Michele è molto attento
al gesto di Ilaria)

Ins.: "In che cosa l'hai TRASFORMATO?"

Il.: "Adesso....." (appoggia sul tavolo il suo filo....lo guarda e alza
gli occhi sull'insegnante come dire: "Vedi un po' tu cos'è")
"....Anche il mio è un pedalò!"

Mat.: "Boing, boing,...." (fa saltare il suo filo sul tavolo ad imitaz=
zione dell'idea di Martina) "Guarda!"

Mi.: c"Il mio è più lungo di così (stende il filo sul tavolo) e mangia
il pesce"

Mar.: "Questo è mio"

Il.: "Ma dove sono i grandi?" (intende i bambini della sezione "C")

Ins.: (sta prendendo appunti) "Sono nella loro sezione"

IL;: "Perchè non ci possiamo andare?"

Ins.: "Saremmo in troppi, e invece qui possiamo lavorare meglio"

Mat.: "Guardxa! ....Te lo dico questo che ho fatto?" (si alza e si
avvicina all'insegnante)

Ins.: "Dimmelo"

Mat.: "Un cu...O....or..."

Ins.: "Un cuore?!....un cuore ragazzi!!!" (rivolta a tutti)
"Ma sentite: PRIMA ponte, ADESSO cuore...."

Mi.: "Guarda io cosa ho fatto!"

Ins.: "Tu Michele eri rimasto alla balena?!"

Mi.: "No"

Ins.: "No?...non è più balena?"
Mi.: "No"

Ins.: "Allora cosa è diventata?"

Mi.: "Un polpo"

Ins.: "Un polipo?"

Il.: "Un polipo? Ma i polipi fanno male!"

Ins.: "Aspetta, voglio provare anch'io...fammi vedere come si fa..."

Mi.: (rivolto a Ilaria) "Ma no, non fanno male....come fanno a fare male"

Ins.: (rivolta a Matteo) "Un altro ponte!"

Ma.: (in silenzio si arrotola il filo intorno ad una mano guardando di
      sottecchi Ilaria)

INs.: (rivolta a Matteo) "Ma come hai fatto che prime era un ponte
       poi è diventato un cuore poi è ritornato ponte, COME HAI FATTO
       Matteo a TRASFORMARE il filo di ferro così?"

Mat.: "Ora di nuovo cuore"

Il;/ "Ma guarda adesso che è!"

Mat. :"Ora di nuovo cuore"

Ins.: "COME FAI?"

Il.: "Guarda me adesso"

Mi.: (ha appoggiato sul tavolo la sua forma a spirale)

Ins.: "Ma ragazzi! (seguendo con il dito la forma sul tavolo di Michele)
       cos'è qui?"

Mi.: "E' un serpente....una lunghezza dixserpente......"

Ins.: "Una lunghezza....."

Mi.: "Una lunghezza di serpente"

IL.: "E adesso fa male!"

Mi.: "NO!"

Il.: "SI'"

Mi.: "Chi?"

Il.: "La lunghezza!"

Ins.: "Fa male la lunghezza?"

Il.: "Ma la balena quando è in mare fa male...quando è in mare"

Mat.: "Delle scale! Ꙃ̶a̶i̶n̶g̶x̶x̶h̶a̶i̶n̶g̶x̶x̶h̶a̶i̶n̶g̶x Bin, bin, bin, (sale con le dita evidenziando la forma a scala del suo filo di ferro)

Mar. (non inquadrata) "Guarda, sembra un pedalò"
(muove in modo alternato i due capi del filo di ferro, movimento a pedalata)

Ins. "Sembra eh?! Assomiglia proprio a un pedalò"

Il.: "Anche il mio è un pedalò"

Ins.: "Come mai Ilaria anche il tuo è un pedalò?" (l'ins. ripete con il suo filo di ferro i movimenti trovati da Martina e Ilaria)

Il./ "Si fa così, guarda! " (muove il filo di ferro come sopra)
I pedalò camminano così"

Ins.: "Provo anch'io!"

Mar.: (si ferma a guardare i gesti di Ilaria) "Questo è un pedalò"

Mi.: "Guarda io cosa ho fatto" (filo di ferro molto arrotolato)

Ins.: "Oh ma come è tutto...." (con la mano fa il gesto di "unito"

Mat.: "Paola...un ....CA VA LUC CIO MA RI NO"

Ins.: "Un cavalluccio marino!"

Mat.: "Un cavalluccio marino"

Mi.: "Zitti, zitti, zitti" (rivolto a tutti)

Ins.: "A me piacerebbe sapere una cosa....ma come hai FATTO Matteo a SCOPRIRE TUTTE QUESTE FORME DIVERSE?"

Mat.: "Le ho fatte x̶x̶x̶i io"

Ins.: "Ma COME hai fatto?"

Mat.: "Ho fatto così...." (mostra con le mani una piegatura possibile del fil di ferro) " E Mi è venuto un cavalluccio"

Mi.: "Guarda cosa ho fatto.....ho fatto una bella.....un piccolo piccolino cucciolino" (il filo di ferro è molto raggomitolato)

Ins.: "Un piccolino?/......"

Mi.: "Un cucciolino che si chiamava cagnolone"

Ins. (comincia ad arrotolarsi il filo di ferro sul dito a spirale, subito imitata da Ilaria, poi, senza parlare, lo appoggia sul tavolo)

Mi.: "(anche lui come Ilaria guarda con attenzione i movimenti della ins. "Anch'io questo devo trasformarlo....in lunghezza.... 'no devo trasformarlo in lunghezza di serpente"

Il.: (rivolta all'insegnante) "Cosa è diventato il tuo?...un pedalò?"

Ins.: "No, non è un pedalò....MI sembra...cosa mi sembra..?...."

Mi.: (con un dito mette in piedi la spirale costruita dall'insegnante) "Guarda!.. "

Ins.: "Oh, sta anche su... sta giù e poi su" (ripete il gesto di Michele)

Mat.: "Un altro cavalluccio marino"

Il.: (si toglie dal dito la sua spirale) "Guarda me...." (appoggia in verticale la spirale sul tavolo e la fa saltare) "Ping poing ping poing...."

Part V. "Children Find a Bug"

A learning encounter led by teachers Magda Bondavalli and Marina Mori with 3 year old children. (It was not discussed at the October meeting, due to time).

A. Annotated account of the encounter by Carolyn Edwards, prepared for *The Hundred Languages of Children, Third Edition: The Reggio Emilia Experience in Transformation*, edited by Carolyn Edwards, Lella Gandini, and George Forman, Praeger Publishers, 2012.

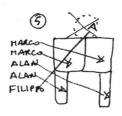

A. Annotated Account of the Episode "Children Find a Bug"

Following is an excerpt from the chapter, "Teacher and Learner, Partner and Guide: The Role of the Teacher," by Carolyn Edwards, in the book, *The Hundred Languages of Children, Third Edition: The Reggio Emilia Experience in Transformation* (pp. 147-172), edited by Carolyn Edwards, Lella Gandini, and George Forman, Praeger Publishers, Santa Barbara, California, 2012.

The episode, "Children Find a Bug," was not discussed during the meetings with Loris Malaguzzi and the Diana School teachers. However, the episode is of great interest, in the opinion of the Editors, and deserves to be included in this volume. The teachers were Magda Bondavalli and Marina Mori.

On the day of this incident, the block area of the 3-year-old in the Diana Preschool has been set up so the two classroom teachers could videotape a "co-operation episode." The teachers have prepared an inviting selection of blocks, tubes, and other lovely construction materials. Then, something unexpected happens, the children discover a bug crawling through the blocks. Instead of interrupting, the teachers follow the children's interest, shaping it rather than canceling it, letting it grow into a problem-solving collaboration involving quite a group of the children. Many questions are posed, implicitly, by the children through their words and actions—questions that could possibly be followed up on another day—about what kind of bug have they found, is it dead or alive, is it dangerous or harmless, how best to pick it up, is it afraid of them, does it have a name, is it weak or strong, is it bad or good, is it disgusting or beautiful, is it a he or she? Even when new children join the group trying to save the bug, they immediately pick up on the original themes and elaborate them, in a circle of cooperation.

At the beginning of the observation, two girls are seen, whom we shall call Bianca and Rosa. To their surprise, they encounter a bug among their blocks.

Their teachers, Magda Bondavalli and Marina Mori, are nearby (one videotaping the scene), watching quietly.

Bianca says, "Yucky! How disgusting. It's a real fly [a horsefly]," and Rosa responds, "It isn't a big fly, because flies fly."

Bianca observes, "Look, it's dead," but Rosa disagrees, "No, it is moving its tail."

Rosa declares, "He has a stinger! Stay far away!" Bianca, also, is worried, as she says, "No, no, let's kill it!" Rosa repeats, "Look, he can sting you," and Bianca embellishes her earlier idea, "Yes, but I said that we kill it. I have a real gun at my house. Let's kill it! He moved! He isn't dead. Help! Help!" Rosa now murmurs, "Yes, he is dead. Try to… Hello, hello."

Bianca commands Rosa, "You kill it! You have pants on." Rosa says, "No, it will sting me," but Bianca counters, "No, not with your clothes he can't." Rosa isn't having it; she says, "It can sting me even through my pants," but Bianca says, "No, he can't sting you through the pants." Rosa insists, "He can sting me through the clothing."

Their nearest teacher intervenes. "In my opinion, he would prefer to be back on his feet. You children try to flip him because he can't flip himself, in my opinion. Why don't you try to take him outside on the lawn? So maybe you could try to save him."

The children accept this reframing. Rosa says, "Don't be afraid. He doesn't sting. Help me bring him outside. Grab the piece of paper [together] so we can carry him outside. We don't have to use our hands."

The commotion has attracted the other children. One child says, "We can carry him with the paper. Can you help me, Agnes?" Agnes says, "Yes, I can."

Rosa now has new thoughts about the bug. She comments loudly, "Oh, how beautiful he is." To the bug, she says comfortingly, "Don't be afraid. We are helping you." The children try to help lift the bug with a piece of paper. They utter various comments, "Not that way. Oh, poor thing. Grab this end of the paper. He even knows how to walk! You ought not to let him die! All right, what the heck, I will help you. Look, it walks! He is able to walk also. Did you see—Was I good? Where did he go? He is inside there [pointing], inside the paper. Here or here? Let's look.

Let's open it [a roll of paper] . Where is it? Oh, it is there." Rosa looks and says, "Where? It is tiny. Oh, there it is!"

The children carry it, but then drop it. The teacher tells one child, "You aren't helping [with the carrying]," but that child protests, "I am helping." Another child cries out, "Help me, fence him in. Come on, help me. Yes, he is fenced in."

The second teacher now speaks up, "For sure, he is getting away. What would you like to do? Try to carry him outside."

The children try to carry the bug outside. Various children call out, "Oh, it fell. It hurt itself. It [the bug] is good. The bug is afraid. No, it is not afraid. Yes, it is afraid. It has fallen. No. He is afraid." Someone declares, "You killed him." This arouses many more comments from the group, "You have to believe, so you can save him. Look, look. You ought not to let him die. Yes, he is beautiful. He is very beautiful and good. I don't want to let him die. Let us put him in here. Put him in here. We must not let him die. Don't step on him."

One girl tries calling the bug, giving it a name, "Come here, beautiful. Beautiful, come here, *Topolone* ("Big Mousie"). Another child responds to her, "He doesn't want to come. Be careful or he will wind up squashed."

The children check on the bug's status. One boy declares, "He is still alive." The second teacher confirms, "He is still alive." She encourages the children, "Well, then, let's get him." A boy says, "He went under the table," and the second teacher guides, "Okay, grab him and take him outside."

The children are triumphant, "We captured him! We captured him. He doesn't want to get down [off the paper]. We got him! We are great!" Once outside, they let the bug go, saying,

"He won't get down. Let's leave him, there, poor thing. Don't squash him. She's beautiful. Where is she?"

(Videotape from the cooperation study of Edwards, Gandini, & Nimmo, 1994).

Part VI. "Children Set the Table for Lunch"

A learning encounter led by teacher Giulia Notari
with 4 year old children. It includes two parts,
first where a small group of boys set the table, and
second where a small group of girls set the table.

A. Transcript of the large group reflection on October 18, 1990 about the children and daily routines. Participating were Loris Malaguzzi, *pedagogista* Tiziana Filippini, *atelierista* Vea Vecchi, co-teachers Paola Strozzi and Giulia Notari, co-teachers Laura Rubizzi and Marina Castagnetti, co-teachers Magda Bondavalli and Marina Mori, and Diana auxilliary staff, along with Carolyn Edwards, Lella Gandini (acting as translator) and John Nimmo, The video was taken the previous spring, when the 5-year-olds were taught by Paola Strozzi and Giulia Notari.

The transcript includes an annotated account of the portion, Boys Setting the Table, prepared by Carolyn Edwards, for a chapter on the role of the teacher in *The Hundred Languages of Children: The Reggio Emilia Approach to Early Childhood Education,* edited by Carolyn Edwards, Lella Gandini, and George Forman, Ablex Publishers, 1993, and reprinted in the Second Edition, 1998. This annotated account is included because it offers a more readable and descriptive version of the episode of the boys setting the table.

A. Children 4-Years Old Set the Table for Lunch

Setting: October 18, 1990, afternoon. Present at the discussion are Loris Malaguzzi, *pedagogista* Tiziana Filippini, *atelierista* Vea Vecchi, co-teachers Paola Strozzi and Giulia Notari, co-teachers Laura Rubizzi and Marina Castagnetti, co-teachers Magda Bondavalli and Marina Mori, and Diana auxilliary staff, along with Carolyn Edwards, Lella Gandini,(acting as translator) and John Nimmo, Video initially translated by Lella Gandini (impromptu) and Carolyn 1/30/91, then by Flavia Pellegrini and Carolyn Edwards 2/15/91. The video was taken in spring 1990, when the 5-year-olds were taught by Paola Strozzi and Giulia Notari. The transcript of this episode is provided in Part 1-C.

Here is a summary of it:

It is just before lunchtime, and two 5-year-old boys, Daniele and Christian, are setting the tables for their class. In this school, children of each succeeding age are given more responsibility in preparing the table for lunch. The 5-year-olds take turns at deciding who is to sit where. The Diana School teachers believe that their system of letting a few children each day set the table and decide upon the seating arrangement, works better and is more in line with their philosophy than either having a fixed seating order (controlled by the teachers) or allowing free choice for everyone at the moment of seating themselves.

Daniele and Christian lay out the tablecloths, plates, and silverware, and decide where everyone is to sit by placing their individual napkins (each in a little envelope with the name sewn on). As they work, another boy comes in and asks to be seated near a certain boy. The table setters agree, and he leaves. Then a girl, Elisa, comes in and asks, "With whom did you put me?" Daniele answers, "Look for yourself." She says, "Well, Daniele, don't you want to tell me where you put me?"

In the meanwhile other children have come in. It is difficult to follow exactly what they say, as they are struggling with the caps on the mineral water bottles. This distracts Daniele and Chris-

tian from Elisa's request. Eventually Daniele says, showing her one of the napkin envelopes, "Is this yours?" She replies yes. Christian comments, "Near Michele." This obviously displeases Elisa, who protests, "And I don't like it."

The teacher, Giulia, enters, and observes the dispute. Daniele asks Elisa, "You don't want to stay near Michele?" She says, "NO! Finally, you do understand!"

Giulia glances toward the second teacher, Paola, who is silently videotaping the scene, and makes a decision not to intervene. "Find an agreement among yourselves," she tells the children, "Elisa, find an agreement with them." She returns to the next room. Christian seeks to find out with whom Elisa wants to sit, then explains to her that she must sit where they placed her. She cries out, "All right!" and leaves, mad, stamping her feet and slamming the door. Christian runs after her, calling her name, and bringing her back into the classroom. He asks twice, "Do you want to sit near Maria Giulia?" She remains angry. "Do what you like!" she shouts. (Later, in discussing this situation, teacher Giulia Notari stated that she thought it appropriate to minimize this situation and let the children take care of it themselves. Elisa often has such reactions, she noted, and it was not really a very painful situation for her.)

—Excerpt from a chapter on the role of the teacher in Reggio Emilia, Italy, published in *The Hundred Languages of Children, Second Edition: The Reggio Emilia Approach, Advanced Reflections*, edited by Carolyn Edwards, Lella Gandini, and George Forman. Greenwich, Conn.: Ablex, 1998, pp. 191–197.

The discussion begins with Paola's opening statement about the segments.

Paola: In any case, all the pieces that we have given you are part of a video that we have planned working with the children with the intention to give it to their parents at the end of the year. Because we want to show and give the parents a memory of the way that these children have learned to live together through three years.

Carolyn suggests looking at all three pieces and discussing them together.

Paola: We are going to see a situation in which the children take care of one of the routines of the day. The idea here is that it would serve you as a context of what you have seen in the other videos. The children working together have this characteristic of exchanges and inventions that we wanted to show to you, because both the adults and the environment appreciate it [their way].

[The group watches the video segments.]

Paola: We thought it was meaningful for you [Lella, Carolyn, John] because you can see the children doing many, many different things. They exchange, they interact, and they invent ways of doing things. And one can see that this happens because there is an adult that appreciates these things and an environment that appreciates them. And so the adults and the environment are all in favor of the children doing these things. [NOTE: Lella's translation: the environment is favorable for these things happening]

Tiziana: What I was saying also to them [the teachers] is that after having worked with the children on activities in which we apply our idea of the child— I don't want to go too far into it, but I mean, the child with high potential for interaction and exchanges, I refer to all that we say about the image of the child and the role of the adult connected with this view, that image has made very interesting and significant working with children on activities—but at the same time, we have seen how that carries on for what concerns the whole day from morning to evening, all the time the child is here. In fact, I think that the organization of routines of the day has become shaped by our image of the child. [NOTE added by Lella: In fact, in other cities the routines are very chaotic or very structured, but in Reggio the children take initiative and make the routines very interactive but also very flexible and enjoyable]. This way, you give to the child a range of possibilities all along the continuum that our schools offer. Even in setting the table or preparing beds and blankets for sleeping, children succeed in

> I think that the organization of routines of the day has become shaped by our image of the child.
>
> — Tiziana Filippini

creating this special atmosphere because the whole school is committed to this image of the child. That is the result, then, of the meaning we give to be together, to offer throughout the whole day a wide range of possibilities to work in a small group, to have relationships individually, to work in a large group, etc.

Carolyn: The children seem to have a keen interest on who sits where at the table, or who sleeps where at the nap, could you comment on that.

Paola: It is a situation where after three years of living together, there are relationships and friendships which are very strong for the children. As everyone knows about these friendships and relationships, who prepares the table or the beds, takes them into account.

Giulia: One interesting aspect is that the children in charge have a power, and the others recognize it and try to bargain with them, respecting however the authority of the organizers. This group which has power succeeds also in creating new relationships. For example, I remember that once they tried to play a trick on a child, placing near him somebody he didn't like, and this kind of "directing" (as a theatre or movie director) is a very powerful possibility for the children. Children take turns in taking this power.

Carolyn: What is the effect of these little alliances or cliques, within the larger group?

Paola: These little cliques produce all sorts of negotiations and dealings among the children.

Marina C.: What about in the case that somebody is excluded? For example, Elisa in the first segment was very upset, and she tried to negotiate but she didn't succeed very well. What happened if she ended up next to somebody she didn't like?

Paola: I think she would continue to negotiate with those children, and even with us, and also with the children next to her.

Lella: This increases their skill of negotiating. It favors their increasing their skill.

Giulia: One thing we did was to change the strategy of forming the organizing group. So we used random groups, using alphabetical order, from the top, from the end, or elections. But the children are often aware early in the morning of who is the organizing group. As a consequence, the negotiations are very intense and often start in the middle of the morning.

Tiziana: I don't know exactly what Carolyn's question was addressing. But if she meant that the forming of couples and little groups could prevent the workings of the large group, from our experience and our daily working, I don't think so. For example, after three years, my daughter Elisa could get along with all 23 or 24 children. Still she had favorites. She particularly loved certain children. That's why she would cry and do all the negotiations that you have seen. But she could really stay with any child and have exchanges with him; and in turn, all the others could do so with her. And I want to stress that— since I meet these children also outside the school—they have knowledge of one another, not only of their favorite friends, which is truly remarkable. Of course they have special friends, and there are variations so that you want to invite one friend to do one thing and another friend to do another thing. That gives a range of many possibilities.

Carolyn: With older children, five or six, you worry about children forming cliques against other children and excluding them.

Vea: I had opportunity to observe these children working intensely and busily exchanging and interacting, while we were working on a project on communication. Something that had struck me at the time was the busy exchange of objects—loans or renting. An incredible set of maneuvering...

Marina C.: or … .

Laura: That continues this year...

> The way we proceed might create exchanges which can be also charged with conflict and pain for the children, but all this intense interaction, is I believe extremely constructive and positive.
>
> — Vea Vecchi

Vea: In Finland we went to see a new school and I was impressed by the way the lunch of the children was set up. There were large tables on which a label with the name of the child was pasted in a specific place. The children would find their place, sit politely, wait for everyone to be seated, and then wait for the teacher to distribute the food. This was some kind of social equilibrium, only apparent, in my view. The way we proceed might create exchanges which can be also charged with conflict and pain for the children, but all this intense interaction, is I believe extremely constructive and positive. Of course, I am convinced that the teacher has to be very attentive about exclusions and that the power of the children organizing should be always mediated by the possibility of negotiation, with the intervention of the adult if necessary.

Someone: It is not that the power of these children in absolute. The teachers are always aware of what is going on.

Carolyn: Another thing that interested us was when Eliaa came in and showed very strong emotion. Two questions. First, Why did Giulia decide to intervene, if only briefly? And second, what is your idea about whether children need to subdue strong emotion in order to solve problems?

Giulia: I don't remember why I took that initiative in that moment. Maybe it was the only time that day. However, sometimes we are called in by the children to be referees or arbitrators of a conflict, and in that case we listen to the different parties and we inquire about who started what and how. We reconstruct the history of the event and in that case I intervene actively in the contest. As Elisa tends to have these problems often—

Tiziana: We call her [at home], Elinore Duze (famous beautiful prima donna of the theatre). [NOTE: Tiziana is Elisa's mother].

Giulia: Therefore I thought it appropriate to minimize the situation and let the children take care of it themselves. As she has often these problems, it was not really a very painful situation for her. Therefore she could easily overcome the problem or pain by herself.

Paola: I remember specifically that incident. Because I was videotaping. Because Giulia and I looked at each other and exchanged some gesture that implied it was better just to let it go and not intervene, with the expectation that this controversy would be solved by the children themselves.

Carolyn: What about the second question? (Lella translates).

Giulia: There are emotions and emotions. There are the ones that are so on the surface and superficial, even if with dramatic effect. [NOTE: Lella, translating afterwards, notes how relaxed the teachers are about describing Elisa in the presence of the mother]. And there are emotions which are very deep and maybe not so easy to read. I certainly don't think a child should be left alone with suffering which is really painful for him, especially not with very strong emotions.

Vea: Children learn also because of this incredible social training that they are obliged to receive. They learn often to communicate with each other, learning to take the point of view of the other. For example, Beatrice and her friend [Elisa] know one another so well that Bea lets the other speak and speak and speak and then she sort of sums up the friend's intention, in a very skillful way. In my view, the children here are very capable of modifying their way of communicating according to the need or the type of the interlocator. Also that is one of the skills that they learn to use very skillfully.

Tiziana: I'm always surprised to realize how much in three years these children have learned to know one another. I don't know if it was because there was a particular group of families that made possible to continue also the relationship at home, so that the children could meet after school or on

Saturdays and Sundays. These children know also what pleases or displeases the ones that are not in their immediate group. For example, I heard two girls talking about a third girl, and one of them said, "Don't tell this to XXX, it would displease her." It is in fact with regard to everybody that they have a cognitive map that is very rich and elaborate, and as a consequence a strategy of behavior that I could say it is individualized. Also toward the boys, it is incredible.

Carolyn: Regarding the second segment [Girls Setting the Table, Part 1-C], Elisa was the leader. How much do the other girls contribute to the outcome, and do they take pleasure in following a leader?

Paola: The dominant situation is a play situation. Elisa gives instructions about where the other girls should position themselves, and the way they respond and handle the objects shows a very strong agreement.

Giulia: We should also say that the children who play with Elisa are not children... completely normal [average]. They themselves are big protagonists. One of the girls is a person who tries to take the center of situations. Giulia fought for three years to have a relevant place in the group. Those are children who accept freely, in that moment, the choreography that Elisa has devised. They like it because they all gain from it, but they are not necessarily children who give in. In fact, they are never that type of child.

Vea: There is a certain kind of balance between Elisa and the other girls.

Tiziana: Elisa and XXX when they were very small in their first year at the preschool, would call each other on the phone and sing each other the songs they had learned at school.

Carolyn: Looking at all these pieces together, we anticipate that other North Americans will notice the drawing apart of the boys and girls. What should we say to them?

All: It is a long speech.

> *It is in fact with regard to everybody that they have a cognitive map that is very rich and elaborate, and as a consequence a strategy of behavior that I could say it is individualized.*
>
> *— Tiziana Filippini*

Paola: We have been observing how children choose to be together, either boys and boys, or girls and girls, or the combination of the two, for many years. We are trying to discover why children do so. And so we have tried different combinations of children. There is a need for children of each sex to find themselves, and to find themselves as a group, and to imitate each other, and this seems to be a need that increases as the children grow older. They need to define themselves through others, and one gets to know oneself more as he or she looks more at the others.

Giulia: I'm going to make a very practical example. Boys play and they choose each other as a group of boys, as they play. The boys keep an eye on the girls, even to organize games with them. And even some games of incursion and some games of entrapment, trying to catch the girls. Boys play together with an eye on that [including the girls]. And girls are a lot more explicit in seeking to attract the attention of boys. They plot in a lot more visible way. They speak about being in love and having crushes, while the boys are a lot more secretive about that. There was one boy who declared himself "in love," but the other boys are much more reticent. The girls are a lot more explicit in these games, and they plot more to have the attention of a boy— to have Daniele, to play a trick on him, or to have him as a friend. In contrast, the boys go on their sorties to the group of girls, but initially they choose their group of boys. But they keep an eye on the girls, to have a feminine element in their games.

Vea: Something that we've never seen in the boys' group. One day we saw all the little girls arrive with their tights on. And Giulia understood that there had been a communiqué (plan) among all the girls that we didn't know about. The little girls often exchange headbands or buttons and pins, all things tied to clothing and dressing—I am, of course, making generalizations. And in the boys, instead, it's more the types of objects that are part of their games. From three-years-of-age, in the boys, we notice it more because it's more visible, we notice a whole series of team games, often coming from the characters that are playing in those days on television. When they are three, sometimes also the little girls participate. Then, at least to us, it seems there is a type of separation that occurs. Given also a series of codes of the squads of communication that follow different strategies. The girls, on the other hand, have always seemed to us more interested in the relationship with the boys, going and trying to get them to come with them. Here, for instance, in this section [of the video] here, there has been a sort of mini-drama that has been going on for months of an amorous type, because two girls were in love with the same boy.

Giulia: You see, there was this little love story between two children; the little boy was very sweet. He was even able to play with the girls, and play house with them, and he was very available to everyone. And so he was very sought after since he was three years old. And he had manifested immediately a preference for one girl classmate. And this had aroused all sorts of jealousies in general, but especially in one little girl. And this affair lasted until the final year, and he was trying to get around it and make everyone happy, because he was a sweet little boy (*bimbo buono*). On the whole he didn't want to hurt the other little girl since he felt courted by her too, so he tried to gain time and say, "Well, I haven't really thought about it yet." And also now the other little boys became involved, who sometimes played the roles of accomplices. We have four tables at which we sit for lunch. The little boys also calculated the seating arrangement. If there were 26 of us, we used four tables of five [six] with some left over. So they did this whole series of mathematical operations. We had an extra table this little table that had been defined as the "lovers' table," (*tavolo di innamorati*) as a trick. And sometimes they would set it with a bouquet of flowers. It's a table for two, while the others are tables for six. And sometimes the little girls who act as accomplices, putting at this table the other little girl who wanted this boy and placing the first one far away. Sometimes they would put all three of them there together. Sometimes these are controlling devices for very big emotions.

Lella: We are interested in aspects of community that supports...

Giulia: It sometimes intervenes in favor, or sometimes takes away from what is happening [with the couple].

Carolyn: We didn't have any more specific questions. We would like to know about any additional ideas you might have about these episodes.

Marina C.: [returns to issue of exclusion raised earlier in the discussion.] There is a question that I wanted to ask before about a little girl named Elisa [Note: not the same Elisa as before], who didn't want to have another little boy. If it's a mechanism that included also the avoidance of exclusion from the group, because, for example, in our class last year a little girl from Egypt started attending the school.[1] So in the beginning there were some curiosity and support from the group on the level of communication and teaching her. Afterwards, progressively they detached themselves from her in the sense that this year when she returned, and she came back with a bigger vocabulary than she had last year and a greater communicative capability, but what she is missing is the support of a relationship with others. So while the others have a network of relationships with each other, a support system, and even mechanisms of listening to each other and understanding each other, she often gets angry. So her attitude is that she gets mad and then she comes to us for help and she wants to know what she can do, because they don't want her near. She feels excluded; she is not a part of this network of relationships.

Laura: It's easily apparent that she is not a little girl of Reggio Emilia, from her clothing and the colors she wears. For example, it's possible that she wears the same sweat suit for two or three days in a row, which is something unheard of for a little girl from these parts. I'm not saying that she is dirty or that she smells. This year she returned with an amazing desire to come back to school, yet it was very late with respect to the other kids [late in time]. So as she came back, she attempted some interactions with the other children. Because she arrives very early in the morning, she tried with whoever was at school. And then she found out that she is able to have relationships with other little girls, but these are relationships that, at a certain point, end. As the other partners arrive at school, they start to form their own little groups, and she starts to wander around in search of a group to join. I saw that she was not very satisfied, and so I spoke with her. So I asked her, "Listen, it doesn't seem to me that you are very happy. Who would you like to have as a friend? Would you like me to help you to do or say some things...?" She told me a series of things that I wrote down, and later when she wasn't there, I told them to some of the children. She said, for example, "Maria Imelda is my friend, *poco cosi*, as little as this." She excludes the boys, because they are not like her, so she wants little girls as friends. And she says, "Only Laura my friend. She knows what to do." But she would like a friend who is more than just a friend such a little bit. Well, this is an extremely complicated, extremely delicate issue. I think it is important that we support her in this search that we help her find some paths, even in regards to the other children, so they realize what the problem is. You can't impose friendship. You can help her, for instance, now she's becoming a little more aggressive. For example, as soon as a little boy bumps against her, she reacts in an aggressive manner. And she is always the victim. The big tension is between following this little girl and these relationships of hers, giving her also a sense of what is going to probably further distance her from the other children, instead of coming closer to them. And to study also what are her aspirations. And attempting these approaches, maybe even with the families, or in any case, to try to create a situation which is a little bit bigger than the one she has first thing in the morning. For instance, she doesn't even nap with us, and I feel that it is going to continue to be a very complex issue.

Loris: She doesn't nap with you?

Laura: No, because she has a very little baby brother, and her mother can't come back later and pick her up every day. And so the father comes to pick her up during his lunch hour. So she goes home then.

Giulia: Well, we had a case that lasted for three years. And unfortunately I have to admit that

---

1. Editors' note: In 1990, Reggio Emilia was just beginning to experience and respond to the increasing arrival of immigrants from North Africa, the Middle East and Eastern Europe. Loris Malaguzzi expressed the desire to learn more about the experience of multiculturalism in the United States. Since that time, Reggio leaders and educators have undertaken systematic and substantive efforts to make the community and schools be culturally inclusive and welcoming, with a focus on active citizenship. See *The Hundred Languages of Children* (3rd edition, 2012), especially chapters 4, 5, and 8; and the DVD *Participation is an Invitation* (Reggio Children, 2014).

when they were three [years old], certain isolations from the group seemed less apparent. Though when they were five or six it was very evident that there were some detached children. I had a little girl who was Egyptian; she looked different because she had different facial structure. And I had a little Iranian boy. So we teachers made some authentic reflections [thought about it], even if they were not very deep. Now I'll tell you about the little girl. She came from a very poor family, while the little boy, even though it was apparent that he had facial structure different from the others, he came from a very elevated family. The little girl also had a more subdued style of dress; she wasn't very well- groomed, even in hygiene. So she didn't have the same odor as the other children. She had a very limited vocabulary, and she was a calm and shy (*mite*) child. She didn't have any domineering or decisive attitudes. She always tried to get into the group in a sweet way; she just tried to come closer to them. I believe that we did a lot. We always tried to keep her in mind when we were creating different groups, or we

> We always tried to keep her in mind when we were creating different groups, or we sometimes let her create the groups. We tried to make her a protagonist.
>
> — Giulia Notari

sometimes let her create the groups. We tried to make her a protagonist. We also tried to work with her family. But these families have very limited communicative abilities. For instance, in our case the mother didn't know how to read in Italian, and so our communication was limited. We also had some social events, not just parties for just one class but general school-wide parties, in which it is easier for people to connect. And then there was another differentiating issue, involving family religious beliefs about eating salami and ham. According to me, all these things reinforced certain negative tendencies. While on the other hand, the other little boy's marginality was less evident. I believe that social marginality has specific features—I'm not referring to marginal-

ity only in school. For example, the father only had Arab friends. We worked a lot on building interrelationships, not only among the children but among the families as well. They lend each other toys and they exchange the children. But with this family, that was never possible. The little girl even went once to the house of a schoolmate, and when she came back she told me she wasn't going to go again because her mother didn't want her to. I don't know what more we could have done. We tried in many careful ways. We even tried to help her appearance a little, to get her to wash and to smell a little better. We even tried giving her a little gift in a way that wouldn't seem a special gift—some little rings or little headband. But even though it wasn't very blatant and everyone was very nice to her, still Sharim wasn't completely integrated with the rest of the children. She was accepted in a civil manner (*civile*) but not as much as the rest of the children. The others sought her out, but I don't know how much social influence she had with the group. Pedran, the boy—I'm not sure, we always have such restricted immigration, usually just one in a class—if there were two children of color, or maybe three, then probably different things would happen. We had two children of color, but one was a girl, one was a boy, and Pedram didn't suffer as much isolation as Sharim. About ninety percent [of the time] he used the same codes [ways of speaking and acting] as the other children. And actually he was even proud of the fact that he was different, that he had this Iranian heritage that he could bring to the classroom. I don't know. I don't think that Sharim suffered a great deal, but I do think that she suffered.

Lella: In the United States these kinds of problems are very common. I brought some material on this problem last year, written by a colleague of Carolyn's who did some studies in this field [Editors' note: Dr. Patricia Ramsey, author of *Teaching and*

Learning in a Diverse World, 1st ed., 1987]. More specifically about the problem of food, in the United States, many times they don't prepare food at school because in a group of children there may be many different styles of eating [e.g. vegetarian] and I find it very amusing that little preschool children are always seen going off with their little lunch bags because their mothers want them to eat vegetarian food, for instance.

Paola: Even though people might like different styles of food, we are not going to give up our traditional cooking in the name of diversity!

Lella: But in any case, pasta is something that is fine for anybody.

Carolyn: I have listened very carefully to everything to all that you have told me the last couple of days, trying to compare what I have heard with what I am familiar with from home. And I think that the goals you have as teachers, and the goals that the teachers in Amherst have, are very similar, but there are some interesting ways in which the means are different, the approaches are different. So I am eager to hear your reactions tomorrow toward what you will be seeing then. Of course, I could try to give my generalizations about how I see these differences, but that would be wrong, that would be to anticipate or to guide your thinking, and I don't want to do that. So I will reserve any final summary remarks until we are all finished tomorrow. But following the methods of Reggio Emilia, I have my hypotheses and my predictions.

All: [Laughter]

Tiziana: She has also picked up our ways!

Loris: We should all thank Carolina [Carolyn] for this great eagerness to develop or to further study problems and we must all take into account the partiality which we all have, the differences between the various camps. There is a difference in fields and interests and studies and different curiosities which push people. For instance, the dif-

> We worked a lot on building interrelationships, not only among the children but among the families as well
>
> — Giulia Notari

ferent experiences—the experience of being a teacher, mother, or daughter, and different social experiences. We don't always have the time, before the eyes of strangers, to appreciate this wide range of interests and differences. I think this is also for us a big occasion to respond, also on diversity, because the diversity is really notable. I would like everyone to keep in mind the deep differences between American culture and European culture, for example, the experience in Amherst and an experience like ours, which is not completely representative of Italy. It is a very particular experience which has been formed through various adventures or events.

Lella: And it's not just chance that people like Carolyn come here.

Loris: This is a reconfirmation of our experience. I think we have had a long journey to get here today. We've been a little bit on Mars, a little bit on Earth...

Someone: A little bit in church...

Loris: America has some extraordinary cultures, and they have profoundly educated even our different ages [throughout the past] For instance, it is extraordinary how much America has brought to us through its movies. But I should say that it is especially the prototype of a certain American that belongs to a big fashion that is like that of the oil drillers [*Dallas*]. Carolyn is also trying to get oil. I know the situation well because I have a nephew who tried to invest in oil, but it seems to me that this culture of always trying to go deeper and find something belongs to them—but also to us, we are also drillers. We never find any.

Someone: We find some methane.

Loris: Yes, a little, it also costs less to look for it. And I just think that these memories of today will also be something that we will remember tomorrow also. Keep in mind that we also live in a situation with a lot of privileges, in our dimension of city and our social level. Carolyn lives in a much more complex area than ours. So we speak about one Egyptian at a time, one South American at a time, one East European at a time, while there a lot of different peoples living together. Different religions and ideas that represent a big question, both for them and for us. America is not only a big cultural force, it is also very strong, and they have many of the social phenomena that they have gone through, we will probably go through, and many forms of violence that we thought were strictly American—for example, gangsters—are forms of violence that we also know today. Do you remember Al Capone? We [Italians] really have some privileges that they [Americans] don't have.

Part VII. Reggio Educators Respond to Video from a Massachusetts Preschool

Large group discussion, led by Loris Malaguzzi, open to the whole system of Reggio early educators.

A. Description of the background and context for the meeting on the evening of 10/17/1990.

B. English translation of the discussion, made by Lella Gandini in Florence on October 27, 1990, from the audiotape.

A. Description of the background and context for the meeting on the evening of 10/17/1990

On the evening of October 17, educators from all parts of the Reggio Emilia early childhood education system were invited to an open discussion where Carolyn Edwards and John Nimmo would show some excerpts of video taken in the preschool classrooms of the Common School in Amherst, Massachusetts. Preliminary discussion about showing this video took place on the morning of October 15 and is found in Part I, B, Stage 3. The preliminary discussion provides insight into the Italian educators' approach to viewing and understanding viewing, including the Amherst video. Present at the October 17 evening discussion were Loris Malaguzzi, Carlina Rinaldi, Giovanni Piazza (*atelierista* at La Villetta Preschool), Laura Rubizzi, Vea Vecchi, Tiziana Filippini (translating), various teachers and staff from the Diana School (including Giulia Notari, Paola Strozzi, Marina Castagmetti, and Magda Bondavalli), educators from other Reggio Emilia schools, Lella Gandini (translating), Carolyn Edwards and John Nimmo.

The idea for this meeting was modeled on the video-reflection methodology of Tobin, Davidson, and Wu's (1989) *Preschool in Three Cultures: Japan, China, and the United States* (as described in Part IA). The goal was for the Reggio educators to get a glimpse of the American preschool and reveal more about their cultural assumptions through their reactions. In fact, this did occur, though the Reggio educators seemed to find it hard to make as much of the Amherst video as they would have liked. They seemed to want to do the same kind of microanalysis of the pedagogy as the group had been doing all week long with their videos. Even so, we get some glimpses of their perspectives in their responses, and also hear interesting comments on the limitations of video as documentation, and the encouraging, affectionate and hopeful concluding remarks by Loris Malaguzzi. During the discussion, first Lella Gandini, then Tiziana Filippini, served as translator. Lella Gandini translated the audiotape in Florence on October 27, 1990.

The edited video used in the discussion included short scenes previously selected by Carolyn Edwards and John Nimmo from video John had taken at the Common School in Amherst, Massachu-

setts between November, 1989 to March, 1990. The Common School is a private progressive early childhood and elementary school with a strong focus on community-building.

B. English translation of the discussion, made by Lella Gandini in Florence on October 27, 1990, from the audiotape

Setting: October 17, 1990, 7:00 p.m. After a brief introduction by Carolyn, the audience of about 50 people viewed the first Amherst video segment which included two scenes from a preschool classroom of 3-4 year-olds. The first scene was of pretend play in the block area featuring four girls and one boy. One girl seems to be particularly directing the play which includes using wood boards as table settings. The second scene involves a carpentry activity facilitated by a teacher, Marcy Sala, in which children are making wooden cars with wheels. Two boys are working at the activity while a third waits. The teacher focuses primarily on the youngest child, Joel, while the third boy, Ben, tries to do the activity for that same child. While we had provided an English transcript and some background at the earlier small group meeting, there was no Italian transcript and very little context provided at this large group gathering. It was thought that viewers would be able to follow the action and the children's expressions without much trouble and the focus was on the educators' reactions to and interpretations of what they saw.

Carlina Rinaldi: It is difficult to enter this conversation for people who have not been participating with you for the past three days.

Watching the tape, I wonder if the situation was favorable for social learning (learning through cooperation). What conversations had John had way before and just before with the teacher? How much did he know of the particulars of this situation and its context? It seems as if in the first situation, the activity was unplanned; the group was spontaneous and the number of children was not preset. While in the second situation, the teacher had chosen two children to participate. Was this number, two, something that they had thought a great deal about, or had it happened just close to the activity?

My second question was: I think the problems concerning the helping in the second activity with the woodworking are connected to the materials themselves. The material is not easy to manage (the wheels) and this makes it hard for Joel to succeed. It seems that this situation was very much structured, so in a sense it seems easier to discuss.

Concerning the first situation, it seems to me that with a few minor differences it could happen spontaneously in our schools too. I could make an observation about the girl who takes leadership. I have been struck by it. Did the teacher give this kind of authorization or direction to one of the children to do so? And was there any indication on the part of the teacher that they should stay in this assigned space? I am struck by the fact that the children choose for their symbolic play such unstructured materials as the pieces of wood [that they use for dishes]...

Laura Rubizzi: These are impressions about the second situation. I am struck by the delicacy of the relationship between this one adult and the two children. It seems a very close relation. I also noticed how the third child, who was more capable in a sense, could and did substitute for the teacher, and in fact, he succeeded more than did the teacher to help the little child (Joel) return with interest and enthusiasm to doing what they were doing. The enthusiasm seems to carry on; they could have gone beyond these particular actions. In my experience it is not too common, this [exclusive kind of] relation between one adult and one child. I would encourage these [Amherst] teachers to trust more the children as cooperators, helping the other children.

[Lella Gandini, note: Interpretation/alternative translation]. It seems the close relation between the adult and the child (Joel) who has difficulty; this relationship seems to become somewhat detached just as the child shows difficulty. And the child (Ben) who helps Joel uses a different modality of intervening than does the teacher. Ben does certain things and that produces a very good effect. It produced participation beyond this particular interaction [pleasantness, etc.]. This relation one-to-one of teacher to child is something I don't

see too much, and I would feel like saying to her, "Have more confidence in the resources of the children to help each other."

But I wonder what we should do now? Should we really talk about cooperation, or about the video itself? It seems that the two issues are slightly different. I know the difficulty of videotaping, and that is why I am asking. A videotape is a construction--the person with the videocamera in his hands has tremendous power of selection.

Voice (unknown speaker): I saw something that disturbed me, the arm of the teacher (Marcy) always between the two children—something that was too much of an intervention. Concerning Lella's question about the teacher having Ben ask permission, yes, I do favor cooperation, but I also thought the teacher was [appropriately] protecting the privacy of this child who was trying to carry through his project and build his car. I see a right of the child to do his own car. I assume there will be one car for each child in the group.

I was also wondering about the fact that the teacher in a sense abandons the child [Joel] with whom she was having such a close relationship, and I wonder why she did that? Maybe the child did not need her any longer? But why, when she started off by being so close, did she then go off?

Carolyn Edwards: Did anyone notice or have anything to say about the fact that there were so many girls playing with just one boy, in the symbolic play segment?

Vea Vecchi: To look at these videos without having a sort of common ground of theoretical analysis and reflection, such as we have had in the last few days, seems to cause people to make remarks that are not completely correct towards the video itself. The video is just a fragment that is not long enough to give people an opportunity to communicate in an appropriate way. So it is not appropriate really to proceed in this way, especially in such a large group that does not share a common experience.

Giovanni Piazza: I have spent much of the last few years working with video, so I would like to make some general remarks about video as a medium. Video has a quality of movement. There is something connected with what was there then at the time that it was taken, another something connected to what you see now, and yet another something connected to what it will mean in some future time. The difficulty, then, for us here is, first of all, that we did not participate in what was there before, and second, that we cannot understand what is being said. So it is very difficult for me to understand what is going on in the video segment. I myself worked for 94 hours, shooting video footage, that over six months was then boiled down to a short edit that had lost completely the meaning it had before. So I am very uneasy about the video as a medium.

In the case of my work, what happened was that, even after working on this material that all of us were familiar with, still people could not agree on its meaning, and these were people from the same culture. So I cannot really make comments about this Amherst video.

However, one thing I could say is that in all of this [Amherst] material that has passed under my eye, I see situations similar to our own. For example, I have seen situations similar to yours where the child spontaneously takes on the role of leader. If the leader then moves off, another will come up, using different "modalities" according to the situation [i.e. be another kind of leader].

Also, speaking about that intrusive arm of the teacher, perhaps it was not really being instrusive, but rather the camera was placed to make it appear so. A related matter is that the process of videotaping can influence teachers' behavior. When videotaping in the *asilo nido*, I myself noticed that the camera influenced the teacher's actions: the arm that was moving in would stop and go no further. Regarding the carpentry scene, I do not think the teacher should make them ask permission but should just let them cooperate. Also, the teacher should not ask permission but should likewise just cooperate.

[He also tells about his own experiences with carpentry where the children made extensive plans before beginning their work.]

> Video has a quality of movement. There is something connected with what was there then at the time that it was taken, another something connected to what you see now, and yet another something connected to what it will mean in some future time.
>
> — Giovanni Piazza

Perhaps instead of speaking so much about the videos, we should spend more time talking about the different views held by each culture.

Loris Malaguzzi: This work is the beginning of an experiment, and it is going in a direction that interests us as well. The preliminary consideration that I would like to make is that this work is very difficult. And we also are in the process of learning and making many mistakes. The video itself has immediately to decide to cooperate with us! That cooperativity has to come through the choice of images. This is very important also in terms of feelings. Unfortunately, we have at our disposal machines that are very primitive--for example, the camera is a fixed point. The video-camera tends to tell its story from a fixed point of view, so it is a strange kind of narrator—not a really good kind. A story should have movement and evolution, but instead with the videocamera it comes from a fixed point. The fixed point of view of the camera presents a contradiction to what we are trying to capture.

An important thing to remember is that the video does not represent, but instead it "reads." It reads, but it does not even read what is there, instead it reads in a situation where the receiver will be somebody other than who was photographing. [Lella's note: He means there is always a discrepancy between the reality of what happened and what comes up in the mind of the viewer.] We have yet to learn lots of things about this medium, and we must keep all of these things in mind in order to read videotape as accurately as possible in terms of what was really happening.

Another question I want to bring up is that when viewing a video such as this, we need information and analysis of the scenario [a script]. We need to know, connected with what we see, information about the space—whether it is a space that allows for action or that stifles action, and whether the space makes things possible or constrains.

For example, referring to the symbolic play scene, I would say that the same child who has been seen as a leader of the others could also be seen as their small slave. Since the space was extremely limited and constrained and created a difficulty for free expression, the children were very restricted, sitting there in Indian fashion. [Lella: this represents a misinterpretation of the boundaries of the space]. So the girl that you call a leader is actually the only one who was in a strategic position to go get other materials; rather than a leader she is at the service of the others. [Carolyn: In fact, this is an interesting observation because I think the other children appear to see the girl not as a boss but as someone making interesting things happen while they sit comfortably and enjoy them]. This girl puts herself in their service in a situation which is absolutely compelling and structured[by how the environment is set up]. In this little drama, there is one figure who has just gained a little sister--and this is a very important event, perhaps the prime event. But in what we see there is no focus on that main character who had evoked or aroused such an important event for the others. So there should have been more focus by the camera on this girl.[Lella: He probably means the camera should have been placed so as to focus more on her, and the editing shouldhave concentrated more on the aspects of interaction that had to do with this event].

The second point is that we assist to a sort of "idle talk"(little background talk you hear when you are in the theater and you hear the talk of people around you as you wait for the performance to start).And of cooperation there is only this kind of physical intensity, as well as the intensity of looks, maybe, but it as if there are the children still waiting for the curtain to go up. [Lella notes: In Reggio, perhaps if the teachers had intervened in a significant way, it would have given re-

> *The videocamera tends to tell its story from a fixed point of view, so it is a strange kind of narrator—not a really good kind. A story should have movement and evolution, but instead with the videocamera it comes from a fixed point.*
>
> *— Loris Malaguzzi*

alization or direction to the potential of the situation]. But as nothing happens, when the curtain finally goes up, all that happens is that they receive wooden plates [Lella: which seems to be unrelated to the birth of the baby sister] and that is very limited. If the potential story which is there has no time and possibility to grow, then cooperative learning does not take place. But since I have seen this scene only once, it is difficult to really interpret what is going on.

Carolyn tells about the teacher role at the Common School.

John Nimmo: Common School teachers are reluctant to intervene for fear of imposing their line of thought on the children.

Loris: Well, I can see that this is the kind of dualism that the teachers at the Common School have expressed in their statement [in the letter, about individualism and cooperation] that you read earlier. In the letter there is that statement. There is a contradiction in the way that they express their ideas.

Lella Gandini: I think that the big difference between Reggio and Amherst is exactly there [concerning the individual and group].

Loris: Yes, it's really a very important point because this discussion on the individual is the Continental Divide of psychological literature.

Lella: One of the goals of this research is to bring to the U.S.A. experiences from here [Pistoia and Reggio] with the question, Could there be a different kind of cooperation between children? Therefore, we have this strong desire to bring some kind of help to the States. Do you understand?

Loris: Yes, yes, yes, I understand that. It is clear from the way that you approach this research. It is evident that for us it is an extraordinary pleasure to try to read different levels of possibility [i.e. with this exchange].

Lella: Keeping in mind also that the multicultural reality in the States is extremely strong, and particularly with the growing presence of Latinos, I would consider that some cultural contributions from Italy would be very relevant there because of the cultural similarities [of Latinos] with Italians [e.g. stress on family connections, physical closeness, attitude of dependency they foster in children].

Loris: Well, I think this multicultural situation is very interesting for us, too, both in terms of what there is similar and what there is different[between U.S. and Italy].

Lella: Yes, there are many differences.

Loris: Because the differences do not concern only our experience of cooperation....

Now the meeting continued with the second segment of the video from the same classroom in Amherst, which included four scenes: (1) The same children from the earlier pretend play scene are conversing at snack time; (2) Children are "reading" books independently and in small groups during a transition to group meeting time; (3) A group meeting of the entire class led by a teacher to brainstorm suggestions for what could be fixed on the playground during a children's work day; and (4) A large group drama-meeting session facilitated by a teacher in which a boy dictates a story and the children act it out.

> This encounter has also helped us to prepare ourselves better and to learn also some things concerning the use of video. Above all, WHY does one take a video, how does one do it, who has to do it, and to whom?
> — Loris Malaguzzi

Carolyn: Would anyone like to comment on what this second segment adds to your understanding?

Loris: This second part [the group meeting time] adds something. I find it very interesting and positive from the pedagogical point of view--this attempt to sum up the day in the group discussion between the adult and children, which I think is a very beautiful thing. The day is finished and she sums up what the day has been and also she prepares the children for the happening of the following day—a sort of preparation. I think this is an op-

timal thing. To exchange ideas with the children, to prepare them for the following day, to see how many children will be involved, what they will be doing—it seems to me I see the children here much more self-assured than I saw them before— much more happy, serene, and vital.

To sum up, the days that we have passed together have been truly cooperative days, very important days in which we have thought very much, and we thought about many things that we still have to go on thinking about. We reflected and worked on material that we found very interesting; therefore, we thank you very much. We are very happy about this connection ("piece of yarn") that there is between us and those at the University of Amherst, because they are vehicles extraordinarily stimulating: extraordinary catalyzers of reflection and thought that allow us to work better. It is very important for us to have these contacts because sometimes we forget about the things we do; thus, it is a stimulus to look at ourselves. These days perhaps have been heavy because we have worked very intensively, but they have certainly been very important days. The promise that you made that you will return is very important to us. It's very agreeable to us. We will even find a way to welcome your [Carolyn's] children!

And in the meantime, say hello to all our friends in Massachusetts, because in November Vea and Tiziana will be coming. We will try to accommodate these things that we say and we will send you other things thought out better, much better. This encounter has also helped us to prepare ourselves better and to learn also some things concerning the use of video. Above all, WHY does one take a video, how does one do it, who has to do it, and to whom? These questions are a major aspect of what we have talked about in these last few days.

And since I cannot embrace you now, I will embrace you later, and now do it symbolically. [Applause].

Part VIII. Initial Reflections on the Material

A. Article (English version). Edwards, C.P., Gandini, L., & Nimmo, J. (1994), "Promoting Collaborative Learning in the Early Childhood Classroom." In L.G. Katz and B. Cesarone (Eds.), *Reflections on the Reggio Emilia Approach. Perspectives from ERIC/EECE: A Monograph Series, No. 6* (pp. 81-104). Urbana, Illinois: ERIC Clearinghouse.

B. Article (Italian version). Edwards, C.P., Gandini, L., & Nimmo, J. (1992). Favorire l'apprendimento cooperativo nella prima infanzia: Concettualizzazioni contrastanti da parte degli insegnanti en due comunita. *Rassegna di Psicologia, 9*(3), 65-90.

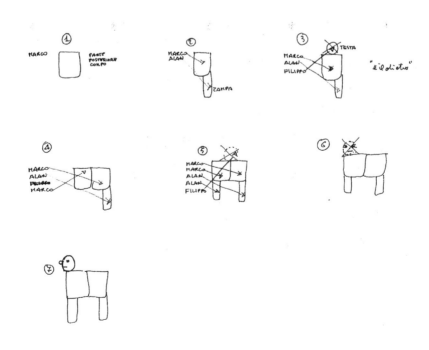

A. Article published in Reflections on the RE Approach

Published in L.G. Katz & B. Cesarone, eds., *Reflections on the Reggio Emilia Approach*. Perspectives from ERIC/EECE: A Monograph Series, No. 6 (pp. 81–104).Urbana, Illinois: ERIC Clearinghouse, 1994.

Promoting Collaborative Learning in the Early Childhood Classroom:
Teachers' Contrasting Conceptualizations in Two Communities

Carolyn Edwards

University of Kentucky
Lexington, Kentucky

Lella Gandini

University of Massachusetts–Amherst
Amherst, Massachusetts

John Nimmo

Pacific Oaks College Northwest
Seattle, Washington

Editor's Note: An earlier version of this paper was presented in April 1991 in the symposium "Italian Young Children in Cultural and Learning Contexts" at the annual conference of the American Educational Research Association in Chicago, Illinois. The paper was published under the title "Favorire l'apprendimento cooperativo nella prima infanzia: Concettualizzasioni contrastanti degli insegnanti di due comunita" in the journal *Rassegna di Psicologia*, published by the University of Rome, 1992, volume IX(3), pp. 65–90.

Italy, with its emerging stature as a European leader in quality public child care, has recently become the site of much research by North Americans. Because many American and Italian psychologists share a goal of advancing new ways of understanding socialization and education in context, it is timely to begin to examine and compare methods and findings. When culturally comparative studies are considered, it is of course necessary to remember that national cultures are not unitary: there is no homogeneous "Italian" or "American" culture. Rather, attention to multiplicity, change, and inter- and intra-locale differences are an essential part of the challenge in analyzing the cultural contexts of learning and development at home and school.

Our study should also be considered part of the endeavor in contemporary social science to transform the individualistic assumptions about science, self, and society that have become deeply ingrained in the thinking of North Americans in particular, and of most peoples of the advanced democracies as well. These assumptions have been found to have severe limits for understanding learning and thinking as inherently social processes, for describing socialization as the collective appropriation, rather than internalization, of culture (Bruner, 1986; Rogoff, 1990; Wertsch, 1991), and even, at the most pragmatic level for working with young children in ways that best promote children's prosocial behavior, empathy, and sense of identification with surrounding reference groups. But just how do we go beyond the individual as the basic unit of analysis in psychology? Theory is slowly being built with key assistance from Vygotskian psychology, cultural anthropology, and interpretive sociolinguistics. At the same time, improved methods of collecting and analyzing data are urgently needed to determine which recommendations will lead in the most fruitful directions. As evidenced by the articles in the journal *Rassegna di Psicologia* (1992, volume IX, number 3), psychologists are on the threshold of finding new ways of seeing and then describing learning and socialization as processes of children's participation in communicative events structured by adults.

Statement of the Problem

This particular study was conducted by an intercultural team at three sites: Reggio Emilia (Emilia Romagna, northern Italy), Pistoia (Tuscany, central Italy), and Amherst (Massachusetts, U.S.A.). All three cities share the features of being small, cohesive cities with progressive political traditions and extensive early childhood services. Of the three, however, only Reggio Emilia and Pistoia have built up city-financed, city-managed systems of preprimary and infant-toddler education. Recognized throughout Italy (indeed, Europe) for their quality and innovative substance, these municipal systems are well known as places where professionals and citizens have joined together and put years of effort into creating distinctive public systems that have many noteworthy features, including (1) the ways in which children, teachers, and parents are connected into operative communities focused on the surrounding city and region; and (2) the ways in which children are stimulated toward cognitive, social, and emotional development through collaborative play and group projects. Such features tend to be quite startling and thought-provoking to the many recent visitors from the United States who arrive with contrasting perspectives based on North American individualist values and Piagetian assumptions about the egocentrism of young children. Far from causing the American visitors to retreat, however, the process of intercultural confrontation and exchange has proved a strong stimulus for research and discussion.

Our study, in particular, focuses on how teachers in three communities seek to promote collaboration and community in their classrooms. We seek to closely analyze the educators' working philosophies in Reggio Emilia, Pistoia, and Amherst and compare them with their preferred methods of structuring children's schedules, organizing small and large learning groups, managing conflicts, dealing with sex role issues, and connecting children to wider communities outside the classroom. It is an extensive study, and in this paper we report preliminary and partial results only. Even from our preliminary analysis, however, it is evident that each of the three research sites has, as expected, a shared language: what anthropologists (D'Andrade, 1984; Holland & Quinn, 1987; Spradely, 1979) call a "distinctive discourse" or "cultural meaning system," and what psychologist Jerome Bruner (1986) calls a "language of education," for framing issues of collaboration and community regarding young children. This shared language, in turn, can be related to objective practices, that is, methods of school organization and grouping of children, as well as to shared beliefs about the roles of the teacher, the nature of the child as learner, rationales for teacher intervention and guidance, and preferred styles of facilitating the learn-

ing process. In this paper we do not address the larger theoretical problem of how psychologists can best describe learning and thinking as a social process and socialization as the collective appropriation of culture. Instead, we begin with a question that is empirical—indeed, ethnographic: namely, how the different communities of educators in our study talk about teaching and learning as co-action and co-creation of meaning, We will demonstrate that the cultural-community differences are not trivial but rather precisely related to those issues in a way that can be informative to psychologists. It is well known that the thinking of most developmental theorists, especially those influenced by the philosophical foundations of Western Europe and North America, is packaged in individualistic categories (Sampson, 1988; Schwartz, 1990; Triandis, 1989: Triandis et al., 1990). In contrast, our Italian informants, especially those from Reggio Emilia, have developed different philosophical categories not only in their minds as sets of beliefs and values, but also in practice, embodied in coherent institutions and functioning routines. These categories, we will demonstrate, posit learning as co-creation of knowledge and posit the child as inherently social. The Reggio Emilia educators have, over the past thirty years, collectively developed a language of education that assumes a co-constructionist view of the child and of teaching and learning that is very close to that proposed by Jerome Bruner (1986) in *Actual Minds, Possible Worlds,* as illustrated in this quotation:

> I have come increasingly to recognize that most learning in most settings is a communal activity, a sharing of the culture. It is not just that the child must make his knowledge his own, but that he must make it his own in a community of those who share his sense of belonging to a culture. It is this that leads me to emphasize not only discovery and invention but the importance of negotiating and sharing—in a word, of joint culture creating as an object of schooling and as an appropriate step en route to becoming a member of the adult society in which one lives out one's life. (p. 127)

Rather than focusing on the developing child as an autonomous learner, Reggio Emilia and Pistoia educators see education as a communal activity and sharing of culture through collaboration among children and also between children and teachers, who open topics to speculation and negotiation (see Bruner, 1986, chapter 9). The Amherst, Massachusetts, educators, in contrast, see education first and foremost as a means for promoting the development of each individual. At the same time, however, as will be shown, although their discourse is guided by Western individualistic categories, it is not exhaustively constrained by those terms. Rather, as they grapple on the theoretical level with issues of collaboration and community, and as they engage on the practical level with an actual classroom of children with its own identity and ongoing history, they too respond to the dialectic between the needs of the individual and those of the group. For all of the teachers in our study, then, we believe that their words, framed within images of everyday practice and decision making, reveal a complex picture of the meaning of collaborative learning. The interviews and discussions in the study communities provide us with alternative models of thinking about how collaboration corresponds to an image of the child, an image of the role of the teacher, and a preferred approach to structuring children's experiences. This paper will illustrate the data and point to the emerging findings by comparing some of the views on collaborative learning of the Reggio Emilia and Amherst educators.

Method

Description of Amherst and Reggio Emilia

Reggio Emilia, a city of about 130,000 people, is located in the Emilia Romagna region. In Reggio Emilia, the municipal early childhood program originated in cooperative schools started by parents at the end of World War II. The city currently supports twenty-two preprimary schools for children three to six years of age, as well as thirteen infant-toddler centers for children under three (Edwards et al., 1993). Children of all socioeconomic and educational backgrounds attend the programs, including special needs children; fifty percent of the city's three- to six-year-olds and thirty-seven percent of the city's children who are under three years of age are served in the municipal schools and centers.

Amherst is a town of about 35,000 people in rural western Massachusetts. Founded in 1755, it is known throughout the United States for its many fine universities and colleges located nearby, as well as for its his-

toric town-meeting form of democratic governance and citizen participation and its long tradition of political progressivism, manifested in abolitionist efforts during the slavery era and antiwar activities during the Vietnam conflict. In terms of early childhood education, nevertheless, Amherst, while very liberal by American standards, has no unified municipal public child care system. Rather, the town is the site of multiple but piecemeal services: a town-financed central office of information and referral; one town-subsidized infant-toddler center that serves town employees' children; numerous high-quality preschools in the private domain; a network of licensed day care homes supervised by the state of Massachusetts; programs or slots for handicapped, disadvantaged, or abused preschool-aged children, financed by the city or the state; and free universal kindergarten education classrooms to serve all five- and six-year-olds as the first year of public primary education (Edwards & Gandini, 1989; Nimmo, 1992).

Interview Methods

Our methodology in all three sites involved a combination of teacher interviews with an adaptation of the "multi-vocal video-ethnography" developed by Tobin, Wu, and Davidson (1989) and described in their book, *Preschool in Three Cultures*. In this method, videotapes of classroom activity are obtained not to document and represent the classrooms, but rather as a stimulus and starting point for a critical and reflective dialogue with the ultimate goal of constructing a *multivocal video-ethnography* (Tobin, 1988; Tobin et al., 1989). Researchers systematically elicit (and record) the reactions to videotaped classroom segments of a series of cultural insiders and outsiders: the focal teachers, colleagues at their school, parents, educators and parents from other cities in their own country, and finally educators and parents from other countries. These reactions are assembled, analyzed, and interpreted by the ethnographer, who thereby takes responsibility for the final product in a report that seeks to preserve the multiplicity of the perspectives or voices of all the people involved.

First, we selected a small group of teachers in each city to be our central informants. We wanted these teachers to be members of an educational community, that is, a coherent group of educators who possessed a shared professional language and set of core values concerning teaching. At the same time, we desired to work with informants who were considered, by their own peers and administrators, to be strong exemplars of their craft and articulate spokespersons for their values and practices. In each city, therefore, we consulted extensively with school administrators, who thereby became deeply involved in the study and indeed made good use of it for their own purposes (incorporating our research in their ongoing inservice staff development endeavors). In Reggio Emilia, where the entire municipal early childhood education system constitutes an educational community, we were directed by the central administration to work with the teachers of one preprimary school, the Scuola Diana, where the *atelierista* was the most experienced in the system and which was favored by a stable teaching staff and outstanding physical environment. In this school, which contained the standard three classrooms for three-, four-, and five-year-olds, we had done extensive slide photography and videotaping in 1988 and therefore had already established good rapport. In Amherst, in contrast, where there was no unified public early childhood system, in order to obtain a group of teachers who belonged to a self-conscious educational community, we interviewed teachers at the Common School, a highly regarded, progressive, independent school serving children ages three to twelve, with three mixed-age classrooms for preprimary children (two classrooms for three- and four-year-olds and one classroom for five- and six-year-olds) and four mixed-age primary classes.

The first stage of data gathering was *initial interviewing* to learn about the teachers' concepts of collaboration and community building. Teachers were given the questions earlier so that they could think about or talk over their answers if they wished. We asked a standard set of open-ended questions, as follows:

- Do you see learning in the age group you work with as a collaborative process? Why or why not? Can you give some examples from your classroom experience?

- How do you as a teacher foster children learning from other children in your classroom? What problems or blocks have you encountered'?

- Do you see children in your age group adopting shared goals in free or structured play? Can you give some examples?

- Do you see children commenting on or responding to each other's work? How do you respond to

this kind of interaction? Is it something you want to encourage or influence in any way?

- Do you see your classroom as a community? If so, in what way?

- How do you connect your children to wider communities? Can you give some examples?

- What are the limitations to the kind of community you can create with your age group of children?

- How about cross-sex relations? What are the limitations to the community and collaboration that can occur between the sexes?

The second, and most extensive, stage of data gathering involved videotaping in the teachers' classrooms during morning activity time on two occasions and then using the videotapes in a playback session called the *video-reflective interview;* this discussion with the teachers was also videotaped. The initial classroom videotapes were collected in Reggio by the teacher participants working with their art director (*atelierista*), but in the other two cities by the research team. The research team then worked together to select a series of segments for video playback, trying to include episodes representative of different kinds of social activity (teacher-child, child-child, conflictual, and cooperative). (In doing this selection, we used information gathered in the prior interviews to be sure to include the kinds of events considered important for collaboration and community building by the relevant teachers, as well as episodes we thought interesting or significant, from our own perspectives.) We also worked together to generate one or more questions to ask regarding each segment, always beginning with an open-ended request, "Tell us about this segment, in terms of the social issues involved," and followed by a specific probe, such as, "Can you comment on this episode in terms of cross-sex relations?" The subsequent video-reflective interviews lasted two to three hours each and took place in a small group that consisted of the teacher (or co-teachers) of the pertinent classroom, sometimes other teachers from their school, sometimes one or more administrators from their system, and two or more members of the research team. They were videotaped for later analysis and later transcribed in full.

In the third and final stage of data gathering, we engaged the educators in *cross-cultural video-reflective discussions.* Gathering together all of the study participants from the city, plus many of their colleagues from other preschools interested in the research, we showed segments from the other research site and asked people to comment on what they saw that was congruent with and discrepant from their professional values, as well as what they saw that was similar and dissimilar to their own classrooms. These discussions, conducted in Reggio and Pistoia concerning Amherst, and in Amherst concerning both Italian sites, were extremely useful in revealing the most deeply held beliefs and values of the different participants, as well as some value-oriented reactions to the other system's practices.

Thus the videotape segments were never intended to capture the objective reality of the classroom: obviously, the segments were not representative in any sampling sense; and furthermore, videotape, with its complex juxtaposition of images and words, has to be interpreted to gain meaning. The meaning necessarily shifts, depending on who is looking and what they are thinking about as they look. Instead, we used video playback in a way similar to, but extending beyond, the format known as *stimulated recall* (a qualitative technique used in research on teaching to investigate individual teachers' interactive thoughts and decision making (Calderhead, 1981; Tuckwell, 1980). That is, by having the videoreflective interview take place in a group setting, we stimulated people to talk and listen to one another, to agree and disagree, and to modify their ideas as the discussion proceeded, and thus to co-construct their descriptions, interpretations, and analyses.

Preliminary Findings

The richness of our data exceeded our expectations and testifies to the strength of the video-reflection methodology as well as the articulateness and thoughtfulness of our informants. We are performing a formal textual analysis of the interview and discussion materials, looking at expressed concepts surrounding issues of collaboration and community understood in their broadest senses. This analysis is guided by the foundational assumption that qualitative analysis should begin as soon as data are collected and continue to emerge throughout the entire project in order to construct "grounded theory" (Glaser & Strauss, 1967; Lincoln & Guba, 1985; Nimmo, 1992). In contrast to *a priori* theory, grounded theory is more responsive to, and able to encompass, the contextual elements and multiple realities encountered in this type of qual-

itative research. Accordingly, therefore, the research team has developed a set of coding categories that refer to all the key words and central themes appearing in the corpus of interviews and discussions and relate to ideas concerning collaboration, cooperation, community, co-action, social exchange and connection, communication, and other related concepts (as well as their contrasts: conflicts, miscommunications, individualistic acts and values, disunities, social segregation, and so forth). The resulting set of approximately one hundred categories has been used to code all interviews and discussions, using a qualitative text analysis program, The Ethnograph (Seidel et al., 1988), which allows segments of text to be assigned multiple codings for later selective retrieval and interpretation. The findings of the study will emerge from the processes of interpretation and comparison.

In this paper, we will provide a preliminary "reading" of the data by demonstrating how distinct the contrast is between ways of approaching young children's classroom collaboration in Reggio Emilia and Amherst. In a future monograph, we will analyze all of the major concepts and themes for the three study communities: Amherst, Pistoia, and Reggio Emilia. Here, we will simply illustrate the directions that analysis will take by showing how different were two of the communities of educators, as revealed in one component of the data: their answers on the initial collaboration interview, in particular, their responses to question one ("Do you see learning in the age group you work with as a collaborative process? Why or why not? Can you give some examples from your classroom experience?"). Almost any segments of the material would have served for these present purposes; however, we have selected for comparison answers to the first question in the interview because they arose from the initial moments of the data-gathering encounter between the teachers and ourselves, and, as such, carry a particularly potent charge in terms of communication of meaning. We consider that these answers offer useful entry points to the systems of meaning that the teachers were seeking to convey to us. Furthermore, by selecting for close analysis the answers to a single question, we are able to reveal the precise differences in the discourse used by the two communities of teachers and begin to understand the similarities and differences in outlook and issues of concern for the two groups of educators. We found that the statements made about collaboration and community in the initial interviews were then clarified, indeed, "acted out" through the social processes of the group discussions in the video-reflective interviews. The cross-cultural video-reflective discussions, finally, brought some closure to the data gathering and revealed core issues of concern to each group within itself as well as a sense of what aspects of the other community's approach were most similar and dissimilar to its own preferred ways.

The Collaboration Interview: Opening Statements of the Reggio Emilia Educators

One of the more senior teachers in the Diana School, PS, made a concise opening statement that put forward several premises we were to hear over and over in Reggio Emilia: the importance of collaboration (she calls it "co-action") to intellectual development; the need for moments of conflict as well as moments of cooperation; the unity of cognitive and affective development; the importance of the physical environment for making collaboration among children possible; and the collaborative model provided by the teachers' collective. When she used the phrase, "Here in Reggio we are convinced ... ," she made clear her sense of identification with the ongoing educational experience in Reggio Emilia. She reemphasized this same idea at the end of her opening statement, describing her own professional formation and sense of affinity with the methods of work in her system.

PS: I do think that the children—each child—gets an advantage by staying with other children. Here in Reggio we are convinced that the cognitive learning and the affective development are tied to co-action of children and also to conflict. We are part of a project that is based on co-action of children and on the sureness that this is a good way of learning. Therefore, I find this question justified, and I see that there is learning as a collaborative process.

I can give examples. One concerns the Oil Project that we did with children. And we should also look at the physical environment [of the school] where children can stay in small groups, and where the teachers, who already cooperate among themselves, form what we call a collective. The teachers cooperate.

Actually, I am a special case [as a teacher] because I studied to be an elementary teacher. ... I must say, I did not have much experience with young children—in fact, none; but I im-

mediately became completely fascinated by the different way the schools are run here. ... From then on, I have been completely taken, and I have decided that this way of working is very congenial to me.

A second senior teacher, LR, opened her reply with a parallel declaration of belief in the validity and correctness of the Reggio Emilia method of working with small groups of children on long-term projects. She then went on to say many significant things about the use of small groups. She noted that small groups allow the teacher to readily enter the children's world and embark with them on an intellectual journey. She defined what this journey is about: asking questions and seeking knowledge. She referred to the working partnership of the fundamental Reggio triangle, teachers–children–parents, in noting how children draw their parents into their inquiries, and then the parents go to the teachers with questions. She then briefly reflected upon the fact that young children actively form their own peer relationships; through observation she has learned how important are these spontaneous groups to the process of children's becoming able to understand (communicate with) one another. Finally, she provided a long example of her project work with small groups of children and explained much about the teacher's role in Reggio, facilitating children's communication by listening for fruitful ideas, acting as the group "memory," and helping children represent their ideas in symbolic form. Here is what LR said to the opening question about fostering collaboration among young children.

LR: It is a way of working not only valid but also right. I, as a teacher, succeed in reading much more and in understanding, in staying within the group as an adult. There is much interest even from me. It is a relationship between me and the children: my staying with them becomes a way to help them to face a problem. I grow up with the children. I work in a state of uncertainty because I do not know where the children can arrive to, but it is a fabulous experience. ...

In the last two years we have assisted the kids who set problems within the group; they ask other children or adults about complex problems. The *whys* they ask are very important and lead to the discovery of being able to solve problems. Kids are always in contact with the work they do; they always ask, "Why?" They inform themselves; they find that what they say and what they do are considered by the adult; they find adults who collaborate with them, for example, their family. Parents are interested in the work children do and come to us with questions.

Last year we had very young children; they had just entered the preschool. We have always observed them, and we noticed that they were inclined to form groups. The children picked out those kids with whom they have lasting relationships. Our work as adults is based also on the observation of these groups, because their staying together in groups permits them to discover one another. Perhaps if they didn't form groups, it would take them longer to understand the others.

[Can you give an example of fostering collaboration?]

Last year, each of the two teachers had to carry on a project which would be brought to an end. We had to be present and absent. We had to catch the right moments to intervene. Kids greatly appreciated the fact of hearing, saying, intervening; and this makes their interest grow within the group, especially in young kids. I had to gather together all the points touched on and remember them. "Where shall we arrive?" I used to ask myself. Children discovered the adult and used her. They used her and her means. "Tell us what we said!" They give, but they want you to give as well. They want to receive.

I then refused to be their memory and proposed a visible form of memory, so we (or better, they) had to translate their ideas into a language comprehensible to them all. The possibilities were many: graphics, simulations, etc.

Since that time, we have always been asking them to do that at once, to give them the opportunity to explain themselves in a better way. And this requires making oneself understood by the others, which is a strong motivation. Other kids often intervene. This is useful as they help the other child to explain himself and to make clear his ideas. For exam-

ple, when studying colored shadows, kids had transparent, colored books. These books made a colored shadow—not a black shadow, as people and animals do. They had to explain this: "Why don't the books make a black shadow?" The experience was really very good.

The younger member of LR's co-teaching team, MC, was interviewed later. Rather than make abstract statements about the place of collaborative learning in the Reggio Emilia pedagogy, she simply sought to describe what the process of collaborative learning looks like, using the example of a videotaped session involving herself and two boys. She described how the children confronted their shared problem, formed a bond, generated a "fan" of ideas, sought each other's opinions and suggestions, and persevered until (rather surprisingly) they achieved the solution of a very difficult problem. She added that this kind of collaborative problem solving is less likely to appear when children are in their entire class of twenty-five.

MC: Certainly the possibilities that a child encounters inside a school are varied and diversified; cooperation understood as a 'system of relations'—not only on the personal level, but in learning to be together with others, facing things together—is an important part because it can increase the qualitative level of one's ideas as compared to others, such as we've observed in the video [in which I work with two boys who are seeking to draw a picture with a computer-activated Logo turtle]. Those two children faced a problem, in which it clearly showed them the meaning of solving together, of how one plus its counterpart confronted the problem and proved how this bond clearly was established, this "fan" of ideas and support—to help one—think and build on ideas, with the support of others. It was actually something of a surprise the way they solved the problem. There is an element of surprise every time one sees and observes such a bond being formed among the children. Their independent decision, "swing of ideas" (exchange), hesitation, and gradual formation of a unified decision, finally turns toward the "house." One is truly amazed, for one could not have suspected such an outcome at the beginning of the episode.

This type of observation we can make not only as in this instance with the two children, but also in all instances of learning, cooperation, and in all contexts. A group of twenty-five children as a unified body may or may not show us this elaborate process of cooperation with one another, such as we may see in smaller groups, such as a group of four children, six, or eight, where the number determines what can be accomplished in respect to cooperation. As in our previous example, with the two children on video, these were children who knew one another and experienced together this new situation in which one could see the diverging thoughts and varied processes, but also the seeking of each other's opinions and suggestions. Though diverging at first, they did not drop their common project but instead arrived at a final decision together.

Finally, in a joint interview with a co-teaching pair, MB and MM, the initial statement addressed issues also frequently raised by the others in later parts of their interviews or in the group discussions, namely, what factors—age, sex, prior experience, group size and composition—influence young children's capacities to collaborate in problem solving. MB and MM noted that for the youngest children (three-years-old), prior friendships formed in the nido (infant-toddler center) are the starting point for collaboration in the preprimary school. Moreover, the collaborative process in three-year-olds looks different, more simple—based on comparison, exchange, and proximity—than among older children. Finally, they referred to two issues then a focus of attention among the Reggio system as a whole: what size of group (two, three, four, five, or more children) works best in project work?; and how do sex differences affect social process and style of problem solving?

MB and MA: In our class there are twenty-five children, three-year-olds, and twenty-three of those twenty-five are coming from the nido. In fact, ten are coming from one nido. We start with that fact because it is a very important element in cooperation. Of course, three-year-olds are very different from four- and five-year-olds, but even at the nido level, especially the last year, they start making friends.

So some of the children who come in [to the preprimary school] at three already have their favorite friends. They arrive in groups that are already quite settled. In fact, for them it is almost more important to be together than to have the same teacher. So this part is very important.

Indeed, the collaborative process is very much in operation at this age. It's very important. It's very—what one does, generally, is close to another child. So although there is not always an exchange, just to be near another person is a very important element.

One should never separate the cognitive and social aspects, speaking of a child, because a child is a whole and when the child learns, he learns as a whole. And it's very important to have a friend nearby when one learns so one can compare, just compare what one learns in a very approximate way. The best relationship at this age is between two children—a couple—that forms spontaneously. One child looks for one other child, not for two or three other children. And at three, the couples can be of the same sex or of different sex. They don't seem to be so aware, or to have problems in playing with children of the opposite sex at this age. But when children become four or five this [sex difference] makes a big difference. And also one thing that is important to keep in mind is that although the children are three years old, actually there is a big range because of the birthdays, some could have the birthday in December or January, so it's quite a wide age range.

In sum, in their opening remarks, the Reggio Emilia educators introduced key aspects of how they view collaboration. Not only what they said was significant, but equally what they did not say. They stressed their identification with the collective nature of their work, and did not differentiate their individual thoughts from those of the larger reference group. Conflict was mentioned as a part of productive communication, rather than as a negative to be avoided, and they did not state any limits to the amount of group work children should do. They noted the importance of small group size in allowing fruitful exchange and dialogue, and did not describe the group as coercive over the individual. They defined the teacher's role in facilitating communication, and did not state any general ways teachers tend to, or should try to, restrain the development of collaborations or cliques between children. Finally, they spoke of the need to observe spontaneous social processes—the natural formation of friendships, the approach–avoidance relations of boys and girls—as a part of understanding children's social possibilities, and they did not volunteer these factors, or developmental or personality factors, as intractable obstacles to any child's participation in collaborative project work. The Amherst teachers, as we shall see, were much more conservative about what they saw as dangers or limitations to collaboration in young children.

The Collaboration Interview: Opening Statements of the Amherst Educators

The teachers in the Common School worked in teaching teams, with each classroom having a head teacher supervising one or two assistant teachers. All of the classrooms are mixed-age, containing the equivalent of two age-grades. This organization is intended to give each child alternating experiences of being one of the older and one of the younger members in the classroom group; to increase the amount of inter-child helping; to reduce competition and invidious comparisons of children's abilities; and to support teachers in giving children one-to-one attention.

One of these head teachers, OS, who worked in one of the three- and four-year-old classrooms, began by affirming that collaboration, in the "social sense," is critical to the mission of early education. In her view, the shared setting of preschool requires that children negotiate how to "get along with each other." Children contribute individual input into this process through problem-solving discussions. However, OS stressed that she and her teaching team do not generally plan for shared projects within the curriculum. Individual ownership of products remains of primary value for both children and teachers. In part, these individual products stand as a representation of each child's activity and even his or her identity.

> *GS:* Well there would be no need to have children to come to school if it weren't that they need to cooper ... ah ... collaborate with each other. You know the whole purpose of a nursery school is that the children have interactions with other children and therefore have

to learn how to get along with other people. In the social sense we totally collaborate all the time. You know, "Who can do what?" and "Who can be where?" and "What is alright to play with who?" and how to be with other people. I mean, everything the whole time has to do with working with other people.

When it comes to actual set-up by teachers, organized work, we do relatively little that is a project that all of them work on at the same time. We might put a project together after each one individually worked on their part. We might then put it together, either as a display together, or we stick it together and make something out of it or, you know, use it in that way, but, when ... in the whole art area most of the time each child works on their own project and takes it home ... eventually.

There is quite a lot of emphasis on bringing a project home: to some extent because you are part of your project, but another extent to communicate with the parents what the children are doing at school. My reason for putting stuff in a bag in the drawer [for parents to pick up and take home], even though the kid might have lost interest at that point, is that it's an easy way to tell the parent that he's been painting today ... you know, so it's nice to let them see it even if they just toss it out. On the other hand, the kids often get attached to what they do and often want to take stuff home. So, there is a lot of emphasis on your own thing, what you make.

But when it comes to getting along with other people and working together and ... so we do a lot of problem solving together. We will have, for instance, on Friday we had a discussion on "What can we do so we don't make the playhouse so messy that we're not able to clean it up anymore?" and then we let the children speak on that subject matter and we try to use their suggestions, if there are any we can agree on. So we talked about it and what we came to on Friday was that we will only have four children there for a little while and see if that makes it better. It's not a finished discussion of the problem, there will be discussion of this for the next six weeks [laughs] ... that happened last year too ... !

The opening statement of MS, head teacher of the other three- and four-year-old classroom, also immediately raised the inevitability of collaboration arising within a shared setting. That MS sees this collaboration as involving the "incorporation of each other's ideas," hints at the Amherst school's attention to perspective taking as a vehicle for both intellectual and social development. While acknowledging her focus on the "individual" (note that she uses the word, "individual," seven times in her first three sentences), MS argued that encouraging children's autonomous action actually makes collaboration possible; that is, through shared knowledge of each peer's contribution of individuality to the "unique group." Finally, MS asserts the much repeated view of the Amherst educators, that collaboration best occurs "naturally" within child-initiated activity" rather than in projects directed by teachers.

MS: I see it [learning] as a collaborative process in the sense that there are twenty individuals in the classroom sharing in activities and social interchange with each other, and within that setting we're bound to collaborate and share with and incorporate each other's ideas. I think we tend to focus more on individual projects and individual strengths of the kids and encourage their self-initiative and confidence in themselves. And in the process, I think that draws our attention to those individual traits—attention to each child as an individual—but in that sense we make up a unique group, with each individual within the group. The kids collaborating together comes out of their knowledge and understanding of each other as individuals.

[Can you give examples?]

There are lots of little groups that gather. For instance, today there was a group playing with Playmobile, with pirates and boats, and collaborating on a shared fantasy theme. We have a marker [pens] area that's pretty much independent where teachers and kids go off and draw together. I've heard kids discussing, "Oh, you make a really nice house. Houses are hard for me, but I can do this well." Kids showing, "Well, I do a house this way," and sort of sharing their different strategies for drawing. At the water tables with different kinds of pumps, I've seen one kid pumping

water and another kid putting a trough underneath and cooperating to catch the water and direct the water in different directions. It tends in our classroom to be child-initiated types of collaboration more than teacher-facilitated, although we do make a conscious effort to set up situations where that can happen naturally—kids collaborating on projects. If we're setting up a corn starch goop activity with different colors and bowls, we'd do it at a round table where kids would have the opportunity to pass and share the colors and mix them, saying, "Can I have some of your green and I'll put in some of my yellow."

Similar to her colleagues, BJ, the head teacher in the five- and six-year-old classroom, held that collaboration is grounded in children having opportunities to contribute their ideas to the group's curriculum. Children take ownership of the curriculum through having this "voice in it." BJ believes that this sense of participation presents the best potential for collaborative effort between children. As a teacher she aims to act as a facilitator. From BJ's perspective, the autonomy she encourages offers the children considerable freedom to truly negotiate ideas with peers. This process involves the (worthwhile) risk of giving over some teacher control of the curriculum. Here is her opening statement:

BJ: I like to give space to the children to interact with the curriculum ... to get their ideas into what we are learning and in that sense I see it as a collaborative effort. Whatever we are studying, the children should have a voice in it in a way that they can feel that they can express their own ideas and influence the way that curriculum goes. It becomes a very variable thing, uneven—some days and some times you feel the need to take charge of what's going on and give it direction, and other times there are many opportunities where you can just go with the flow, with what the children are suggesting to you.

[Can you give examples?]

I guess, as an example: one of the things I love to do is plays, and we did a play this fall that involved insects, because we were studying them and the children made up the play and decided what part they would play in it. The children are not at the point where they work wonderfully well at accepting each other's ideas, but they were able to sustain what came out of the group as a whole, and I helped them put it together. But it was their ideas, and they bought into it, and they worked together and did a slightly crazy ... but it was their ideas and it was childlike in its conception and fun and successful. My own experience has been that feeding kids lines in a play is never half as successful, particularly with young children, as saying, "Who would you like to be in this play?" And people know what they want to be and what they can be doing and [in that way] build the play from the ground up.

The final opening statement comes from RA, presently the head teacher of the six- to eight-year-old classroom but for many years the head teacher of three- and four-year-olds. She distinguished between projects that foster collaboration and those that do not. Yet, even when children are focused on "personal goals," RA still identifies collaboration as happening in the "give and take" of individual perspectives that occurs in a group setting. This process is reminiscent of the "incorporation of ideas" noted by MS earlier. As teacher, RA supports this exchange through modeling. With these older children, though, RA also plans curricula that will necessitate children coming together collaboratively in pursuit of "common goals," such as when making a large group sculpture. She also describes clearly the way in which the organizational feature of a mixed-age group plays a key role in promoting inter-child nurturance and cooperation. Even when talking about these activities, however, RA still emphasizes the individual when she discusses the process of peer "consultation" in collaborative projects and the way mixed-age grouping allows teachers to provide children with "individual attention."

RA: I think it depends on what they are doing. There are certain things we plan with collaboration in mind. For instance, this past semester we studied the culture of Indians, and there were certain things the children worked on on their own and were their [individual] projects. However, even in those situations they worked at tables in groups, and there's a lot of give and take. There's a lot going back

and forth, and the teachers will model a lot of this. Because very often a teacher will be doing a similar sort of project and might lean over and say to a child], "Oh, how did you get that to do that over there'?" and modeling that kind of questioning and answering, so the children will do it with each other. But, the end result is something they own themselves and take away with them, and that tends to be something that happens a lot.

And so what we try to do is think of things that necessitate them all working toward a common goal as opposed to working toward a personal goal. One of the parents came in who works a lot with clay and they built a huge clay horse modeled on Indian terra-cotta sculpture. And they all knew that it was something that no one was going to take away with them, and they all had to work on it together. And there was a lot more consultation, "Oh, what do you think would look good here? How should we make the legs?" So there was a lot more collaboration that went on with something like that. So I think that learning can be [collaborative], depending on the task.

[Is this a mixed-age group you are working with?]

Yes, there are six-, seven-, and eight-year-olds. So that also changes the dynamics, because the older children know the ropes and are very often called upon to help the new fledglings coming in and show them what to do and how to do it. I think the older children tend to be more collaborative. They seem to feel like they know what is going on, and it's their role—it's built into the operation of the classroom—that in order to provide the individual attention that we like to give children, they need to assume a role in which they are helping [younger children].

Together, the Common School teachers introduced key aspects of how they view collaboration. Their use of "we," speaking of the teachers' perspective, was reminiscent of the Reggio educators and reflected the strong sense of collegial partnership within each of the teaching teams and within the school as a whole. In defining collaboration, they talked about the impact of the shared ecology of the classroom and the mixed-age grouping that promote spontaneous collaboration through play, mutual helping, and exchange of ideas. They made a distinction that we never heard in Reggio Emilia: between this kind of child-initiated collaboration, rooted in spontaneous social interaction, and a kind that is teacher-initiated, taking place in the context of group problem-solving discussions or teacher-initiated projects like doing a play or building a large sculpture. Teachers preferred the spontaneous, child-initiated collaborations and the group problem-solving discussions as the most valuable and appropriate experiences for young, preprimary children.

It is interesting that, in spite of coming squarely out of the politically and pedagogically leftist Progressive Education tradition, these teachers followed the common American habit of using many words and phrases that originated from the domain of property relations and transactions: BJ says that children "bought into" the play idea; RA talks about children doing work they "own themselves" and offering ideas in "consultation." They talked on several occasions about "investment" and "input" into the curriculum "owned" by all. This can be seen as complementary to their Deweyian vision of the school as a democratic community in which each individual has an equal voice and active participation. In general, their emphasis is on children's individual self-development and how this can be enhanced through friendship, mutual helping, play, perspective taking, group problem solving, and as children grow older, genuine collaborative project work. These issues (and others) emerged repeatedly in subsequent interviews in the data gathering: in the dialogues held with each teaching team and the two large meetings for cross-cultural video-reflection.

Conclusion

Beginning with shared assumptions about the nature of the child and of schooling as a "system of relations and communications embedded in the wider social system" (Rinaldi, 1990), the educators in Reggio Emilia have developed over the past thirty years a distinctive approach to early education. The concrete features of this approach include, as key components, small group collaborative learning; continuity over time of child-child and child-teacher relations; a focus on problem solving and long-term projects involving mastery of many symbolic media; fostering of

the connections between home, school, and the wider community; and awareness and appreciation of cultural heritage (city, region, and nation). Accompanying these concrete organizational features is a shared discourse or language of education that allows the Reggio teachers to collaborate, that is, in their own terms, to exchange ideas, listen to one another, and engage in meaningful conflict over ideas. Their language of education is readily apparent in their statements in the collaboration interviews, as well as the subsequent group video-reflection discussions. It is based on a theory of knowledge that defines thinking and learning as social and communicative events—co-constructive experiences for both children and adults.

The Amherst educators, members of a school community founded in the 1960s and based on Deweyian principles of progressive education, likewise have developed a shared language of education. Central to their goals are promoting the development of each unique individual, within a strong community stretching backward and forward in time and containing children, their families, and all the staff at the school—director, librarian, teachers, assistant teachers, and others. This community is conceived as democratic, diverse, and drawing strength from the ties of cross-age relationships. Their language of education, very different from that heard in Reggio Emilia, is based on a theory of knowledge that sees thinking and learning as a matter of each child gaining knowledge of self, others, and the wider world through social interaction, research, and discussion—processes that stimulate the development of mature autonomy and self-realization. Placing the two perspectives in juxtaposition, it is easy to see how each language of education constrains or directs the thinking of its teachers, but at the same time packages ideas economically to make communication and dialogue possible for the community. The language of education preferred in Amherst focuses teachers' attention on individuals and how they develop and change over time. The preferred discourse makes it difficult for them to regard groups as the always desirable context for intellectual work and supports the view that teachers should closely monitor social interactions between children and be available to work closely in short, one-on-one or one-on-two spurts, with children engaged in intellectual work, so that children have opportunities for both guided and independent learning. In contrast, the language of education preferred in Reggio Emilia focuses teachers' attention on children always in relation to the group, and makes it difficult for them to speak systematically about the value of their program in terms of what the children gain from it, year by year, across specific domains.

At the same time, the educators in each community seem to be aware of more dimensions and more complexity than what their language of education structures for them. As we shall discuss in future writings, both groups of teachers are highly aware of the unique personality of each child and also highly knowledgeable about the group processes in their classroom. Indeed, it appeared that the interviews and discussions involved in our research, particularly the cross-cultural video-reflection, provoked the teachers to consider the limitations of both their own and the other community's discourse and practices.

References

Bruner, J. (1986). *Actual minds, possible worlds.* Cambridge, MA: Harvard University Press.

Calderhead, J. (1981). Stimulated recall: A method for research on teaching, *British Journal of Educational Psychology* 51 (2, Jun):211–217. EJ 251 802,

D'Andrade, R. G. (1984). Cultural meaning systems. In R. A. Shweder and R. A. LeVine (Eds.), *Culture theory: Essays on mind, self, and emotion* (pp. 88–118), New York: Cambridge University Press.

Edwards, C., L. Gandini, and G. Forman, (Eds.). (1993). *The hundred languages of children: The Reggio Emilia approach to early childhood education.* Norwood, NJ: Ablex. ED 355 034.

Edwards, C. P., and L. Gandini. (1989). Teachers' expectations about the timing of developmental skills: A cross-cultural study. *Young Children* 44(4, May):15–19. EJ 391 009.

Glaser, B. G., and A. L. Strauss. (1967). *The discovery of grounded theory: Strategies for qualitative research.* Chicago: Aldine.

Holland, D., and N. Quinn, (Eds.). (1987). *Cultural models in language and thought.* New York: Cambridge University Press.

Lincoln, Y. S., and E. G. Guba. (1985). *Naturalistic inquiry.* Beverly Hills, CA: Sage.

Nimmo, J. W. (1992). *Classroom community: Its meaning as negotiated by teachers of young children.* Unpublished doctoral dissertation, School of Education, University of Massachusetts, Amherst.

Rinaldi, C. (1990). *Social constructivism in Reggio Emilia, Italy.* Paper presented at the annual conference of the Association of Constructivist Teachers, Northampton, Massachusetts, October. Translated into English by B. Rankin, L. Gandini, and K. Ellis.

Rogoff, B. (1990). *Apprenticeship in thinking.* New York: Oxford University Press.

Sampson, E. E. (1988). The debate on individualism: Indigenous psychologies of the individual and their role in personal and societal functioning. *American Psychologist* 4(1): 15–22.

Schwartz, S. H. (1990). Individualism-collectivism: Critique and proposed refinements. *Journal of Cross-Cultural Psychology* 21(2, Jun): 139–157. EJ 411 278.

Seidel, J. V., R. Kjolseth, and E. Seymour. (1988). *The Ethnograph: A user's guide (version 3.0).* Littleton, CO: Qualis Research Associates.

Spradley, J. P. (1979). *The ethnographic interview.* New York: Holt, Rinehart, and Winston.

Tobin, J. J. (1988). Visual anthropology and multivocal ethnography: A dialogical approach to Japanese preschool class size. *Dialectical Anthropology,* 13(2): 173–187.

Tobin, J. J., D.Y.H. Wu, and D. H. Davidson. (1989). *Preschool in three cultures: Japan, China, and the United States.* New Haven, CT: Yale University Press.

Triandis, H.C. (1989). Cross-cultural studies of individualism and collectivism. In I. Berman (Ed.), *Nebraska Symposium on Motivation.* 1989 (p. 41-133). Lincoln, NE: University of Nebraska Press.

Triandis, H. C., C. McCusker, and C. H. Hui. (1990). Multimethod probes of individualism and collectivism. *Journal of Personality and Social Psychology* 59(5):1006–1020.

Tuckwell, N. B. (1980). Stimulated recall: Theoretical perspectives and practical and technical considerations. Center for Research in Teaching, University of Alberta. Occasional Paper Series, Technical Report 8-2-3.

Wertsch, J. V. (1991). *Voices of the mind: A sociocultural approach to mediated action.* Cambridge, MA: Harvard University Press.

B. Article published in *Rassegna di Psicologia*

FAVORIRE L'APPRENDIMENTO COOPERATIVO NELLA PRIMA INFANZIA.
CONCETTUALIZZAZIONI CONTRASTANTI DEGLI INSEGNANTI DI DUE COMUNITÀ

Carolyn Edwards
Lella Gandini
John Nimmo
University of Kentucky, Lexington

La prospettiva teorica entro cui si muove questa ricerca guarda all'apprendimento e alla formazione del pensiero come a processi essenzialmente sociali (Bruner, 1986; Rogoff, 1990; Wertsch, 1991). Obiettivo di questo studio è di evidenziare e caratterizzare, attraverso un confronto interculturale, somiglianze e differenze nell'approccio ai processi di apprendimento/insegnamento in specifici contesti culturali. In particolare, sono state analizzate le opinioni delle insegnanti di tre città (due italiane e una nordamericana). I dati sono stati raccolti ricorrendo ad una complessa metodologia che ha consentito di sollecitare le riflessioni delle educatrici sulla propria esperienza a partire da videoregistrazioni compiute in precedenza nelle proprie classi (Tobin, 1989; Tobin, Wu, Davidson, 1989). I risultati della ricerca evidenziano, accanto ad interessanti analogie, l'esistenza di due differenti modelli educativi, l'uno basato sullo sviluppo dell'individuo, l'altro sulla centralità del gruppo, espressi mediante un linguaggio condiviso sull'educazione, proprio di ciascuna delle comunità analizzate.

La socializzazione come appropriazione collettiva di cultura

Da alcuni anni vari ricercatori nordamericani hanno scelto l'Italia come campo di ricerca sull'educazione della prima infanzia grazie al ruolo guida che in questo paese hanno acquisito i servizi educativi sviluppatisi nei comuni di alcune regioni. Poiché l'interesse ad individuare modi nuovi per accrescere la conoscenza della socializzazione e dell'educazione infantile considerate nel loro contesto, viene condiviso da molti tra gli psicologi nordamericani ed italiani, questo è il momento propizio per iniziare ad esaminare e paragonare

metodi e risultati. Quando si considerano i risultati di studi culturali compa-
rativi, è necessario ricordare che le culture nazionali non sono unitarie né
omogenee. Occorre piuttosto prestare attenzione alle molteplicità, ai cam-
biamenti, alle differenze all'interno di una zona e tra zone diverse. Sono proprio
questi aspetti complessi parte essenziale dell'interesse insito nell'analisi di
contesti culturali dell'apprendimento e dello sviluppo sia a casa che a scuola.

Il nostro studio (così come gli altri inclusi in questo numero di *Rassegna
di Psicologia*) partecipano dell'impegno preso dalle scienze sociali contem-
poranee di trasformare le premesse individualistiche sulla scienza, la personalità e la società che si sono radicate nel pensiero degli studiosi nordamericani in particolare, ma certamente non solo tra loro. Queste premesse
individualistiche, come si è notato, creano forti limitazioni per la comprensione dell'apprendimento e della formazione del pensiero come processi essenzialmente sociali e per la descrizione della socializzazione come appropriazione collettiva piuttosto che come interiorizzazione della cultura
(Bruner, 1986; Rogoff, 1990; Wertsch, 1991); a livello più pragmatico, li-
mita la possibilità di educare i bambini in modo da promuovere al meglio il
loro comportamento proto-sociale, l'empatia e il senso di identificazione con
il gruppo di riferimento. Ma come procedere al di là dell'individuo considerato come unità base dell'analisi psicologica? La teoria in proposito viene
costruita con l'assistenza della psicologia vygotskiana, l'antropologia culturale e la sociolinguistica interpretativa. Allo stesso tempo occorre trovare
urgentemente metodi migliori di raccolta e di analisi di dati per stabilire quali
scelte potrebbero portare in direzioni più fruttuose. Come appare evidente
dagli articoli in questo numero, gli psicologi sono alle prese con il tentativo
di trovare nuovi modi di vedere e descrivere l'apprendimento e la socializzazione come processi legati alla partecipazione dei bambini ad eventi comunicativi che sono stati favoriti dagli adulti.

Somiglianze e differenze dei contesti culturali

Questo particolare studio à stato condotto da un gruppo interculturale in
tre luoghi diversi Reggio Emilia, Pistoia ed Amherst [1]. Tutte e tre queste

---

1. Il gruppo inter-culturale include Lella Gandini e Donatella Giovannini (Italia), John
Nimmo (Australia) e Carolyn Edwards (Stati Uniti). Amherst si trova nel Massachusetts,
USA.

città hanno aspetti comuni: sono città relativamente piccole, coese, con una tradizione politica progressista ed estesi servizi per l'infanzia. Di queste tre città Reggio Emilia e Pistoia hanno costruito un sistema di educazione 0-6 anni finanziato ed amministrato dal comune. Questi progetti educativi sono conosciuti per la loro qualità e contenuti innovativi in tutta Italia e sono noti nel resto dell'Europa. Vengono in particolare riconosciuti come luoghi dove educatori professionisti e cittadini si sono uniti ed hanno investito anni di lavoro e di energie per creare un sistema pubblico di servizi educativi per la prima infanzia. Tra i numerosi elementi portanti di queste esperienze educative va sottolineato: 1) il modo in cui i bambini, gli insegnanti e i genitori contribuiscono a formare delle comunità che operano strettamente collegate alla città e con la regione circostante; 2) il modo in cui i bambini vengono stimolati, sostenuti e guidati nello sviluppo cognitivo, sociale e affettivo attraverso l'attività e il gioco cooperativo nonché i progetti di gruppo. Questi aspetti tendono ad essere sorprendenti per molti dei visitatori che sono venuti di recente dagli Stati Uniti con un loro bagaglio di idee e valori individualistici e con idee preconcette piagetiane sull'egocentrismo dei bambini. Ma piuttosto che scoraggiare tali visitatori, la possibilità di iniziare un processo di scambio e confronto tra culture ha dimostrato di essere un forte stimolo per la ricerca e la discussione.

Il nostro studio, in particolare, mette a fuoco come gli insegnanti in tre comunità cercano di promuovere cooperazione e senso di comunità tra i bambini nelle loro scuole. Cerchiamo di analizzare da vicino la filosofia portante che sostiene il lavoro degli educatori a Reggio Emilia, a Pistoia e ad Amherst e di paragonare le loro idee ai metodi da loro scelti per strutturare le giornate dei bambini, per organizzare gruppi piccoli e grandi, per regolarsi nei riguardi dei conflitti, per esaminare le questioni legate ai ruoli sessuali e per collegare i bambini alla comunità più ampia al di fuori della scuola. La nostra ricerca è ampia ed in questo articolo ci limiteremo a presentare solamente risultati preliminari e parziali.

Tuttavia, perfino da questa analisi preliminare è evidente che in ciascuno dei tre luoghi in cui si è svolta la ricerca, viene usato un linguaggio comune. È quello che gli antropologhi (D'Andrade, 1984; Holland, Quinn, 1987; Spradyly, 1979) chiamano un «discorso distinto» o « un sistema culturale di significati» e che lo psicologo Jerome Bruner (1986) chiama un «linguaggio dell'educazione». Gli educatori che hanno partecipato a questo studio lo adoperano per inquadrare, riguardo ai bambini, le questioni relative alla cooperazione e al senso di comunità. Questo linguaggio comune, a sua volta, può essere messo in relazione a pratiche oggettive, per esempio al metodo di organizzazione della scuola e al modo di raggruppare i bambini. Inoltre, può essere messo in relazione a convinzioni condivise per quello che riguarda il ruolo dell'insegnante, l'immagine del bambino nel processo di apprendimento, la logica che detta l'intervento e la guida da parte degli insegnanti e gli stili scelti allo scopo di facilitare il processo di apprendimento stesso.

In questo articolo non esaminiamo gli aspetti teorici più ampi relativi ai modi in cui gli psicologi possano descrivere nel modo migliore l'apprendimento e il pensiero, visti come processi sociali, e la socializzazione come appropriazione collettiva di cultura. Piuttosto, partiamo con una questione empirica - di fatto etnografica - vale a dire ci chiediamo *in quale modo* in queste diverse comunità gli adulti, che partecipano al nostro studio, parlino di questi due importanti elementi dell'educazione; e più precisamente di insegnamento/apprendimento come co-azione e co-creazione di significati. L'intento è di dimostrare che le differenze dovute alla comunità culturale non sono ovvie, o futili, ma piuttosto precisamente collegate a quegli elementi, pensiero ed apprendimento, in modo tale da fornire utili informazioni per gli psicologi. È noto che la maggior parte delle teorie dello sviluppo, specialmente quelle influenzate dai fondamenti filosofici occidentali e nordamericani, è immerso in categorie individualistiche. In contrasto, i nostri informatori italiani, in specie quelli di Reggio Emilia, hanno sviluppato categorie filosofiche differenti, non solo a livello teorico come convinzioni e valori, ma anche a livello della pratica educativa, inserite in istituzioni coerenti e pratiche educative funzionanti. Queste categorie, tenteremo di mostrare, pongono l'apprendimento come co-creazione di conoscenza e il bambino come intrinsecamente sociale. Gli educatori di Reggio Emilia hanno, durante un periodo di circa trent'anni, collettivamente sviluppato un linguaggio dell'educazione che parte da una visione co-costruttivista del bambino e dell'insegnamento/apprendimento molto vicina a quello proposto da Jerome Bruner (1986):

«... ho finito per riconoscere sempre più che, in gran parte delle situazioni, l'apprendimento è quasi sempre un'attività comunitaria: è il processo per il quale si perviene a condividere la cultura. Non si tratta solo di far sì che il bambino si appropri davvero delle sue conoscenze, ma che se ne appropri in una comunità di persone che condividono il suo senso di appartenenza ad una cultura. È questa convinzione che mi porta ad enfatizzare l'importanza non solo della scoperta e dell'invenzione, ma anche del confronto e della compartecipazione; in una parola, l'importanza di creare una cultura collettiva che sia oggetto di insegnamento e che riesca a costituire un momento efficace nel tragitto che porta il bambino a diventare membro della società adulta in cui vive la propria vita».

Piuttosto che mettere in luce il coinvolgimento autonomo nell'apprendimento del bambino in via di sviluppo, gli educatori di Reggio Emilia e Pistoia, considerano l'educare come un'attività da intraprendere in comune e come una condivisione di cultura realizzato attraverso la cooperazione sia tra bambini che tra bambini ed educatori che a loro volta aprono nuovi argomenti all'indagine e alla negoziazione (vedi Bruner, 1986, cap. 9).

Gli educatori di Amherst, al contrario, vedono l'educazione prima e soprattutto come mezzo per promuovere lo sviluppo di ogni individuo. Allo stesso tempo però, come si vedrà, per quanto guidato da categorie occidentali individualistiche il loro discorso non viene del tutto collocato all'interno di tali categorie. Piuttosto, mentre a livello teorico gli educatori di Amherst si cimentano con questioni legate alla cooperazione e al senso di comunità, e a livello pratico si impegnano con una classe di bambini reale con la sua particolare identità e con la sua propria storia, anche loro cercano di rispondere in modo adeguato alla dialettica tra bisogni individuali e i bisogni del gruppo.

Per tutti gli insegnanti che hanno partecipato al nostro studio quindi pensiamo che le loro parole, inquadrate dalle immagini della pratica giornaliera e delle decisioni da prendere, rivelano una tessitura complessa dei significati da loro dati all'apprendimento cooperativo. Le interviste e le discussioni nelle comunità dove ha avuto luogo lo studio ci forniscono modi alternativi di pensare la cooperazione, che corrispondono: a un'immagine del bambino, a un'immagine del ruolo dell'insegnante e ad un approccio scelto con cura nello strutturare l'esperienza dei bambini stessi.

Questo articolo illustra i dati e sottolinea i risultati che stanno emergendo, in questa fase dello studio, attraverso il paragone di alcuni aspetti delle valutazioni degli educatori di Reggio Emilia e di Amherst riguardo all'apprendimento cooperativo.

69

Metodologia

Descrizione dei due luoghi di ricerca

Reggio Emilia è una città di circa 130.000 abitanti nella regione Emilia Romagna. Il programma comunale per l'educazione della prima infanzia ha origine dalle scuole autogestite iniziate da gruppi di genitori alla fine della seconda guerra mondiale. Attualmente il comune gestisce 22 scuole dell'infanzia e 13 asili nido (Edwards, Gandini, Forman, in stampa). I bambini che frequentano queste istituzioni provengono da tutti gli strati sociali e includono bambini portatori di handicap. Le scuole dell'infanzia comunali accolgono il 50% dei bambini tra i 3 e i 6 anni e gli asili nido circa il 37% dei bambini da 0 a 3 anni di età.

Amherst è una città di circa 35.000 abitanti, situata nella zona rurale dell'ovest del Massachusetts. Questa città fondata nel 1755 è nota negli Stati Uniti per l'alta concentrazione di Università e College di ottima fama e per la forma di governo democratico e con una forte partecipazione cittadina attraverso gli storici *town meetings* (democrazia diretta), e la lunga tradizione di progressismo che si era manifestata nella scelta dell'abolizionismo e in un passato più recente nelle attività contro la guerra in Vietnam. Per quello che riguarda l'educazione della prima infanzia, mentre questa città viene considerata molto avanzata per gli standard americani, non ha un programma comunale unificato. Vi sono molte istituzioni ma frammentarie; tra queste, un ufficio centrale che raccoglie e distribuisce informazioni riguardo i servizi per l'infanzia, istituzioni educative per i bambini dei dipendenti comunali, molte scuole private di ottimo livello, una rete di famiglie che provvedono alla custodia e cura di bambini e hanno sia una licenza che il controllo dello stato, programmi statali o comunali per bambini con handicap e bambini maltrattati, ed infine l'educazione pubblica gratuita a partire dai cinque anni nei giardini d'infanzia che sono parte delle scuole elementari (Edwards, Gandini, 1989; Nimmo, 1992).

Interviste iniziali e interviste di riflessione sul video

La metodologia, in tutti e tre i luoghi studiati, consta di interviste di vario tipo con le insegnanti. Si tratta di un adattamento della metodologia sviluppata da Tobin, Wu e Davidson e descritta in *Preschool in Three Cultures*. Con questo metodo si ottengono videotape dell'attività quotidiana delle classi, non per documentare ma piuttosto come stimolo per impostare un dialogo critico e di riflessione con l'intento principale di costruire una *video-etnografia a più voci* (Tobin, 1989; Tobin, Wu, Davidson, 1989). I ricercatori sistematicamente sollecitano e registrano le reazioni da parte degli insegnanti, sia tra quelli che fanno parte della cultura rappresentata che di quelli al di fuori di essa, sui segmenti video scelti tra quelli che descrivono le attività dei bambini. Tra le persone invitate a partecipare al dialogo vi sono gli insegnanti della classe studiata, i loro colleghi, i genitori, educatori e genitori di altre città nello stesso paese, ed infine educatori e genitori di altri paesi. Queste reazioni vengono messe insieme, analizzate, e interpretate da etnografi che si prendono la responsabilità della compilazione dell'analisi finale presentata in un rapporto che cerca di salvaguardare la molteplicità delle prospettive e delle voci delle tante persone coinvolte.

Abbiamo cominciato col selezionare come informatori principali un piccolo gruppo di insegnanti in ognuna delle tre città scelte. Era nostra intenzione che queste insegnanti fossero membri di una comunità educativa, vale a dire, parte di un gruppo di educatori impegnato in un progetto educativo coerente e che possedessero e condividessero un linguaggio professionale ed una serie di valori base riguardo l'educazione dei bambini. Nel contempo desideravamo lavorare con informatori che venissero considerati dai colleghi e dagli amministratori degli esempi forti della loro professione, nonché fossero delle persone in grado di esprimere in modo articolato i loro principi e le loro pratiche educative. In ogni città, dunque, abbiamo avuto ampie consultazioni con gli amministratori, che attraverso questo processo si sono coinvolti con interesse, e a volte profondamente, nello studio e hanno trovato utile incorporare la nostra ricerca nel loro programma di aggiornamento degli educatori. A Reggio Emilia, dove tutto il sistema comunale di educazione della prima infanzia fa parte del progetto educativo siamo stati indirizzati dall'amministrazione a lavorare con gli insegnanti della scuola dell'infanzia Diana. In questa scuola suddivisa come di norma in tre sezioni per i bambini di 3, di 4 e di 5 anni, avevamo fatto nel 1988 delle riprese video e fotografiche e avevamo inoltre stabilito un buon rapporto professionale, anche attraverso i numerosi contatti di lavoro, con uno dei membri del nostro gruppo di ricerca.

Ad Amherst, al contrario, dove non c'è un sistema unificato di educazione pubblica per la prima infanzia, per poter trovare degli insegnanti che appartenessero a un gruppo che fosse deliberatamente parte di una comunità educativa, abbiamo scelto ed intervistato le insegnanti di una scuola tenuta in grande stima, una scuola progressista ed indipendente che educa bambini dai 3 ai 12 anni. In questa scuola, *The Common School*, vi sono tre sezioni di età mista per i bambini di livello pre-elementare, due sezioni per i bambini di 3-4 anni e una per i bambini di 5-6 anni, oltre alle 4 classi di età mista a livello elementare.

La prima fase della raccolta dei dati è stata *un'intervista iniziale* per dar modo alle insegnanti di esprimere le loro idee relative alla cooperazione e alla formazione di un senso di comunità tra bambini. Le domande venivano date in anticipo agli amministratori e alle insegnanti, così che potessero pensare alle risposte se lo desideravano. Abbiamo posto una serie di domande aperte come segue:

* Consideri l'apprendimento come un processo legato alla cooperazione per i bambini del tuo gruppo d'età? Se è così, puoi dare qualche esempio legato all'esperienza della tua sezione?

* Come fai, come insegnante, ad incoraggiare nella tua sezione l'apprendimento dei bambini da altri bambini? Quali problemi o quali ostacoli hai incontrato a questo proposito?

* Noti che i bambini, del livello di età della tua sezione, adottino finalità condivise nel gioco libero o nel gioco strutturato? Se sì puoi dare qualche esempio?

* Noti che i bambini facciano commenti o rispondano l'uno al lavoro dell'altro? Come rispondi a questo tipo di interazione?

* Consideri la tua sezione come una comunità? Se è così, in che modo?

* Come colleghi i bambini a comunità più ampie? Puoi dare degli esempi?

* Quali difficoltà pensi di incontrare nella formazione di un senso di comunità con i bambini di questo livello di età?

* Che cosa puoi descrivere a proposito delle relazioni tra i due sessi? Nei termini di un senso di comunità e di cooperazione, quali sono i limiti?

La seconda, e più estesa fase della raccolta dei dati include video riprese nelle classi delle insegnanti partecipanti durante l'attività della mattina in due occasioni diverse. A queste è seguita, dopo qualche tempo, una sessione definita *intervista di riflessione sul video*; anche questo scambio con le insegnanti è stato video registrato. I video iniziali erano stati ripresi a Reggio Emilia dalle stesse insegnanti partecipanti, che avevano lavorato con l'atelierista, ma nelle altre due città anche le video riprese iniziali erano state fatte dal gruppo di ricerca. Lo stesso gruppo di ricerca ha poi selezionato con cura una serie di segmenti da utilizzare nell'intervista di riflessione sul video con le insegnanti (nonché una serie di segmenti per la presentazione nelle situazioni culturali diverse), cercando di includere episodi rappresentativi di diversi tipi di attività sociale (scambi insegnante-bambino, bambino-bambino, momenti di conflitto e momenti di cooperazione). Nel fare questa selezione abbiamo usato informazioni raccolte nelle interviste iniziali per essere sicuri di includere il tipo di eventi considerati significativi per la cooperazione e la formazione di un senso di comunità da parte delle insegnanti; abbiamo anche incluso episodi che pensavamo fossero significativi secondo la nostra prospettiva. Inoltre abbiamo formulato domande aperte relative ad ogni segmento seguite da una domanda più precisa, relativa all'episodio in questione. L'intervista di riflessione sul video, di solito di circa due ore di durata, si svolgeva in un piccolo gruppo composto dall'insegnante o dalle insegnanti della classe particolare, qualche volta altre insegnanti della stessa scuola, qualche volta alcuni degli amministratori e due o più membri del gruppo di ricerca. Le video riprese di queste interviste sono servite a documentare questo incontro; in seguito i dialoghi completamente trascritti sono stati sottoposti ad un'analisi accurata.

Nella terza fase della raccolta dei dati, quella finale, abbiamo coinvolto le educatrici in una *discussione-riflessione, sul video, di tipo inter-culturale.* In questa occasione abbiamo riunito tutti i partecipanti allo studio del luogo, ed educatori di altre scuole che erano interessati al tema della ricerca. Abbiamo mostrato loro segmenti selezionati relativi all'altro luogo e chiesto alle persone presenti di commentare se quello che notavano fosse congruente o discordante dai loro principi professionali ed inoltre di esprimersi su quello che consideravano simile o dissimile dalla esperienza quotidiana nelle loro scuole. Queste discussioni, condotte a Reggio e a Pistoia osservando un video che illustrava vari segmenti riguardanti la scuola di Amherst e condotto ad Amherst presentando le scuole di Pistoia e di Reggio Emilia, sono risultati molto utili a mettere in luce valori e convinzioni dei diversi partecipanti e ad esprimere alcune reazione dettate dai propri valori sulle pratiche portate avanti negli altri sistemi.

Ribadiamo che i segmenti di videotape non erano destinati a raccogliere la realtà oggettiva delle classi e non erano ovviamente una campionatura rappresentativa. Inoltre il mezzo di comunicazione video, con le sue complesse sovrapposizioni d'immagini e di parole, deve essere interpretato per acquisire significato. Il significato necessariamente si sposta secondo chi guarda e secondo ciò che pensano le persone che guardano. Invece, facendo in modo che *l'intervista con riflessione sul video* avesse luogo in una situazione di gruppo, conducevamo i partecipanti a parlare e ascoltarsi l'un l'altro, a cercare di mettersi d'accordo e manifestare il loro disaccordo, a modificare le proprie idee man mano che la discussione procedeva e così facendo costruire insieme descrizioni, interpretazioni ed analisi comuni [2].

Una lettura preliminare dei risultati

La ricchezza dei dati raccolti ha superato le aspettative e testimonia sia la positività di questa metodologia sia la capacità di riflettere e di esprimersi con chiarezza da parte degli educatori che hanno partecipato. Stiamo procedendo ad un'analisi formale del testo delle interviste e delle discussioni, rilevando concetti espressi relativi alla cooperazione e al senso di comunità considerate in senso ampio. Questa analisi viene guidata dalla convinzione di base che l'analisi qualitativa dovrebbe iniziare appena i dati sono stati raccolti e continuare ad emergere attraverso l'intero progetto per costituire *una teoria costruita sul campo* (Glaser, Strauss, 1967; Lincoln, Guba, 1985; Nimmo, 1992). Al contrario di una teoria stabilita a priori, una teoria costruita sul campo risponde meglio ed è più atta a includere elementi del contesto e realtà multiple che si incontrano in questo tipo di ricerca qualitativa. Seguendo questa linea, dunque, il gruppo di ricerca ha sviluppato una serie di categorie per codificare i dati che si riferiscono a tutte le parole chiave ed ai temi centrali che appaiono nel corpus delle interviste e delle discussioni. Parole e temi, relativi alle idee che si riferiscono alla cooperazione, il senso di comunità, la co-azione, gli scambi e i collegamenti sociali, la comunicazione ed altri concetti connessi, nonché il loro opposto come: conflitti, disguidi di comunicazione, azioni e valori individualistici, disunità, segregazioni sociali, ecc. La risultante serie di circa 100 categorie è stata usata per codificare tutte le interviste e le discussioni usando un programma di analisi qualitativa testuale, THE ETHNOGRAPH (Seidel, Kjolseth, Seymour, 1988), che per-

---

2. Abbiamo usato la proiezione dei video in un modo simile, ma che andava oltre, a quello che viene chiamato *ricordo sollecitato*: una tecnica qualitativa usata nella ricerca sull'insegnamento per studiare i pensieri interattivi e il processo attraverso cui gli insegnanti prendono decisioni. (Calderhead, 1981; Tuckwell, 1980).

mette di assegnare a segmenti di testo un codice per poterlo rintracciare, e interpretare selettivamente al momento dell'analisi. I risultati dello studio emergono dai processi di interpretazione e di confronto.

In questo articolo forniremo una «lettura preliminare» dei dati mostrando quanto si presenti con evidenza il contrasto tra l'approccio alla cooperazione tra bambini nelle scuole di Reggio Emilia e di Amherst al di là delle differenze ovvie. In una monografia futura analizzeremo i concetti e i temi principali per quello che riguarda tutte le tre comunità studiate: Amherst, Pistoia e Reggio Emilia. Qui illustreremo semplicemente la direzione dell'analisi, mostrando come siano differenti due delle comunità di educatori, come questo venga sottolineato da una sola componente dei dati: la loro risposta alla prima domanda dell'intervista iniziale («Consideri l'apprendimento come un processo legato alla cooperazione per i bambini del tuo gruppo d'età? Se è così, puoi dare qualche esempio legato all'esperienza nella tua sezione?»). Altri segmenti del materiale potrebbero essere usati a questo scopo; tuttavia abbiamo selezionato questa prima domanda perché il momento iniziale dell'incontro con le insegnanti a nostro avviso ha una forte carica di comunicazione e di significato. Queste risposte offrono un utile ingresso al sistema di significati che le insegnanti cercavano di trasferirci.

Le affermazioni fatte a proposito della cooperazione e del senso di comunità nelle interviste iniziali venivano poi ulteriormente chiarite, e quasi «drammatizzate», nelle interviste di riflessione sul video, attraverso i processi sociali della discussione di gruppo. In seguito, la riflessione interculturale sul video, è servita a stabilire una conclusione alla raccolta dei dati e ha sottolineato ancora una volta le questioni di base che impegnano le educatrici all'interno di ogni gruppo. Inoltre questa ultima discussione ha messo anche in luce quali aspetti dell'approccio dell'altra comunità fossero giudicati simili o diversi da quello scelto nel proprio ambito.

Reggio Emilia: centralità del collettivo e valore cognitivo del conflitto

Una delle insegnanti che da molto tempo lavora alla scuola Diana, PC, ha fornito un'introduzione concisa ed ha elencato numerose premesse che abbiamo sentito ripetutamente enunciate da parte delle educatrici di Reggio Emilia: l'importanza della cooperazione (da lei definita come co-azione) per lo sviluppo intellettuale, l'importanza di momenti sia di conflitto che di cooperazione, l'unità dello sviluppo cognitivo e sociale; l'importanza dell'ambiente fisico per rendere possibile la cooperazione tra bambini e il modello cooperativo che viene offerto dal collettivo degli insegnanti. Quando PC ha usato la frase: «Qui a Reggio siamo convinti…» metteva in evidenza la sua identificazione con il progetto educativo in continuo sviluppo a Reggio. Inoltre è ritornata su questo aspetto verso la fine della sua introduzione quando ha descritto la sua formazione professionale e il senso di affinità da lei provato con il metodo di lavoro che è parte del sistema di Reggio.

PC: «Non solo l'apprendimento o lo sviluppo cognitivo ma anche quello affettivo e quello motorio traggono vantaggio dalla cooperazione. E forse invece che cooperazione, che fa pensare a qualcosa di «morale», che va tutto bene, direi co-azione, essere insieme magari anche in conflitto. Noi siamo qui dentro a un progetto che è nato e si struttura sullo stare insieme dei bambini, sulla co-azione e anche sulla scommessa che questo è un modo buono per crescere.

Il primo esempio che mi viene da fare è quello dello spazio fisico della scuola e delle sezioni. Non ci sono 25 bambini nei banchi o in una situazione assembleare, ma all'interno della sezione vi sono tre stanze per loro e possono stare insieme in piccoli gruppi. Il fatto che ci siano due insegnanti invece che una mette in evidenza anche una cooperazione tra gli adulti. Poi, già durante l'orario di lavoro, tutte le insegnanti della scuola comunicano tra loro. Non sono solo i bambini coinvolti in questo progetto di cooperazione ma anche le insegnanti. Penso che l'apprendimento sia un processo legato alla comunicazione e quindi alla cooperazione tra bambini, tra bambini ed insegnanti ed insegnanti e famiglie.

Io sono insegnante elementare; quando ho cominciato questo lavoro stavo facendo un corso per assistente sociale e ho preso questo posto come supplente. Quando sono entrata non conoscevo i bambini piccoli, non avevo fatto grosse esperienze con loro. Ma sono rimasta subito affascinata e mi ha colpito la diversità con la scuola che avevo conosciuta. Qui i bambini erano impegnati in centri d'interesse a fare, parlare, giocare e trafficare in modo molto diverso dalla mia esperienza di bambina piccola a scuola. Da allora ho condiviso questo progetto anche per la sua flessibilità inevitabilmente legata al senso stesso dei termini: comunicazione, cooperazione e progetto».

Un'altra insegnante, LR, ha aperto la sua intervista con una dichiarazione parallela di convinzione riguardo la validità e correttezza del metodo di lavoro con piccoli gruppi di bambini su progetti a lungo termine. A questa dichiarazione ha fatto seguire molti commenti significativi sul lavoro fatto in piccoli gruppi. Ha notato che un piccolo gruppo permette all'insegnante di entrare più facilmente nel mondo dei bambini e «imbarcarsi» con loro per una esplorazione cognitiva. Ha anche definito in cosa consiste questo viaggio: porre domande e cercare conoscenza. Si è riferita al funzionamento del triangolo di partner nel fondamentale modulo di lavoro a Reggio: insegnanti, bambini e genitori, notando come i bambini inseriscano i genitori nella loro ricerca e in seguito i genitori si rivolgano agli insegnanti per porre loro delle domande. Poi ha riflettuto sul fatto che i bambini costruiscono attivamente le relazioni tra pari, e come attraverso l'osservazione avesse appreso quanto fossero importanti questi gruppi spontanei nel processo della crescente capacità dei bambini di comunicare e capirsi reciprocamente. E per finire ha offerto un lungo esempio del suo lavoro attraverso progetti con piccoli gruppi di bambini e ha spiegato come si intende il ruolo dell'insegnante a Reggio. Tra l'altro ha sottolineato che l'insegnante ha il ruolo di facilitare la comunicazione tra bambini, ascoltando con attenzione idee fruttuose, funzionando come memoria del gruppo e aiutando i bambini a rappresentare le loro idee in forma simbolica. Ecco quello che LR ha detto all'inizio, a proposito di incoraggiare la cooperazione tra bambini.

LR: «Non solo la ritengo una possibilità valida ma anche adatta a tutti e non solo ai bambini del mio gruppo di quest'anno. Attraverso gli ultimi anni, come persona e come insegnante, ho imparato a «leggere» molto di più e capire le dinamiche stando all'interno del gruppo dei bambini e a quello degli adulti. Lo stare con i bambini in modo da accompagnarli gradatamente ad affrontare un problema che pongono o che mi sembra importante che affrontino è un modo di crescere con loro. Ci sono momenti di incertezza, che danno un po' di disorientamento all'adulto, specie nei primi tempi, ma è un'esperienza assolutamente stupenda, nel senso che rinnova ogni volta e non delude le aspettative. Nel corso degli ultimi due anni abbiamo visto che i bambini stessi sono propositori di problemi all'interno del gruppo. Sono essi stessi che interrogano gli altri per sapere qual è il loro parere. Oppure, l'adulto propone un problema e i bambini ne pongono un altro che può essere connesso al primo o può seguire percorsi non preventivati o preventivabili. I bambini si pongono dei «perché» molto grossi e scoprono di essere capaci di inquadrare i problemi e di poter contare sugli altri per provare a risolverli. Lo stesso tipo di rapporto, vale a dire il gruppo come presenza forte è importante anche tra gli adulti. I bambini vedono che gli adulti fanno un lavoro parallelo al loro lavoro e che considerano ciò che loro fanno importante, lo documentano e lo ripropongono, lo estendono alle famiglie. I bambini vedono che quello che si fa nella scuola è importante e riverbera a tutti i livelli.

77

L'anno scorso avevamo i bambini piccoli, erano appena entrati nella scuola dell'infanzia. Come sempre li osservavamo e ci siamo accorti che tendevano a riunirsi in gruppi tra i quali si stabilivano rapporti più duraturi. Su questa osservazione, di come i gruppi di bambini si formano e si sciolgono, noi basiamo il nostro lavoro. Questo stare insieme in piccoli gruppi consente il massimo della scoperta dell'altro.

Un esempio. L'anno scorso la mia collega ed io eravamo organizzate in modo che ognuna di noi portasse avanti anche un progetto con un gruppo di bambini. Eravamo nello stesso tempo presenti ed assenti. Dovevamo decidere di volta in volta quando intervenire e quando non intervenire; quando lasciar andare lontano l'iniziativa dei bambini. È possibile fare ipotesi su quello che avverrà all'interno del gruppo, ma solo entro certi limiti. Comunque è uno stare insieme molto complesso, molto ricco, fatto di tutte le caratteristiche delle persone. Si passa da un momento molto serio in cui i bambini costruiscono delle teorie ad un altro i cui ridono come pazzi perché la situazione è umoristica. A volte sembrano completamente persi e mentre io magari mi chiedo: «Da qui dove andiamo?» I bambini si rivolgono a me, si rivolgono all'adulto, e chiedono: «Dimmi che cosa ho detto prima?» Vedono che noi prendiamo degli appunti, che registriamo e sanno che possono fidarsi. Mi sembra che sappiano di poter contare su di noi come risorsa, sanno che entro certi limiti possono anche usarci come memoria. Danno molto all'adulto ma si aspettano anche di ricevere. Poi abbiamo proposto al gruppo di trovare altre forme di memoria, più visibile, di tradurre le loro idee in altri linguaggi rileggibili, comprensibili a tutti loro. I bambini elaborano teorie, quasi sempre chiediamo loro di tentare di chiarire meglio a sé e agli altri, attraverso altri linguaggi (grafica, simulazioni,...)

È importante dare ai bambini la possibilità di spiegarsi e comunicare meglio e chiedere anche l'aiuto necessario degli altri per arrivare allo scopo. Per esempio mentre uno sta cercando di rappresentare, se uno degli altri bambini chiede: «Perché fai così?» Questo porta il primo bambino a tentare di argomentare, cercando di chiarire meglio il suo pensiero per l'altro e per se stesso».

Una delle insegnanti che lavora in coppia con LR è stata intervistata più tardi. MC piuttosto che fare delle affermazioni astratte a proposito dell'apprendimento cooperativo nella pedagogia di Reggio Emilia ha pensato di descriverlo usando l'esempio tratto da un segmento di video che riprendeva un'esperienza di due bambini seguita da lei. MC descrive nella intervista come i bambini affrontavano il loro problema comune, come stabilivano di conseguenza un legame tra di loro, come generavano un ventaglio di idee, chiedevano l'opinione e suggerimenti l'uno all'altro e continuavano attraverso difficoltà e successi fino a quando, in modo piuttosto sorprendente, riuscivano a superare un ostacolo particolarmente difficile. Tra i commenti, MC sottolinea che sicuramente questo tipo di cooperazione, nella soluzione di problemi, difficilmente avrebbe avuto luogo nel caso in cui i bambini fossero stati nel gruppo intero di 25 nella sezione.

Un'altra intervista si è svolta, per loro scelta, con entrambe le insegnanti dei bambini di 3 anni, MB e MM. All'inizio hanno introdotto questioni frequentemente dibattute da altri nel corso delle varie interviste e anche nella discussione di gruppo. Un aspetto riguarda questi fattori: età, sesso, esperienza precedente, dimensione e composizione del gruppo e come questi fattori influenzino la capacità del bambino di cooperare nella soluzione dei problemi. MB e MM hanno notato che per i bambini più piccoli le amicizie precedenti, stabilite all'asilo nido, sono il punto di partenza della cooperazione nella scuola dell'infanzia. Inoltre hanno osservato che la cooperazione tra bambini di tre anni ha aspetti diversi, è legata alla vicinanza, al confronto, allo scambio; ha una base più semplice di quella che si verifica tra bambini più grandi. Queste insegnanti hanno anche sottolineato due questioni a cui tutto il sistema di Reggio in quel momento dava una particolare attenzione. Quale dimensione del gruppo funziona meglio quando si lavora su progetti: due, tre, quattro, cinque o più bambini? Come influiscono le differenze di età e le differenze sessuali sul processo sociale e sullo stile della soluzione dei problemi?

MB e MM: «Pensiamo che con i bambini di tre anni il modo di cooperare sia diverso da quello dei bambini di 4 e 5 anni. Però se consideriamo che in fondo il bambino appena nato ha la capacità di cooperare occorre esaminare questo aspetto con cura. Nella nostra classe ci sono 25 bambini di 3 anni, e 23 di loro provengono dall'asilo nido. Infatti 10 bambini provengono dallo stesso asilo nido. Questo è un importante elemento per la cooperazione, perché già a quel livello iniziano a formare delle amicizie. Arrivano in gruppi che sono già abbastanza stabili. Si potrebbe dire che forse è per loro più importante stare insieme che avere di nuovo la stessa insegnante.
Pensiamo che il processo collaborativo sia davvero già attivo a questa età. Quello che i bambini scelgono è di giocare e «fare» vicino ad un altro bambino; e sebbene non ci sia sempre uno scambio, essere vicino è sempre un elemento molto importante. Non si dovrebbe mai separare l'aspetto cognitivo e l'aspetto sociale, quando si parla di un bambino, perché il bambino è uno, è intero e quando apprende lo fa con tutto se stesso. Inoltre quando si impara è molto importante avere un amico vicino per paragonare quello che si fa. La relazione migliore che si forma a quest'età è tra due bambini, una coppia che si forma spontaneamente. Un bambino generalmente cerca un altro bambino non due o tre bambini e a

quest'età di tre anni le coppie possono essere dello stesso sesso o di sesso diverso; non sembrano dare attenzione a queste differenze. Ma sappiamo che a 4 o 5 anni le differenze sessuali sono molto importanti. Però un aspetto che occorre tener presente a 3 anni è che c'è una grande varietà di capacità poiché alcuni bambini hanno il compleanno a settembre altri a gennaio».

Nell'insieme le educatrici di Reggio Emilia hanno introdotto degli aspetti chiave riguardo la loro visione della cooperazione. Non solo quello che hanno detto era significativo ma anche quello che non hanno detto. Hanno messo in luce la loro identificazione con l'aspetto collettivo del loro lavoro, e non hanno differenziato i loro pensieri individuali da quelli del gruppo più ampio di riferimento. Il conflitto veniva da loro delineato come parte importante della comunicazione produttiva, piuttosto che un evento negativo da evitare; inoltre non hanno posto limiti alla quantità di lavoro di gruppo che i bambini dovrebbero poter fare. Hanno sottolineato l'importanza dei piccoli gruppi per determinare scambi fruttuosi e dialoghi, non hanno descritto il gruppo come una forza coercitiva nei confronti dell'individuo. Hanno anche definito il ruolo dell'insegnante come atto a facilitare la comunicazione e non hanno menzionato in modo generale che le insegnanti dovrebbero controllare lo sviluppo della cooperazione o i «gruppetti» tra bambini. E per finire hanno caldeggiato la necessità di osservare i processi sociali spontanei, la formazione di amicizie, l'approccio-evitamento nelle relazioni bambino-bambina come parte del processo di comprensione delle possibilità sociali dei bambini e non hanno considerato volontariamente fattori come lo sviluppo, la personalità come ostacoli insormontabili alla partecipazione dei bambini nel lavoro su progetti. Le insegnanti americane, tendevano a vedere di più come vedremo, pericoli e limitazioni alle possibilità di cooperazione tra due bambini.

Amherst: partecipazione e autonomia individuale nella cooperazione

Le insegnanti nella scuola di Amherst lavorano in gruppo; in ogni classe c'è un'insegnante che sovraintende, coadiuvata da due insegnanti-assistenti. Tutte le classi sono miste per età nell'arco di due anni. Questa scelta organizzativa intende dare ad ogni bambino l'esperienza alternata di essere uno dei grandi e uno dei piccoli membri della classe, accrescere le occasioni di aiuto tra bambini, ridurre la competizione e i confronti invidiosi riguardo alle capacità dei bambini ed essere di sostegno all'insegnante nel dare attenzione individuale ai bambini.

Le osservazioni di apertura di MS, l'insegnante responsabile di una sezione di bambini di 3-4 anni partono dall'inevitabilità della cooperazione che MS vede determinata dalla condivisione dell'ambiente. Tuttavia MS considera che la cooperazione implica l'incorporazione delle idee dell'altro. Questa osservazione indica che viene data attenzione, nella scuola di Amherst, a prendere in considerazione il punto di vista degli altri come veicolo sia allo sviluppo intellettuale che a quello sociale. Mentre MS riconosce di dare attenzione all'individuo (vi è da notare che questa insegnante usa questo termine sette volte nelle prime tre frasi), afferma che è incoraggiando l'azione autonoma dei bambini che si rende la cooperazione possibile. Vale a dire, questo avviene attraverso la conoscenza condivisa del contributo dell'individualità di ogni coetaneo a quel «particolare gruppo». Inoltre MS asserisce, manifestando il punto di vista che viene ripetuto più volte dalle educatrici di Amherst, che la cooperazione riesce meglio quando si verifica all'interno dell'attività iniziata dai bambini, piuttosto che nei progetti diretti dalle insegnanti.

MS: «Considero l'apprendimento come un processo collaborativo nel senso che vi sono venti individui nella classe che condividono attività e scambi sociali reciproci; all'interno di questa situazione siamo tenuti a cooperare, a condividere ed ad incorporare le idee uno dell'altro. Penso che tendiamo più a mettere a fuoco progetti individuali e doti individuali dei bambini ed incoraggiare la loro iniziativa individuale e la fiducia in sé. Penso che in questo processo la nostra attenzione di educatrici vada alle caratteristiche individuali - l'attenzione ad ogni bambino come individuo - ma in questo modo noi formiamo un gruppo particolare, con ogni individuo all'interno di quel gruppo. La collaborazione dei bambini viene dalla loro conoscenza e comprensione uno dell'altro come individui.
[Puoi dare un esempio? chiede la ricercatrice]
«Vi sono molti piccoli gruppi che si riuniscono. Per esempio, oggi c'era un gruppo che giocava con Playmobile, con pirati e navi, e giocando collaboravano su un tema fantastico comune. Noi abbiamo uno spazio dove i bambini usano i pennarelli, uno spazio un po' autonomo dove insegnanti e bambini vanno a disegnare insieme. Ho sentito i bambini che dicevano: «Tu fai delle case molto belle. Per me le case son difficili, ma questo lo faccio bene». I bambini si mostravano i disegni «Beh, io faccio le case così» e mostravano uno all'altro le proprie strategie per disegnare case. Un altro esempio. Alla tavola che contiene l'acqua per

giocare con diversi tipi di pompa, ho visto un bambino che pompava l'acqua e l'altro che metteva un recipiente sotto e lo aiutava a raccogliere l'acqua e poi a convogliarla altrove. Nella nostra classe succede che ci siano più casi di collaborazione iniziata dai bambini che facilitata dagli insegnanti, anche se noi facciamo una scelta deliberata di organizzare situazioni dove possa avere luogo una cooperazione in modo naturale - per esempio su un progetto di manipolazione con diversi materiali colorati».

Una delle insegnanti responsabili di una delle due classi per i bambini di 3-4 anni, GS, inizia la sua intervista affermando che l'aspetto sociale della cooperazione è parte essenziale della missione educativa della prima infanzia. Secondo GS condividere l'ambiente scolastico richiede ai bambini di negoziare per trovare il modo di andare d'accordo tra loro. I bambini contribuiscono individualmente a questo processo attraverso discussioni in cui risolvono i problemi. Tuttavia, GS sottolinea che lei e le sue colleghe non pianificano generalmente progetti comuni all'interno del curricolo. La proprietà individuale dei prodotti rimane un valore primario sia per i bambini che per le insegnanti. In parte questi prodotti individuali servono a rappresentare l'attività di ogni bambino ma anche l'identità di ogni bambino o bambina.

In modo simile alle sue colleghe, BJ, l'insegnante responsabile della classe dei bambini di 5 e 6 anni, pensa che la cooperazione sia basata sull'opportunità per i bambini di partecipare con le loro idee al curricolo di gruppo. I bambini prendono possesso del curricolo attraverso la loro voce. BJ pensa che questo senso di partecipazione offra il potenziale migliore per lo sforzo cooperativo tra bambini. Come insegnante vede il suo ruolo soprattutto come facilitatrice. Secondo la prospettiva di BJ l'autonomia che incoraggia nei bambini offre loro una libertà considerevole per poter negoziare veramente le proprie idee con i coetanei. Questo processo implica il rischio, che vale la pena di correre, che l'insegnante debba rinunciare a qualche aspetto del controllo del curricolo. Ecco come BJ ha iniziato la sua intervista.

BJ: «Mi fa piacere dare spazio ai bambini per interagire con il curricolo, mi piace raccogliere le loro idee su quello che stiamo imparando e in questo senso lo vedo come uno sforzo collaborativo. Qualsiasi cosa si studi dovrebbe essere possibile per i bambini avere una voce in modo da poter esprimere le loro idee e influenzare il modo in cui il curricolo procede. Diventa una cosa molto variabile, qualche

volta - certi giorni - si sente il bisogno di prendere carico di quello che succede e di dare una direzione ai bambini, altre volte ci sono molte opportunità di seguire semplicemente il flusso di quello che i bambini suggeriscono.
Puoi dare un esempio? Ad esempio, poiché mi piace fare le commedie, ne abbiamo organizzata una quest'anno che trattava di insetti, perché li stiamo studiando. I bambini hanno inventato la commedia e deciso le parti che avrebbero recitato. Non sono ancora al punto di lavorare benissimo insieme e accettare le idee l'uno dell'altro ma sono stati capaci di sostenere quello che è venuto fuori dal gruppo e io li ho aiutati a mettere la commedia insieme. Ma erano le loro idee e loro ci si sono dedicati, hanno lavorato insieme e hanno fatto una cosa piuttosto folle...ma erano le loro idee e anche se la commedia era infantile nei concetti era buffa e divertente ed ha avuto successo. La mia esperienza personale è che suggerire le battute adatte ai bambini non funziona tanto, è meglio chiedere loro: « Chi vorrebbe partecipare a questa commedia?» E allora sanno che cosa vogliono essere e che cosa possono fare e così costruiscono la commedia dal principio alla fine».

L'ultima intervista introduttiva condotta ad Amherst è quella con RA, che è adesso l'insegnante della classe dei bambini di 6-8 anni ma che è stata per molti anni responsabile di una delle classi di 3 e 4 anni. RA inizia distinguendo tra i progetti che incoraggiano la cooperazione e quelli che non l'incoraggiano. Tuttavia, dice RA anche quando i bambini sono assorbiti dalle loro mete personali, vi è cooperazione negli scambi di punti di vista individuali che si verificano in una situazione di gruppo. Questo processo ricorda quello descritto come «incorporazione d'idee» notato da MS in precedenza. Come insegnante RA incoraggia questo scambio come modello incentivandolo nei bambini. Con questi bambini più grandi, però, RA pianifica anche un curricolo che rende necessario per loro di mettersi insieme e cooperare al fine di raggiungere mete comuni, come quando per esempio costruiscono una grande scultura. Questa insegnante descrive anche chiaramente come l'età mista serva a promuovere tra bambini attenzioni, aiuto e cooperazione. Perfino quando parla di questo, tuttavia, continua a dare importanza all'individuo quando, per esempio discute il processo di «consultazione» tra pari in progetti collaborativi e il modo in cui l'età mista permette agli insegnanti di dare ai bambini attenzione individuale.

RA: «Penso che dipenda da cosa stanno facendo. Ci sono certe cose che pianifichiamo pensando alla cooperazione. Per esempio, il semestre passato abbiamo studiato la cultura degli indiani e c'erano certe cose su cui i bambini hanno lavorato da soli: erano i loro progetti individuali. Tuttavia, perfino in queste situa-

zioni, lavoravano intorno alla tavola in gruppi, c'erano molti scambi, e la possibilità per l'insegnante di incentivare questo comportamento di scambio. Questo è
possibile anche perché spesso l'insegnante porta avanti contemporaneamente un
progetto simile a quello dei bambini e chiede:» Come hai fatto a far funzionare
quello in questo modo?» Ma il risultato finale è qualcosa che loro posseggono da
soli e portano con sé a casa. Un'altra cosa che cerchiamo di fare è di pensare ad attività che necessariamente devono essere eseguite con la partecipazione di tutti o
molti bambini; così piuttosto di raggiungere una meta personale penseranno a
raggiungere una meta di gruppo. Uno dei genitori che lavora con la creta è venuto
a lavorare con i bambini e loro hanno costruito un enorme cavallo di creta, mo-
dellato su di una scultura indiana di terra cotta. Sapevamo che era qualcosa che
nessuno si poteva portare a casa e che occorreva che lavorassero tutti insieme.
C'erano molte consultazioni durante il lavoro: «Che cosa pensi che andrebbe
bene qui? Come dovremmo fare le gambe?» La cooperazione era evidente e molto
più che con altri progetti. in sostanza penso che l'apprendimento possa essere
cooperativo secondo il compito che i bambini svolgono.
«Lavori con un gruppo misto per età?» Sì sono bambini di 6-7-8 anni. Anche
questo cambia la dinamica perché i bambini più grandi sono più esperti e spesso a
loro viene richiesto di aiutare i «novellini» appena arrivati e mostrare loro che
fare e come farlo. Penso che i bambini più grandi tendano ad essere più coopera-
tivi. Sembra infatti che si rendano conto che per contribuire al buon funzionamento della classe, cioè all'attenzione individuale necessaria ad ogni bambino, il
loro ruolo sia di aiutanti dei bambini più piccoli».

Nell'insieme delle loro risposte le educatrici di Amherst introducono degli
aspetti chiave di come vedono la cooperazione. Il loro uso del pronome
«noi» parlando del punto di vista degli insegnanti, ricorda lo stesso approccio
da parte delle educatrici di Reggio Emilia e riflette il forte senso di collegia-
lità all'interno di ogni gruppetto di insegnanti ed all'interno dell'intera scuola.
Nel definire la cooperazione, parlano dell'impatto dell'ecologia condivisa della
classe e del raggruppamento per età mista che promuove spontaneamente la
cooperazione attraverso il gioco, l'aiuto reciproco e lo scambio di idee.

Queste insegnanti hanno fatto delle distinzioni che non abbiamo udito a
Reggio Emilia. Per esempio, tra il tipo di cooperazione iniziata dai bambini,
che ha radici nell'interazione sociale spontanea, e quella che viene iniziata
dall'insegnante, che si verifica nella discussione sulla soluzione di problemi
all'interno del gruppo o partecipando a un progetto che è stato avviato dal-
l'insegnante, per esempio come preparare una commedia o costruire una
grande scultura. Le insegnanti preferivano la cooperazione spontanea iniziata

dai bambini e la discussione di gruppo per risolvere dei problemi. Le considerano come le esperienze più valide e appropriate per i bambini in età prescolare.

È interessante notare che anche se queste insegnanti provengono direttamente da una tradizione di educazione progressista, politicamente e pedagogicamente di sinistra, tendono a seguire un'abitudine comune negli Stati Uniti come quella di usare molte parole e frasi che provengono direttamente dal linguaggio tipico dei passaggi di proprietà. Per esempio BJ diceva che i bambini si fossero «appropriati... dell'idea del gioco»; RA parla dei bambini che fanno del lavoro di cui sono proprietari e di offrire delle idee come consulenza. Le insegnanti in varie occasioni parlano di investimento o input nel curricolo, un curricolo di cui tutti sono proprietari. Questo può essere visto come complementare alla loro interpretazione di Dewey, vale a dire della scuola come comunità democratica in cui ogni individuo ha una voce uguale e partecipa attivamente.

In generale le loro attenzioni si concentrano sullo sviluppo individuale dei bambini e si preoccupano dei modi in cui possa essere incoraggiato, attraverso l'amicizia, l'aiuto reciproco, il gioco, l'assumere la prospettiva degli altri, il risolvere problemi in gruppo, e quando i bambini diventano più grandi, nell'impegnarsi in progetti di lavoro genuinamente collaborativi. Questi punti e altre ancora sono emersi ripetutamente nelle interviste seguenti e durante le altre fasi della raccolta dei dati, nei dialoghi che abbiamo avuto con ogni gruppo di insegnanti e nei due grandi incontri che sono stati organizzati per la riflessione video tra culture.

Un confronto conclusivo tra centralità del gruppo e crescita dell'individuo

Partendo dalle premesse condivise sull'immagine del bambino e della scuola come un «sistema di relazioni e comunicazioni inserite in un sistema sociale più ampio» (Rinaldi, 1990), gli educatori di Reggio Emilia hanno sviluppato durante i 30 anni passati un approccio all'educazione della prima infanzia assai peculiare. Gli aspetti concreti di questo approccio includono come componenti essenziali: l'apprendimento cooperativo in piccoli gruppi, la continuità attraverso il tempo della relazione sia con l'insegnante che tra bambino e bambino; una grande attenzione alla soluzione di problemi e ai progetti a lungo termine che coinvolgono la padronanza di molti linguaggi e mezzi d'espressione simbolici, il favorire il collegamento tra casa scuola e la comunità più ampia; e l'apprezzamento del proprio bagaglio culturale come città, regione e nazione.

Gli aspetti concreti e organizzativi sono accompagnati da un linguaggio condiviso o un «linguaggio dell'educazione» che permette agli educatori di Reggio Emilia di cooperare. Vale a dire, nella loro stessa definizione, di scambiare idee, di ascoltarsi reciprocamente, di dibattere sui conflitti che nascono dalle idee. Il loro linguaggio relativo all'educazione è direttamente palese nelle affermazioni contenute nelle interviste sulla cooperazione e anche nelle seguenti riflessioni e discussioni sui video. Questo linguaggio è basato su di una teoria della conoscenza che definisce il pensare e l'apprendere come eventi sociali, comunicativi ed esperienze co-costruttive sia per i bambini che per gli adulti.

Per gli educatori di Amherst, che sono membri di una comunità scolastica fondata negli anni sessanta e basata sui principi di Dewey sull'educazione progressiva, si è sviluppato nello stesso modo un linguaggio condiviso sull'educazione. Punto centrale delle loro mete educative sono: promuovere lo sviluppo di ogni singolo individuo, all'interno di una comunità forte che si estende nel tempo passato e futuro, che contiene i bambini, le famiglie, tutto il personale e il direttore della scuola. Questa comunità è democratica e integrata, ricava forza dai legami delle relazioni tra età differenti. Il linguaggio dell'educazione di questi educatori è molto diverso da quello udito a Reggio Emilia ed è basato su di una teoria della conoscenza che vede il pensare e l'apprendere in termini della crescita di conoscenza di sé e degli altri e del mondo più ampio da parte di ogni bambino, attraverso l'interazione sociale e i processi di ricerca e di discussione. Questi processi stimolano lo sviluppo di un'autonomia matura e la realizzazione di sé.

Confrontando le due prospettive è facile vedere come ciascun linguaggio dell'educazione costringe o dirige il pensiero delle insegnanti, ma allo stesso tempo contiene le idee in modo da permettere la comunicazione e il dialogo nella comunità. Il linguaggio dell'educazione preferito ad Amherst mette a fuoco l'attenzione delle insegnanti sugli individui e come questi si sviluppano e cambiano attraverso il tempo. Il loro linguaggio preferito rende difficile considerare il gruppo come un contesto sempre desiderabile per il lavoro intellettuale. Rende invece più facile esprimere il parere che le insegnanti dovrebbero seguire da vicino l'interazione sociale tra bambini ed essere a disposizione per lavorare insieme in brevi intervalli; in questo modo i bambini impegnati nella loro attività avranno possibilità di fare sia lavoro guidato sia lavoro indipendente. Per converso il linguaggio dell'educazione preferito a Reggio Emilia mette a fuoco l'attenzione delle insegnanti sui bambini in relazione con gli altri bambini (e con gli adulti), rende facile considerare il gruppo come insieme da seguire da vicino, parlare della sua dimensione, composizione e delle dinamiche di comunicazione ed attività al suo interno. Rende difficile per loro dilungarsi su quello che un bambino particolare ha raggiunto oppure di parlare in modo sistematico a proposito del valore del loro programma in termine di quello che i bambini imparano anno per anno in campi di conoscenza specifici.

Allo stesso tempo, le educatrici in ogni comunità sembrano essere coscienti di altre dimensioni ed altre complessità al di là di quello che il loro linguaggio dell'educazione struttura per loro. Come discuteremo nella monografia in preparazione, tutti e tre i gruppi di insegnanti danno grande attenzione alla personalità unica di ogni bambino e sono anche molto preparati sui processi di scambio nei gruppi delle loro classi o sezioni. In verità, le interviste e le discussioni, che erano parte integrante della nostra ricerca, e in particolare la riflessione video di tipo interculturale hanno sollecitato le insegnanti a considerare sia i limiti sia i punti forti, propri e degli altri, relativi ai principi e alle pratiche professionali delle due comunità.

Bibliografia

Bruner J. (1986). *Actual Minds Possible Worlds*. Cambridge, Massachusetts: Harvard University Press (tr. it., *La mente a più dimensioni*. Bari: Laterza, 1988).

Calderhead J. (1981). Stimulated recall: A method for research on teaching. *British Journal of Educational Psychology*, 51, 211-217.

Corsaro W.A., Emiliani F. (1992). Child care, early education and children's peer culture in Italy. In M.E. Lamb, K.J. Sternberg, C.P.Hwang, A.G. Bromberg (Eds.), *Child Care in Context: Cross-Cultural Perspectives* (pp. 81-115). Hillsdale, NJ: Lawrence Erlbaum.

D'Andrade R.G. (1984). Cultural meaning systems. In R.A. Shweder, R.A. LeVine (Eds.), *Culture Theory: Essays on Mind. Self. and Emotion* (pp. 88-118). New York: Cambridge Univ. Press.

Edwards C.P., Gandini. L., Forman G. (Eds.) (1992, in press). *The Hundred Languages of Children: Education for all the Child in Reggio Emilia*. Norwood, NJ: Ablex.

Edwards C.P., Gandini L. (1989). Teachers' expectations about the timing of developmental skills: A cross-cultural study. *Young Childre*, 44, 15-19.

Gandini L. (1984). Not just anywhere: Making child care centers into «particular» places. *Beginnings*, 1, 17-20. Reprinted in *Child Care Education Exchange*, 1991, march/april, 5-7.

Gandini L. (1988). Children and parents at bedtime: Physical closeness during the rituals of separation. Unpublished doctoral dissertation, School of Education, University of Massachusetts, Amherst.

Gandini L., Edwards C.P. (1988). Early childhood integration of the visual arts. *Gifted International*, 5, 14-18.

Glaser B.G., Strauss A.L. (1967). *The Discovery of Grounded Theory: Strategies for Qualitative Research*. Chicago: Aldine. Holland D., Quinn N. (Eds.), *Cultural Models in Language and Thought*. New York: Cambridge University Press.

Lincoln Y.S., Guba E.G. (1985). *Naturalistic Inquiry*. Beverly Hills, California: Sage.

Nimmo J.W. (1992). Classroom community: Its meaning as negotiated by teachers of young children. Unpublished doctoral dissertation, School of Education, University of Massachusetts, Amherst.

Pistillo F. (1989). Preprimary education and care in Italy. In P. Olmsted, D. Weikart (Eds.), *How Nations Serve Young Children: Profiles of Child Care and Education in 14 Countries* (pp. 151-202). Ypsilanti, Michigan: High Scope.

Rinaldi, C. 1990. Social constructivism in Reggio Emilia, Italy. Paper presented at the annual conference of the Association of Constructivist Teachers, Northampton, Massachusetts, october. Translated into English by Baji Rankin, Lella Gandini, and Kristin Ellis.

Rogoff B. (1990). *Apprenticeship in Thinking*. New York: Oxford University Press.

Sarnpson E.E. (1988). The debate on individualism: Indigenous psychologies of the individual and their role in personal and societal functioning. *American Psychologist*, 4 (1), 15-22.

Schwartz S.H. (1990). Individualism-collectivism: Critique and proposed refinements. *Journal of Cross-Cultural Psychology*, 21 (2), 139-157.

Seidel J.V., Kjolseth R., Seymour E. (1988). *The Ethnograph: A User's Guide (Version 3.0)*. Littleton, Colorado: Qualis Research Associates.

Spradley J.P. (1979). *The Ethnographic Interview*. New York: Holt, Rinehart, & Winston.

Tobin J.J. (1989). Visual anthropology and multivocal ethnography: A dialogical approach to Japanese preschool class size. *Dialectical Anthropology*, 13,173-187.

Tobin J.J., Wu D.Y. H., Davidson D.H. (1989). *Preschool in Three Cultures: Japan. China. and the United States*. New Haven, Connecticut: Yale University Press.

Triandis H.C. (1989). Cross-cultural studies of individualism and collectivism. In J. Berman (Ed.), *Nebraska Symposium on Motivation. 1989*, pp. 41-133. Lincoln, Nebraska: University of Nebraska Press.

Triandis H.C., McCusker C., Hui C.H. (1990). Multimethod probes of individualism and collectivism. *Journal of Personality and Social Psychology*, 59(5), 1006-1020.

Tuckwell N.B. (1980). Stimulated recall: Theoretical perspectives and practical and technical considerations. Center for Research in Teaching, University of Alberta, Occasional Paper Series, Technical Report 8-2-3.

Wertsch J.V. (1991). *Voices of the Mind: A Sociocultural Approach to Mediated Action*. Cambridge, Massachusetts: Harvard University Press.

Whiting B.B., Edwards C.P. (1988). *Children of Different Worlds: The Formation of Social Behavior*. Cambridge, Massachusetts: Harvard University Press.

Abstract

The study involves comparison of teacher assumptions, choice and interpretations of child interaction in Reggio Emilia and Amherst, which present parallel features.

The method is adapted from the «multi-vocal video ethnography» of Preschool in Three Cultures (Tobin, Davidson, Wu, Yale, 1988) designed to bring the representations of «cultural insiders» and «outsiders» into critical juxtaposition. First, classroom (one each at 3-, 4-, & 5- year - old levels) were videotaped during morning activities. Second, head teachers were given a structured interview about collaborative learning, social cooperation, and community-building at school. Third, teachers viewed their videotapes, responding to specific segments previously selected by the inter-cultural research team. Fourth, the tapes were reviewed by the teachers from the other cities to elicit their interpretations of some of the same events.

Each of the study communities has a distinctive discourse for describing collaborative learning and community (i. e. different key concepts as determined by textual analysis). These are discussed in terms of contrasting patterns of social organization and grouping of children, as well as the emphasis teachers place on different child «needs», rationales for intervening and preferred styles of facilitating learning.

Articolo ricevuto nel marzo 1991; revisione ricevuta nel giugno 1992.

Le richieste di estratti vanno indirizzate a Carolyn Edwards, University of Kentucky, 315 Funkhouser Building, Lexington, Kentucky 40506-0054 (USA).

Additional Material

DVDs of the following resources have been deposited in the Documentation Center of the Loris Malaguzzi International Center in Reggio Emilia:

Videorecording of 3 original cooperation episodes:
"Clay Animals"
"Children at the Computer"
"Children Set the Table for Lunch"
[In Italian] Also includes transcript (English) of children's words, prepared by Reggio educators for October 1990 meeting.

Videorecording of 4 more original cooperation episodes:
"Children with Wire"
"Children Find a Bug"
"Drawing a Castle with a Logo Turtle"
"Children and Boxes"
[In Italian] Also prepared for the October 1990 meeting by Reggio educators.

Videorecording of **Videoreflection of "Drawing a Castle with a Logo Turtle,"** originally taped on 10/16/90.

The University of Nebraska–Lincoln does not discriminate
based on gender, age, disability, race, color,
religion, marital status, veteran's status,
national or ethnic origin,
or sexual orientation.

Lightning Source UK Ltd.
Milton Keynes UK
UKHW05f2238240518
323179UK00004B/122/P